ANGEL THERAPY

The Complete Practitioner's Guide

ANGEL THERAPY

The Complete Practitioner's Guide

by Hazel Raven

Raven & Co. Publishing

Disclaimer

This book is not intended to be a substitute for medical advise or treatment. Any person with a condition requiring medical attention should consult a qualified medical practitioner or suitable therapist. Neither the author nor the publisher accept liability for readers who choose to self-prescribe. Also, do not hesitate to consult a veterinary specialist if your pet seems unwell or aggressive.

ISBN 0 9538890 2 5

First Published in 2003 by
Raven & Co Publishing
Apartado De Correos 223
Alora, 29500
Malaga, Spain

Cover Illustration by Martyne Raven
Illustrations by Hazel and Martyne Raven
Front and Back cover designed by Graham and Hazel Raven
Printed by T. Snape & Co. Ltd., Boltons Court Preston Lancs. England

For information on purchases, bulk purchases or group discounts for this and other titles by Hazel Raven or details of Angel Therapy or Vibrational Medicine courses – please contact the European College of Vibrational Medicine or Raven & Co Publishing at:

http://www.raven.org.uk

For information on Martyne Raven's art work, jewellery designs and cards please contact the ECVM at http://www.raven.org.uk and go to the links page.

Other Books by Hazel Raven

Crystal Healing – A Vibrational Journey Through the Chakras

Crystal Healing – The Complete Practitioner's Guide

Dedication

This book is dedicated to my life partner and husband Graham. His unconditional love, support and sense of humour throughout the extensive research, exploration and development of the Archangel essences and the writing of this book and Angel Therapy course has made it all not only possible but a reality.

Secondly, this book is dedicated to my daughter Martyne for all her artistic skill in being the visionary artist behind the Archangel labels and front and back cover illustrations of this book.

Thirdly, to the rest of my family, especially Marc, Gary and Andrea and my spiritual sister Jacqui Malone, who 'discovered' my Angelic essences. Her belief in me, my books, courses and Angelic essences is one force in the universe that is truly awesome!

And finally to 'the Source', and all his Angelic messengers...who traverse the cosmic web and act as its guardians and guides.

To Metatron for jumping up and down on my head...until I took notice of him.

To Seraphiel, the 'gambler', for teaching me the game of life, including synchronicity.

To Gabriel, who cradled me in his arms when I felt defeated and called me his 'little brother'.

To Haniel, who destroyed my ego and then rebuilt me in the image of God.

To Michael for protecting me.

To Raphael for teaching me to slay the demons that cause dis-ease.

To Sandalphon for guiding me each step of the way.

To Chamuel, the essence of God's love.

To Uriel, alias Don Poco Tarde.

To Shamael, the initiator.

To Jophiel, who carries me onwards and upwards.

To Raziel, may your flames of enlightenment descend on earth.

To Tzaphkiel, who loves us all like the perfect mother.

To Zadkiel, long may your violet flame transmute all that is mis-qualified.

To Joseph in his technicolour dream coat, my dream interpreter and Guardian Angel.

And finally to all the Assisting Patron Angels – the Angel of the Animals, you make me weep with the beauty of your unconditional love and support.

About the Author

Hazel Raven, the being of love and light who gave birth to this book, is the founder member and course director of the International Association of Crystal Healing Therapists. The association was formed in 1986 and has been instrumental in gathering information and in practical research; it has also been involved with setting the United Kingdom standards for crystal therapy. This led Hazel to offer the knowledge in the form of seminars, training courses and lectures to the wider public. She has been running these courses since 1988 and has trained a dedicated team of professional crystal therapists and qualified tutors.

An acclaimed therapist in the disciplines of crystal, Angelic and vibrational healing, Hazel is also an accomplished teacher and lecturer, running courses and giving talks throughout the UK and in the USA. Her work with Crystals, Celtic Shamanism, Meditation, Yoga, Angels and Ascended Masters has brought her into contact with many people in all walks of life, awakening them to their spiritual purpose and true potential in this lifetime.

She can see auras and uses this gift to enhance her therapy work. Her style of teaching is inspirational and she has been instrumental in setting the standards which have furthered the cause of crystal healing as a recognised complementary therapy in Britain and a number of European countries. Hazel is a qualified educationalist, who is a former vice-chair of the Affiliation of Crystal Healing Organisations and was previously treasurer for four years, is well respected by her colleagues in the field of complementary therapies and has served on the Inner Council of the British Complementary Medicine Association for many years as its crystal therapy representative for education.

Initiated as a Reiki Master in 1994 and Karuna Master in 1995, Hazel served on The Reiki Federation's Steering Committee as representative for obtaining validation for courses.

In May 1999, Hazel was asked to attend the Foundation for Integrated Medicine conference at the Commonwealth Institute in London, which was also attended by HRH The Prince of Wales, the Foundation's patron. Hazel has always been aware of the vibrational healing and spiritual powers of flowers, trees, crystals, herbs, colour and sound. Of all the places she has visited, she feels her heart remains in Stonehenge, sacred to the Ancient Celts, and regards it as her spiritual home.

Hazel has been approached by several well-established and reputed multi-discipline therapy schools to co-ordinate a vibrational healing course. She has had a series of articles published and has appeared on television and radio, in the press and national women's magazines, including the Christmas 1997 edition of Cosmopolitan magazine, which featured her Angelic experiences.

Hazel founded the European College of Vibrational Medicine to promote vibrational therapy. So far the ECVM distance learning courses have attracted students from every continent.

For more details of the ECVM courses please contact:

http://www.raven.org.uk

http://www.angeltherapy.org.uk

Table of Contents

**Part Five:
Breathing, Meditation
and Relaxation** 129

Part One

Angels

Introduction

My own experiences of Angels has been life-long in fact I can not remember a time I was not aware of the Angelic realm. As a child I saw beautiful Angels in my bedroom every night. These were the most exquisite creatures you could imagine, they 'gifted' to me a serenity and deep sense of peace. I was frequently comforted by them throughout my difficult childhood. I know I am alone in this childhood experience as one of my students recently shared her first Angelic encounter with me. I felt honoured that she choose to share it with me, as I know she had never told anyone before. Her encounter happened when she was 9 years old and going through a very bad time at home, her early life had been difficult to say the least, and one night as she lay on her bed she said "the ceiling dissolved and she saw before her the most exquisite Angel carrying a sword of blue flame". The sense of protection and guidance from this beautiful being changed her young life and she has been able to grow to adulthood whole and healthy despite many negative family situations. The *amazing* thing is I *knew* she had experienced an encounter with Archangel Michael even before she told me, because she carried his Angelic signature within her energy field. I noticed it the first moment she walked into the room, I could feel it, we smiled and instant Angelic recognition passed between us. I say *amazing*, but really I should not, for in truth when you open your heart to the Angelic realms it is a miraculous way to live. Each and everyone of us can open ourselves to the Angelic realm as we do so our lives will be filled with wonder, love and miraculous joy.

My Angel 'experiences' have been featured in Glennyce Eckersley's best-selling book 'Angel at my Shoulder', also in 'Cosmopolitan' magazine (Christmas edition) and other women's magazines and I have appeared on television over 40 times. I have facilitated many peoples opening to the Angelic realm through my courses, seminars and Angelic crystal essences. The first combination gemstone essence I made for the Angel seminars I have been running since 1990. Very early on I devised a crystal and gemstone energy web, 'Angel of Light', that would adjust the human energy field to the Angelic frequencies. The crystal web allows for easier contact with your Guardian Angel and other beings from the Angelic Realm of love, light, wisdom, truth, compassion and healing.

The workshops have always been a huge success and many thousands of people have attended and gained insight, protection and healing from the Angelic Realm. But I still felt something was missing. When people attended the Angel seminars they very quickly would adjust their perception to the Angelic Realms, but on returning home they would find it more and more difficult to maintain the energy shifts. Slowly their vibrations would return to their previous level. After meditating on this problem I was guided by the 'Angels of Light' (who are in fact a group of Angels called the Seraphim) to make a gemstone essence using the crystals from the 'Angel of Light' energy web. This I did and the results have been not only dramatic, but very positive. Initially I just made an essence, then the Angel essence cream was born and finally the aura spray. Each method of using the original essence brought immediate and positive results. These varied from dramatic spontaneous healings to space clearing of negative energies to easily attainable meditative states to balancing geopathic stress.

The Angel seminars and 'Angel of Light' essence, cream and aura spray have been featured on television and in the national press, as well as women's magazines. The 'Angel of Light' aura essence began to be in such great demand we had to find a distributor so that it could be made available through shops and therapy centres. 'Angel of Light' was quickly followed by the 'Angel of Ascension' (also developed from my Angel Seminars) then followed Archangels Michael, Gabriel, Raphael, Uriel, Chamuel, Zadkiel, Jophiel, Haniel, Raziel, Zaphkiel, Sandalphon, Shamael and the Angel of the Animals.

This book is designed to pass on the exploration and wisdom gained in my investigation of the Angelic realm – much of the information has never been available in this format before. As an angelic aspirant I wish to share with You my perceptive powers of investigation and information gathered – which is beyond the level of individual personal consciousness. This rare information is offered through my Archangel Enlightenment Therapy course and through this book. I haven gathered of wealth of knowledge, wisdom and understanding into the therapeutic aspect of Angels and Archangels which has been applied in therapy sessions, Angel seminars, meditation and group initiations.

At the core of this therapeutic approach is the ancient underpinning wisdom of the ancients, the mystic traditions of the ages. We can not be sure where Angelic tradition began on earth but the earliest writings of Sumeria, Egypt, Persia and India recognised winged beings or messengers of the Gods. On a Sumerian stele (a stone column) a winged being an inhabitant of the seven heavens is depicted pouring 'the water of life' into the Kings cup. The teachings of Islam and the Judaeo-Christian traditions are still concepts that persist to this day they all have at their core the seven heaven ideology. I will explore further the idea of seven heavens in the chapter on the Angelic hierarchy.

If you do not have personal experience of the Angelic realm the principle of Angels may seem ludicrous, whimsical or even threatening. The theologians define Angels as a class of spiritual being, a divine messenger. In fact there are many mis-conceptions about Angels, their function and their role in human evolution. In this book I wish to set the records straight. Angels are for everyone, some of you are probably aspiring to be Angels and live your life in joy, truth, wisdom and peace. In ancient times people were less bound into rigid mental attitudes and demanding stressful timetables, they were subsequently more in tune with the rhythm of the earth and natural cycles of the universe, this allowed the mystical side of their nature to be nurtured and guided by their 'higher selves'. Their revelations and divine inspiration have come down to us through ancient manuscripts. So I invite you to cross the bridge and open your mind to the mysteries of the ages and claim your true birthright as you step into your souls maturity and enlightenment.

Perception of Reality

The way your body and aura (personal energy signature) are organised gives you your perception of reality. Your perceptive ability is fixed or 'tuned in' to certain energy bands or frequencies by your past conditioning and belief system. You are most familiar with those we call sound, light, touch, taste and smell (third dimension). If you were able to alter at will your own bioelectromagnetic signature it would be possible to connect your individual pattern to a slightly different pervading omnipresent model or pattern, consequently altering your experiences, comprehension and ultimately realisation.

We are surrounded by energy and energy patterns. Depending on our awareness, culture, expectations, intellect and perceptive abilities, this gives us our personal reality profile. Any time that changes occur, we become aware of the many billions of different energy currents and energy flows that live alongside us and the different sorts of beings that also inhabit our universe. All energy is omnipresent and all-pervasive; it only requires the correct energy shift or awareness to find it.

As a child I was aware of the myriad different energies and energy systems: in fact, I could not understand why others were not aware of these energies. I did not realise that they were not 'tuned in' to the frequencies that were my reality, my birthright. From an early age I have studied these energies and energy realities. The mystical traditions of many native peoples are very unlike those of the average westerner: their belief systems are vastly different. The more I studied, the more I became aware of the limitations we inflict upon ourselves.

All energy begins with a central point which is the source of 'all'. In the Tantric view, sound, as a vibration of undifferentiated intelligence, is the catalyst that sets into motion the unfolding of the manifest cosmos. This nothingness is comprised of all the energies and forces of the Divine universe, existing in harmony beyond our understanding at a time before our existence. It has neither mass nor form, but it has the potential to become everything and anything. It is that first point from which we came and to which we will some day return.

Imagine, if you will, the first primal movement that awakens the sleeping equilibrium of the Divine Intelligence and arouses the two active principles to carry out creation. This great cosmic vibration splits the Divine Intelligence into two streams of magnetic force, as two aspects are projected outward, male and female. The centrifugal positive male force is the ground from which the centripetal negative feminine energy springs. It is the female that unfolds the universe into manifestation. They are the Father (Bindu) and Mother (Nada) aspects of the supreme power. The act of creation, the act of Divine Intelligence manifesting from a place beyond physical reality and thus beyond our comprehension, as seen within the Kabala, gives a way of perceiving how we can each evolve and attain higher and greater knowledge or gifts.

The Divine Intelligence began to manifest through stages its energies, acquiring greater density, much as steam condenses into water and then can change into ice: it is still the same, but different. Everything at some level or another is energy in motion; the electrons and protons that make up every atom of every substance and form have motion. According to quantum theory, matter is never quiescent but always in a state of motion. Macroscopically the materials around us may seem dead and inert, but modern physics pictures matter not as passive and inert, rather as continuously dancing and vibrating.

This vibrational movement continues as the energy moves further and further away from its source. It becomes heavier and denser and vibrates more and more slowly, but it does have the potential and the content of all the higher and finer vibrations within it. We, as human beings, contain this energy of the all within our energy field. Through meditation and conscious attunement, we can cause our reality to shift into any desired frequency or vibration. This ability will become much more prevalent and the frequencies will become available to all within the earth vibration. This has been prophesied by many peoples in many countries to take place over the next twenty years. We, who choose to work with multiple frequencies or select the frequency reality of our choice, are the forerunners of the evolution into cosmic consciousness. It is no longer appropriate to just go along with the reality map we have been 'tuned in' to through our sentimental tribal conditioning.

Our thoughts and expectations create our reality, whether we are aware of this or not; what we think about or our mind dwells on day after day is brought into existence. When we are experiencing joy, happiness, peace and health, our vibratory pattern will be high. The real challenge is to gain control of the internal world we call the mind. This will facilitate our human evolution on a return journey home from the gross physical plane back to our source.

It is my sincere wish that this book helps you to become one with your true source of power, love and wisdom, which is your Divine birthright…your higher self, this energy that exists in each being, yet exists independently also. Some call it God. Others call it Goddess, Great Spirit,

Jehovah, Allah, Brahma, Cosmic Consciousness, Atman, Holy Spirit or Universal Mind. The names and paths are numerous, but there is one Divine essence which pervades all beings, the one-thread-soul.

In this book I wish to show you how the Divine Intelligence used the 'frequency' we call Angels.

Out of the simplicity of God came the complexity we call creation.

As the energy of Divine Intelligence moved further and further away from the point of harmony and perfection, Archangels were used to underpin the foundation of the manifest world. Each Archangel holds a special place on the web-of-creation and each holds a specific frequency or attribute. Angels hold lesser energies and can move freely without vital loss of structure in the web; indeed Angels can adjust the frequency of creation, allowing our personal Divine vision to manifest into our everyday normal waking reality.

Archangels are arches or gateways into dimensions or spheres of different vibrations: they can't move – if they did, creation would no longer exist. Archangels will hold the gateways open for all sentient beings until all beings become enlightened and make their return journey home, through all the levels of God's emanations, back to the source.

Angels

Angels are winged messengers: in fact the word Angel is derived from the original Greek word *angelos*, which translates as 'messengers of the gods'. They act as bridges between the higher refined vibrations or emanations of God (spirit) and the physical material world. As Angels are older than civilisation, we find records of winged beings in all mystical traditions acting as a channel for the Divine Intelligence.

These channels for the Divine Intelligence do not have the same vibratory rate as 'normal rational humans' and so have no defined form, so they can appear to a human in whatever shape that human's awareness can perceive. This perception requires an altered state of awareness. These shifts in perception can be induced by many different situations, which include meditation, dreams, spiritual development, stress, life-threatening situations and, of course, actively asking to see or work with Angels.

Most people are familiar with religious art where Angels are depicted with wings, but Angels are pure spirit and therefore have no gross physical manifestation. Each person who encounters the Angelic vibration will do so in whatever form is most appropriate to them at any given time or situation. Some people sense or feel the presence of Angels, others hear them, others smell beautiful aromas, others encounter them in deep meditation, visions or dream states. The most profound encounters are full perceived physical manifestation, which can take the form of winged beings, spinning mandalas or a beautiful light show. Still others encounter Angels as saviours who rescue them from difficult, often life-threatening situations. In these encounters the Angel appears as an ordinary man or woman dressed in present-day clothes.

As Angels are genderless beings of a vibration that is pure light, they obviously are in perfect balance. This means their male and female qualities are perfect and complete in themselves – they are androgynous. One person may perceive a particular Angel or Archangel energy signature as male, while another person will perceive it as female; yet other people perceive them as having a twin flame or female partner to manifest the male energy into the earth vibration. This is just the 'human' mind trying to rationalize the human experience of reality onto an Angel or Archangel's energy signature. In fact, throughout history, Archangels have been portrayed almost exclusively as male; this is not surprising when we live in a society that denigrates the female human form and expression.

Religious dogma, rational scientific thinking and a society geared towards the profit and loss mentality are a guaranteed recipe for spiritual oblivion and soul loss. This nothingness pervades all areas of most people's lives and it is only in times of great stress that the soul searching begins – yes, we truly search for our souls – to reconnect ourselves with the one-thread-soul of the universe, the Divine Intelligence that pervades all.

I believe, as do many others, that the 'normal rational human' consciousness is evolving and this is where the Angels can help us throw a little light onto our true eternal nature that has been obscured for centuries by veils of illusion. In fact mystics have not been welcome for many centuries in the Western world. As any free-thinking individual will tell you, mystics by nature are very hard to control and our present-day Western view of the world requires us all to be manageable; free thinking and free minds are a danger to an orderly profit and loss society. Angels have no allegiance to any particular religion or belief system.

People who are aware of Angels have a different view of the world: they believe we are surrounded by legions of Angels. In fact Angels are always at our side, they await your awakening! The miracle of working, seeing and understanding Angels is available to everyone, regardless of any core belief system you may adhere to. Angels are a pure emanation of the God-force. This Divine Intelligence only knows perfection in its pure expression as an Angel, so Angels only transmit love and positive attributes. When you work with the Angelic realm you only experience positive emotions and experiences. If you experience something that is not loving and uplifting or is trying to control you, you are definitely not tuned in to the Angelic vibration and need to look at your own life to purge it of any negative traits you may be harbouring within your own personal energy system.

Sometimes, though people do experience feelings of anger, hatred, resentment, bitterness, sorrow or fear as they arise, they will be projections from your own deep subconscious that the higher refined vibration of the Angel has brought to the surface for you to heal. This healing will raise your vibration and allow you access to more and more higher refined vibrations. Angels are always with you, they only await your call, but you do have to ask because human beings have free will. This means Angels can never interfere with your own free will.

Angelic Inspiration

Keep an Angelic journal. Essential knowledge and personal Archangel or Angelic experiences can dissipate like a dream unless they are written down. After each meditation or therapy session permit yourself assimilation time. Sit and write down your experiences, however fragmented, vague or nebulous they may have seemed to you.

Enter fully into the experience with all your faculties; how did it make you feel?

What was the most salient, prominent or striking feature of the meditation or therapy session?

Do not be overly concerned if you cannot fully understand the experience right away; fragmentary information is often referenced again in subsequent meditations or therapy sessions with the same Archangel or Angel. Some experiences make no sense to you for weeks, months or even years, and so your Archangel journal becomes a special way of assimilating understanding. If you are more of a pictorial person, you might decide to draw pictures of your experiences, or if you are verbal to record them in written form. Choose any hard-backed notebook which you find beautiful, one that you will treasure for the rest of your life. You could customise a plain notebook with Angelic pictures. Never be concerned with your spelling or writing style; allow yourself literary freedom.

Sense the presence of Angels on a daily basis; you do not need to be clairvoyant or a medium to experience the joy and delight of Angelic contact. As more and more of us become aware of Angels, the veil between our world and theirs becomes thinner. Also, some people never actually see an Angel: they are just aware of their Angel(s) by the change in atmosphere of the room, or a beautiful aroma or fragrance, or feelings of love or an overwhelming sense of deep peace or protection. Coloured lights may appear from nowhere, shafts of brilliant light or even spheres of colours may dance in front of you (especially when working with Angels for healing ourselves and others). Some people feel the presence of Angels, even Angelic hands on their shoulders.

Remember we all have a Guardian Angel who journeys with us through this lifetime and in fact all our incarnations. This guardian loves you unconditionally and is always with you, so making contact is very easy.

Make an Angelic altar as an angel therapist or angel aspirant it is good to have something tangible to focus on. It is also vital to establish a powerful connection with the Angelic realms. An angel altar is your own personal sacred space, somewhere you can create an Angelic celebration. Creating an Angelic healing altar – no matter how tiny – offers valuable grounding to your work and a chance to explore your creativity and express yourself emotionally, artistically and spiritually. Angels are attracted to places of joy, harmony, love and peace. Personal selection of items inspired by the angels through meditation and inspiration will help you become more mindful of the issues and challenges concerning the particular aspect of your life you are currently working on.

Once you have got into the routine of attending to the Angelic altar daily – whether to clean, purify or reorganise it, or change some of your sacred objects – it will be much easier to include a set amount of time for meditative thought. Remember, this is your sacred space and you should only include items which have meaning for you. It can be a valuable exercise to meditate on what you might like to include before you start, allowing your Angels to guide you. Experiment with the layout; if an item irritates or upsets you, or is less than inspiring, remove it. You could place crystals, Angelic art, photographs of loved ones, shells, bells, incense, candles, flowers, oils, religious icons, Angel cards, affirmation cards, wind-chimes, feathers, a small notebook, pencil etc. on your altar. Remember to place a representation of anything you want to bring into your life, such as love, spiritual wisdom, compassion or abundance.

Your Angelic altar need not be indoors. There is no limit to this exercise…one of my students created an Angelic room. In 1990 I decorated my New Age crystal shop with Angels, commissioning my daughter (a well-known Angel artist) to decorate the walls and ceiling with Angels. Everyone who entered felt the heavenly vibration. Even today I have Angel pictures in every room! Remember, Angels raise the vibration and each time you focus on your Angelic space it gathers and focuses more Angelic energy. Many people find that their flowers last longer on their Angelic altar. One of my most Angelic students found her roses lasted months…and one of the roses even changed colour after an especially profound Angelic encounter!

Practise being an Angel yourself and behaving as though you are already enlightened.

Make friends with other Angels here on the Earth plane, through the Internet if need be. Organise Angel gatherings or Angelic support groups.

Ask the Angels to help you in all areas of your life. You never pray to Angels (only God), so just communicate respectfully with your Angels as though they were your best friends.

Mentally ask your Angels for help; call them mentally in any situation when you need immediate assistance.

Invoke Angels. This is very easy. Remember Angels can never interfere in your life…if you need assistance, just ask. On special occasions, when you are in danger, a guardian Angel may have special dispensation from God to intervene and help you. This happens frequently with children when they are in life-threatening situations.

Invocation: A decree to the Angels should always be positive.

Archangel Haniel, warrior and protector of the dharma, keep my feet forever on the path towards full enlightenment of my soul. Encourage me when I feel weak, disillusioned or beset by obstacles. Reveal to me the glory of God and renew my spiritual armour so that my soul will find true salvation.

Archangel Zadkiel, teach me the righteousness of God. Teach me to trust in God. Use your violet flame of transformation and freedom to transmute all my lower energies and negative karma into positive life-affirming energy.

Archangel Sandalphon, guardian of planet Earth and holder of the sacred presence, teach me to bridge heaven and earth, so I too may hold the energies as a sacred guardian of this beautiful planet. Teach me to plant my feet gently on the earth while my head is in the heaven of heavens as I fulfil the destiny of being a gateway, an arch others can pass through towards enlightenment.

When you have a problem(s) write a letter to the Angels. Open your heart to the Angels…do not hold anything back, just allow the feelings to pour through you and onto the paper. Really let go and ask them to resolve the problem(s) to your highest good and the good of all, then leave it up to the Angels…do not try and manipulate the situation. You may be surprised at how quickly your problem(s) is resolved and very often it will not be in the way you expected. This is because the Angels do not have a limited human mind set and can work in ways you would not even dream of! Angelic contact is often experienced in your dream state, especially if you practise the Angelic temple meditation.

The 'calling card' of the Angels is a white feather. You can ask for one as physical proof of your Angelic contact. You may be surprised as to how this white feather manifests in your life. I always mention this 'white feather' calling card at my seminars…one student who attended was talking to a few others after a seminar when she said she was not truly convinced of the concept of Angels…just at that moment one of the other students noticed that stuck to her cardigan sleeve was a pure white feather!

Visualise your Angels. Use your imagination; even if you feel you cannot see them, what would they look like if you could? Write down what you think your Angel looks like. This exercise frees your imagination, this in turns frees your intuition. When you become adept at working with Angels, you simply go into a meditative state, quiet your conscious mind, tune in and be still. If you have a specific question, ask it, make your mind blank and wait for an answer. But when you are just developing this skill it helps to follow a meditation ritual, like the Angelic Guidance Meditation.

Angel Hierarchy

"For He shall give His angels charge over you, to keep you in all your ways. They shall bear you up in their hands, lest you dash your foot against a stone."
(Psalms 91:11,12)

In the New Testament there are references to seven ranks of heavenly beings, hence the old saying of 'being in the seventh heaven' when you feel deliriously happy. From heaven to earth there are three levels or spheres of Angelic influence, according to the fifth century scholar Dionysius. The first and closest to God are the Seraphim, Cherubim and Thrones.

Sphere One

Seraphim – are angels of love, light and fire. Their purpose is to inflame humans to Divine love. They are closest to God and are considered the highest order of all the Angels, maintaining the integrity and purity of the Divine essence of love. They are also collectively known as the 'Angels of Light' and bring forward a healing energy known as 'brilliance'…it is pure 'Cosmic Iridescent Rainbow Light' and contains all the colours and 'rays'. The Seraphim, whose essence is perfect love, direct the 'Divine' energy which emanates from the first creative source. Seraphim means 'the inflamer', from the Hebraic root word *saraph*, which means burning. They are the angels of 'Divine' fire. In the Bible, they bring a glowing coal to cleanse Isaiah, by placing it on his lips. In that moment he is cleansed of all karma. The Seraphim have six wings: two cover their face, two cover their feet and they fly with the other two. Continually singing 'Holy, Holy, Holy' they surround God's throne. It says in Revelation 4.8 that if we call on their power, our being is flooded with infinite love, light and joy. In fact working with the Seraphim is like becoming pure iridescent cosmic light. Their speciality is miracles, joy and the path of ascension. In medieval symbology they are red and carry fiery swords. Dante said seraphim are related to the presence of "gladness of God." Ruled by: Archangel Seraphiel who is dazzling and sometimes called the Prince of Peace and Archangel Metatron.

Cherubim – are the next closest to God and hold the energy signature of the stars and galaxies. They therefore keep the celestial records and give out knowledge. They are vast cosmic beings who direct the perfect light of God in the form of love. They hold the responsibility of spreading this love energy and they must maintain the purity and perfection of God's love. This they magnify and radiate, expanding it outwards into the entire cosmos. They praise God constantly, day and night. Cherubim are not the cupid-like beings often portrayed in art, although it is understandable when one considers how this loving energy feels. Perhaps this is due to their childlike quality, or simplistic childlike trusting perfect love. I personally feel this energy as the hand of God reaching down and uplifting us. This energy can carry us heavenwards into the 'arms of God'. I have also seen this energy bathing those who work with the Angelic realm; I see it as if 'God has smiled on them'. This was clearly expressed by Rainer Maria Rilke when he wrote: "Who, if I cried out, would hear me among the angels' hierarchies? And even if one of them pressed me suddenly against his heart; I would be consumed in that overwhelming existence" (Duino Elegies, I). The name Cherubim means 'fullness of God's knowledge,' from the Assyrian *karibu* meaning 'one who prays' or 'one who communicates'. In Assyrian art they are depicted as winged creatures with human or lion faces and the bodies of eagles, bulls or sphinxes. In the Middle Ages they were often described as being blue or wearing blue, a fitting colour for those who are wise and dispense wisdom. Sometimes they are considered to be equivalent to the order of wheels. Satan was one of the Cherubim before he fell from grace. Ruled by: Zophiel, Ophaniel, Rikhiel.

Thrones – bring us the justice of God. They oversee the planets and carry the loving energy further outwards. They maintain the purity of the vibration and ensure every planet is bathed in God's perfect love. They act to carry out God's desires. God desires that we are all evolving into loving beings of pure light so we can make the return journey home through all the levels of creation…back to the perfect heart of God and his boundless love. Humans were created from the mind of God and as we evolve into Angels (who were created from the heart of God) we take our place in Angelic hierarchy. Thrones are also called wheels, as they have a pure formless energy, like huge fiery spheres. The Virgin Mary is said to be a Throne. They are referred to as chariots or the merkabah in the Jewish Kabbala. The Zohar (occult book) puts wheels above seraphim; others put them as cherubim. Ruled by: Zaphiel/Zabkiel/Oriphiel.

"The man form is higher than the angel form; of all forms it is the highest. Man is the highest being in creation, because he aspires to freedom" – Paramahansa Yogananda (Autobiography of a Yogi).

Sphere Two

Dominions – or Dominations – oversee the Angelic hierarchy and act as channels for God's love through the vibration of mercy. They manifest God's majesty. Their emblem of authority is a sceptre or orb which they carry in their left hand and a staff of gold which is in their right hand. They regulate the duties of angels (organise the rotas!). Ruled by: Zadkiel/Hashmal.

Virtues – are 'Lords of Light' who hold and channel immense Divine light. They give out valour and grace. They also work miracles on earth. Sometimes they are referred to as the 'shining' or 'brilliant' ones. Their energy has speeded up the ascension process and allows you to have the courage, resolve and fearlessness to make your 'ascension in the light'. Jesus was accompanied by two of this order of angels when he made his ascension.

Powers – are 'Karmic Lords' who protect our souls and are the keepers of the Akashic records. They have the task of keeping demons under control. In this capacity they prevent them from overthrowing the world. They are often seen as the Angels of death and rebirth. Ruled by: Sammael/Camael/Ertosi.

Sphere Three

Principalities – are in charge of nations, towns, cities and sacred sites. They also protect religion.

Ruled by: Anael/Cerviel/Requel.

Archangels – are Divine bridges, our personal first route to God within the Universal Web of Consciousness. Each will be described in great detail later in this book. Each Archangel has a chapter dedicated to them and the legions of angels they lead.

Guardian Angels – personal helpers who record all your incarnations.

Angels – millions of them helping in lots of different tasks. They guard all physical things and people. They include the Angels of Joy, Love, Courage, Peace, Hope, Faith, Freedom, Harmony, Balance, Abundance, Creativity, Inspiration, etc.

Angels and Archangels have different roles or tasks. In fact much has been written down the centuries of the seven Archangels of Jewish lore. They each have a spiritual fire or colour. There are references to Angels in the Old Testament and the New Testament, but usually they are not identified with a particular name.

Elemental Kingdom

These are nature spirits who create balance and abundance on the Earth plane, where they are honoured and appreciated. They often appear to humans as coloured dancing lights. They can be subdivided into their elements.

Fairies, elves, gnomes and goblins are earth spirits and rule over the flowers, plants, trees, soil, sand and crystals. They teach us how to nourish ourselves and live in abundance as co-creators in balance and harmony. This means living responsibly with regard to all life on the Earth plane. The earth spirits' message is 'harmonize with, do not disrupt, nature'. We all know tampering with nature not only disrupts the harmonious flow of the weather but also damages the environment. When we work in harmony with the elemental forces, rather than combating them, we create positive energy in our living and working environments. By focusing on the powerful energy that flows around us, we can begin to bring balance and harmony to every area of our lives.

Undines and mermaids are water spirits who rule over the water and tend to the creatures that dwell within the water realm. A vast part of the Earth is covered with water. The water spirits teach us to go with the flow. Water has many forms: just as ice, water and steam are all the same substance, they may appear different, but in truth they are all the same chemical composition. So the water spirits have a lot to teach us about adapting to many different situations without losing our basic stability and eternal divine nature.

Salamanders are fire spirits who guard the secrets of the transformational fire energy. They can be found in abundance around volcanoes. The fire spirits teach us about our life force, this dynamic energy that dwells within each of us. Fire also purifies, burns and destroys the old so that new may emerge. Creative fire teaches us spiritual fortitude. Fire spirits teach us how to remove old blocks and traumas as their energy quickly burns away the blocks or negative energy in the auric shell.

Sylphs are the spirits of the air; they carry our higher thoughts and prayers to the Angels. Air is light, flexible and free. Most life forms need air to live. Working with the sylphs increases our intuition and communication. It teaches us the power of our thoughts.

Devas are more evolved than the elementals and they work with humans, especially as guardians of sacred sites. Very often they can also be found dwelling in beautiful quartz crystals. If you are lucky enough to find a 'devic temple crystal' it will become a great mentor. It has the ability to teach you how to connect the higher spiritual vibration with matter to manifest heaven right now here on earth. The devas who dwell in quartz crystals also have the ability to teach you about healing, both personal and planetary.

The Seven Heavens

Angelology (the study of Angels) is an extremely perplexing and complicated field of endeavour with many scholarly perspectives written over aeons by different mystics, visionaries and theologians, none of whom seem to agree!... at least not in every detail. However, the belief that there exists not one but seven heavens or seven celestial mansions is integral to the monotheistic religious traditions – Islamic, Christian and Jewish. The seventh heaven or most refined sphere is where the perfect essence of God dwells. In fact the seven heaven tradition goes back some 7,000 years to Sumeria. On a Sumerian stele (a stone column), a winged being – an inhabitant of the seven heavens – is depicted pouring 'the water of life' into the King's cup. The Sumerian civilization of Mesopotamia gave birth to the Assyrian, Babylonian and Chaldean civilizations, which in turn were highly influential in all Near Eastern religions and angelology. The seven heavens are not the astronomical crystal heavens of Ptolemy, but rather spiritual realms. The names of the seven heavens are found in the Old Testament and are derivatives of the word heaven.

The First Heaven

Vilon (from the Latin 'velum' meaning veil). This is not a biblical word. Sometimes called Shamajim or Shamayim (common word in the Bible for heaven). This is the lowest heaven and is associated with planetary angels and angels that rule the stars and natural phenomena such as the atmosphere, wind, water etc… in fact everything that is related to the third-dimensional plane of human scientific existence.

The Second Heaven

Raqia ('expanse' in Genesis 1.6, 1.14, 1.18). Zodiac angels rule over this sphere. It is considered by some to be the holding place of sinners awaiting the 'Day of Judgement'. Fallen angels are also held prisoner in this heaven. It is the dwelling place of John the Baptist in Islamic tradition.

The Third Heaven

Shechakim or Shehaqim (the 'skies' in Psalms 18.11). This is a strange heaven, as hell is found in the northern region. A river of flame flows through this cold icy land and it is here that the wicked are punished by the angels. The Angel of Death rules over this domain. In the southern half lies the 'Garden of Eden', a Paradise. The southern half also houses 'The Tree of Life', which is guarded by three hundred angels of light. The celestial garden, which has a gate of gold, is where all perfected souls go at death. Two rivers flow through it: the river of milk and honey and the river of oil and wine. Having heaven and hell in the same heaven may seem odd to us, but in keeping with sacred lore they do dwell side by side. Saint Paul was lifted to this heaven in a vision.

The Fourth Heaven

Zebul (the 'lofty place' in Isaiah. 63.15) is ruled over by Archangel Michael. It is where the "heavenly Jerusalem" is located… the Altar and Temple of God. It is the 'City of Christ' from Saint Paul's Apocalypse vision. The city was all gold, with twelve walls encircling it, and there were twelve walls inside. There were also twelve gates of great beauty. The city was encircled with four rivers: a river of honey, a river of milk, a river of wine and a river of oil.

The Fifth Heaven

Maon (the 'dwelling' in Deuteronomy 26.15) where the angels sing the praise of God by night and God's chosen people sing his praises by day. Some of the fallen angels are also held here.

The Sixth Heaven

Makon (the 'habitation' in Psalms 89.14, 97.2). This is where the Akashic records are stored (all the happenings on earth, including the deeds of every individual who has ever lived on earth) and their punishment or reward (karma).

The Seventh Heaven

Arabot (the 'clouds' in Psalms 68.5). This is the abode of God, the Throne, the absolute Holy of Holies. The highest orders of Angels, Seraphim, Cherubim and Thrones dwell here. It is the home of the blessed spirits and unborn souls.

Planetary Angels

The seven planets which were widely known to the ancients (at least as far back as the Roman era) were each attributed to archetypal energetic beings who also related to the days of the week they were said to rule over. In twelfth century Moorish Spain the cross-cultural fertilization of Christian, Arab and Jewish heritages brought about the birth of the golden age of the Renaissance, heralding the end of the Dark Ages, and it was from Spain during this time period that the first documentary evidence of planetary angels also emerges. This knowledge was stifled and condemned by Protestant Puritanism in Europe from the sixteenth century onwards, but the synthesis of astrology, religion, mysticism and alchemical magic has surfaced once again in the New Age movement. Listed below are the planet, day, virtue and corresponding appropriate gemstones to help you invoke and petition the planetary angel of your choice. For instance, if you wish to bring love, beauty and harmony into your life you would petition Archangel Hagiel on a Friday night and wear a rose quartz pendant around your neck.

Archangel Michael – Sun – Sunday – Vitality – Ruby and Garnet

Archangel Gabriel – Moon – Monday – Nurturing – Moonstone and Pearl

Archangel Camael – Mars – Tuesday – Courage – Carnelian and Red Coral

Archangel Raphael – Mercury – Wednesday – Communication – Emerald, Green Jade, Aquamarine

Archangel Zadkiel – Jupiter – Thursday – Abundance – Yellow Sapphire, Citrine, Topaz

Archangel Hagiel – Venus – Friday – Love, Beauty and Harmony – Rose Quartz and Diamond

Archangel Cassiel – Saturn – Saturday – Wisdom – Blue Sapphire, Lapis, Amethyst

Kabalistic Tree of Life

The Kabala is essentially a process of instilling wisdom which was passed from Master to pupil. Kabalists say it originated as the revelation of a secret mystical teaching of Judaism. It is a Hebrew word meaning to receive inner wisdom, from mouth to ear, as an oral tradition. There is no single book called the Kabala, rather it is a body of information. Two original texts are: *The Zohar* "The Book of Splendor" and *The Sepher Yetzirah* "The Book of Formation", the latter being accredited in legend to Melchizedek, a priest king of Salem (later Jerusalem), which was given as a revelation to Abraham, the father of the Jewish nation.

The structure of existence as described by Kabalists shows the descending logical stages through which the Divine One-Thread-Soul of the Universe brought the original Divine scheme into manifestation. The Kabala has been used by initiate mystics for centuries as a means of experiencing the different aspects of creation. The practical validity of the Kabala as a map, route or pathway to God has been evaluated by each initiate over the centuries through spiritual revelation and direct personal experience. As no-one knows the true mystical history of the Kabala, although some Kabalists say it dates back to the time of Adam in the Garden of Eden, the mystical Kabala is as alive, fresh and unique as you are, as a portion of the Divine One-Thread-Soul of the Universe. Only *you* can truly understand and interpret your experience of the Kabala, as each journey home to God will be unique and always perfect for your own individual comprehension.

Various spellings can be found for the Kabala: they correspond with different historical periods and traditions. The expression "Tree of Life" was popularized in the Middle Ages. The Kabalist mystics understand that the vision is a manifestation of a cosmic core reality which underpins the various elements symbolising the structure of existence. The Divine energy descends from above and gives birth to the ten sephiroth. (The singular form of sephiroth is sephirah). You can view them as emanations, vessels, spheres, circles, points of light or mandalas. Each mandala or sephirah (the name actually means a vessel) represents an energy signature. Energy signatures across from each other balance one another. *Severity* must be balanced with *Mercy* or it is cruelty. *Mercy* must be balanced with *Severity* or it is weakness.

The Tree of Life is a visual representation or map of the return pathway of *ascension to God consciousness*, by ascending from bottom to top in reverse order (ten back to one) through the sephiroth or preferably by a more direct path through the centre pillar.

Amazingly, the Tree of Life can be used as a template or blueprint for a multitude of systems that give us understanding of the processes we can use to access the Divine within our own life and ego-centred personalities and this allows us to arrange and order life in the manner in which we see and understand the world.

Once the ten sephiroth spheres are in place, plus the twenty-two interlocking paths, it equals the thirty-two paths of wisdom in the archetypal world. Between the ten spheres and thirty-two paths are the fifty gates of inner light. The spheres, paths and gates of light form the Tree of Life pattern. Each sphere has a name which relates to its function. Each sphere also has an Archangel which holds the energy signature. Each of the twenty-two interlocking paths is assigned a letter from the Hebrew alphabet.

The Creative Power of Sound

The Hebrew alphabet is considered sacred and it consists entirely of consonants. These consonants have a vibration or energy signature, which means they are alive with *creative cosmic* power. This cosmic power is latent and can only be activated by the human voice when it provides the vowel sounds through Divine understanding. Kabalists emphasize that prayer is not effective unless it is spoken aloud: this releases the cosmic force of God to flow down through the sephiroth and then through you, which allows the 'Will of God' or 'Light of God' to be made manifest on earth. For although God is omniscient, he gave us all free will. This means that he and his Angels (Angels do not have free will) can only act to help us if we specifically ask. God has given us freedom (free will) as an evolutionary experiment. We are each allowed to experience good and bad. These good and bad experiences can be seen as a series of life lessons or soul initiations. The life lessons are specific spheres on the Tree of Life (stages on the path of ascension) which we access by means of the thirty-two paths of wisdom. When we fully balance and integrate the attributes of the spheres or sephiroth into our daily life, we come closer to the restoration of our original Divine blueprint and in so doing step onto the path of ascension – the journey of love. Each Archangelic chapter in this book has an *invocation* which is designed specifically to be spoken *aloud*, which then fully activates the attribute of that Archangel and corresponding sphere on the Kabalistic Tree of Life.

The Absolute

In the beginning God created the heaven and the earth. And the earth was without form, and void; and darkness was upon the face of the deep. And the Spirit of God moved upon the face of the waters. And God said, "Let there be light": and there was light. And God saw the light, that it was good: and God divided the light from the darkness.

Beyond the spheres at the top of the Tree of Life is the Divine, which is perfect, pristine and Absolute. The Divine generates a sequence of veils of negative existence.

Ain = Void

Ain Soph = Limitless All

Ain Soph Aur = Infinite Light

These are the stages the Divine must go through to bring about manifestation or point of light. This point of light is omnipotent and omnipresent: it is limitless and without dimension, containing all possibilities. It is everything. This point of light in the Kabala is called *Kether* or Crown: it is the beginning of the Tree of Life and the point from which all the other spheres flow downwards.

In the Kabalistic scheme there are *Four Worlds of The Tree of Life*.

Atziluth is 'The World of Emanation' – the realm of unity and perfection, which is archetypal.

Briah is 'The World of Substance' – representative of form and the physical plane.

They are also representative of fire, water, air and earth. Some people who work with Archangels use the Kabalistic teaching and tradition, as they form the basis of Western esoteric mysticism. However, it is not at all necessary for those wishing to work with Angels and Archangels to subscribe to this system or indeed any system. Perhaps, though, it is interesting to understand its basic principles, as all paths eventually lead back to God.

The Archangels and Ten Divine Names of the Sephiroth

Kether or Crown – Archangel Metatron (Divine)
Chokmah or Wisdom – Archangel Raziel *(Ratziel)* (Cosmic Father)
Binah or Understanding – Archangel Tzaphkiel *(Zaphkiel)* (Cosmic Mother)

Daath or Knowledge – Holy Spirit *(Shekhina)*. *Daath* is a non-*sephirah* and the external aspect of *Kether*. Some Kabalists consider it to be a place of mysterious powers and miracles.

Geburah or Judgement – Archangel Chamuel *(Khamael)*
Chesed or Mercy – Archangel Zadkiel *(Tzadkiel)*
Tiphareth or Beauty – Archangel Raphael

Hod or Glory, Majesty – Archangel Michael or Archangel Jophiel
Netzach or Victory – Archangel Haniel
Yesod or Foundation – Archangel Gabriel

Malkuth or Kingdom – Archangel Sandalphon or Archangel Uriel *(Auriel)*

The Three Triads

The first triad starts with *Kether* (Crown) and begins the activity: it has all the power and potential of creation. It then forms *Chokmah* (Wisdom) and *Binah* (Understanding). These first three spheres are the Divine trinity and traditionally relate to the realm of the intellect. These first three spheres also form pillars, which act as support for the next seven spheres to bring the energy of the Divine down to *Malkuth* or Kingdom.

The second triad consists of *Geburah* (Judgement), *Chesed* (Mercy) and *Tiphareth* (Beauty). It traditionally represents the realm of the soul as it seeks incorruptible perfection, righteous power and the beauty of compassion.

The third triad consists of *Hod* (Glory), *Netzach* (Victory) and *Yesod* (Foundation). It traditionally represents the realm of nature and the lower aspect of the second triad.

The final sephirah and the lowest on the Tree of Life is *Malkuth*, the Kingdom. It corresponds to the physical body and is our gateway to the Divine and the Divine's gateway to us.

The Three Pillars

The Tree of Life has three columns or pillars.

The left-hand column is *Boaz*; it is water, passive and made up of *Binah*, *Geburah* and *Hod*.

The right-hand column is *Jachin*; it is fire, active and contains *Chokmah*, *Chesed* and *Netzach*.

The middle column is *Zohar*; it is air, balance and contains *Kether*, *Tiphareth*, *Yesod* and *Malkuth*.

The Divine energy then descends from above and uses these pillars as structure: this is how the formless takes form. The three pillars also take on characteristics and energy signatures of their own. The middle pillar of *Zohar* embodies compassion: once you have integrated this energy into your being, the direct route to God is open to you.

The Three Parts of the Soul

Kabalists believe that the soul has three soul parts and each comes from a different sephirah. Each part is not necessarily active in all people.

Nefesh is sourced from *Malkuth* and sustains the body, giving it life and allowing it to participate in the material world.

Ruah originates from *Tiphareth* and is the spirit. It is the aspect that allows us to transcend the lowly human condition by using our intellect and reason. It is the aspect of your soul which stirs you into the deep contemplation of God.

Neshamah is an emanation of *Binah*, the 'Cosmic Mother'. It is the super-soul, pure spirit, and can never die or be corrupted: it is the eternal aspect of God.

The Lightning Flash

Kabalists also describe the emanation and descent of the Divine light through *Kether* into *Malkuth* as a lightning flash which flows constantly from left to right and back again. The energy flows from *Kether* into *Chokmah* and *Binah* and then into the 'non-*sephira*' *Daath*. Duly charged with cosmic power, it then moves to the sephirah of *Chesed* and on to *Geburah*, flowing finally through *Tiphareth*, *Netzach*, *Hod* and *Yesod* and being earthed in *Malkuth*.

Daath

The lower seven sephiroth are also separated from the top three, the 'Divine Trinity', by the 'non-*sephira*'. This is known as the abyss or veil and its name is *Daath*, the place of knowledge; it is a non-place, as it is transpersonal. There is no sideways path to this sphere: the only access to it is from above or below on the middle pillar of *Zohar*, which is balance.

The Merkaba

The path of the mystic and those who study the *Kabala* hopefully allows us to have direct personal experience, contact and on-going revelations with God. For too long it appears that organised religions have wanted their congregations to abide by their 'laws', which mostly do not allow ecstatic encounters of a personal nature with God. These man-made anti-mystical 'laws' are the basis for the mystical traditions to have been practised in secret. The quest of the mystic throughout the ages was fuelled by the prophet Ezekiel's vision of the *Merkaba*, or throned chariot of God.

The early Jewish mystics practised *Merkaba* mysticism. Today more and more 'ordinary' people are studying the *Kabala* and the *Merkaba* in order to have direct personal experience of God. Perhaps this shift in consciousness is due to the raising of planetary awareness, which recognizes that there are many pathways to God and abiding by man-made antiquated laws is no longer appropriate or desirable.

The word *Merkaba* is made up of three sections or smaller words: *Mer-Ka-Ba*.

Mer translates as the 'Light of God' or 'Super-Soul'.

Ka symbolises the individual spirit which dwells in your heart centre.

Ba is the spark of life that animates the physical body and gives us our personal reality or perceptive ability.

The way our body and aura are organised links our perceptive ability to certain energy bands or frequencies. You are familiar with those we call sound, visible light, touch, taste etc. If we were able to alter at will our own bioelectromagnetic signature in some way, it would be possible to link our individual pattern to a slightly different all-pervading omnipresent, omnipotent model or pattern, thus altering our experiences, signature and comprehension and ultimately realisation.

The *Merkaba* symbolically is comprised of two three-dimensional three-sided pyramids. One pyramid is pointing upwards, symbolizing the *yang* aspect of duality, while the other is pointing downwards, symbolizing the *yin* aspect of duality. As the energy integrates, it creates the star tetrahedron. This geometric structure represents wholeness. It is the Merkaba vehicle we 'came in' with and it is the vehicle we shall use to leave this physical reality. By using the *'Star Merkaba'* it acts as a portal (transmitter/receiver) connecting us to our own Divine essence and the energy of 'All That Is'. The way to access the *Merkaba* vehicle is through visualization and using the sacred Hebrew alphabet.

The *Merkaba* is also represented as two interlocking triangles in the centre of the *Anahata* or heart chakra (although Kabalists do not use the Sanskrit terms for the energy centres embedded in your etheric spine) and as the symbol of your 'Holy Guardian Angel'. This is symbolic of the upper (spiritual) and lower (physical) trinities coming together to create wholeness and unity, which expands the threefold flame in your heart.

Archangels

As the energy of Divine Intelligence moved further and further away from the point of harmony and perfection, Archangels were used to underpin the foundation of the manifest world. Each Archangel holds a special place on the web of creation and each holds a specific frequency or attribute. Archangels are arches or gateways into dimensions or spheres of different vibrations: they cannot move – if they did, creation would no longer exist – but Archangels can appear on every level of the web of creation. Just as God is omnipotent and omnipresent, Archangels have this attribute as well, because unlike humans they are complete and in constant awareness of God. When humans gain this constant awareness of God they become enlightened. Archangels do not have free will: they are God's messengers – they are the 'markers' (the gateways) on the path; they light the way home. Archangels will hold the gateways open for all sentient beings until all beings become enlightened and make their return journey home, through all the levels of God's emanations, back to the source. In their unique way the Archangels make it possible for humans to experience the Divine Intelligence, in all its facets. They bring down to us with our limited human perspective aspects of the pure force we call God.

We, as humans, deal in concepts or ideas. The force we call God is beyond concepts, but we can begin to work towards a thinning of the veil of illusion, where the rational mind will limit our perspectives, by working directly with the Archangels. As each Archangel holds up to us a mirror reflection of the God force – the light of God – we can slowly assimilate this vast knowledge which is sometimes called the 'language of light'. This light will dissolve blocks in our energy field and clear our karmic debris, opening us to our true potential. This enlivens the Divine spark within us, which we all contain. We are not separate from our creator, but intimately link into the very heart of God.

We can never work with Archangels with our rational mind, which is full of concepts. We need to approach the Archangel realm with our hearts and with our soul. This will feed our spirit and free us from the rational mind's concepts that bring feelings of separation, pain, duality and illusion. God is perfect and complete in itself, God does not know separation or duality.

When you start working with the Archangelic realm you will get many messages in the form of dreams, visions, revelations and coincidences which are designed to *wake up* your consciousness. This *awakening consciousness*, as we shall call it, is a lifelong journey towards wholeness. This means we need to own our emotions and learn our spiritual lesson gained from each Archangel and apply these insights in our everyday lives. The degree to which an individual is successful in understanding the particular spiritual lesson and applying the insights gained will determine the amount of subtle energy flow which can move into the body to maintain correct physical health, emotional well-being, mental stability, spiritual growth and Divine understanding. The Archangels will help us to remove the old dead layers of our psyche which have caused our vibrational rate to become low. When our vibrational rate is low, or its functioning is abnormal, this is because of improper attitudes, old self-deprecating message tapes, sentimental tribal conditioning, fear, guilt, hatred, etc. We shall explore each of the Archangelic gateways to help our awakening consciousness emerge into the light of God, by feeding our Divine nature. This will be done chapter by chapter as we work through the essences or webs of light devoted to each major Archangel. First I would like to present you with an overview of the kabalistic tree of life and introduce you to the major Archangels that are holding the gateways open for you, so you can journey home not only in safety but in good company too.

Archangel Metatron

Brings enlightenment and spiritual growth. He is the Angel of Ascension, known as the Prince of the Angels. Archangel Metatron is the guardian of the threshold. Behind him stands the void; under him are all the other Archangels. The void contains all possibilities and when we traverse this 'space', the void…we come face to face with the 'Godhead'. This is the ultimate goal of human existence. On our path 'home' to the 'one heart', Metatron is our most important guide to initiation. Metatron is keeper of the Akashic records. He is said to have taken human form as the prophet Enoch. He works with Lord Melchizedek (also known as Archangel Melchizedek). Melchizedek also took human form as a priest and king of Salem (present day Jerusalem) to form the order of Melchizedek…this was to co-ordinate the work of the Christ energy on Earth. Archangel

Metatron's colours are brilliant white 'light' that contains all colours and pure gold. Archangel Melchizedek's colour is gold. Archangel Metatron's retreat centre/temple of light is over Luxor, Egypt. Melchizedek has his temple of light over Jerusalem.

Shamael

Is the Archangel of sacred sound, utilizes the transformational healing energy of sound in its sacred aspect. Shamael carries the colour vibrations of indigo, violet and gold. He represents the first impetus of creation and is depicted as an aspect of Archangel Metatron in Western spiritual mystical tradition (the Kabala).

Tzaphkiel (Zaphkiel)

Is the Archangel of deep contemplation of God, representing the Divine feminine watery aspect of creation, the Shakti of Shiva. Tzaphkiel has the power to nurture all things and gives us glimpses of other realities. Tzaphkiel will catch us if we fall, for God's love is unconditional and non-judgemental. Allow Tzaphkiel to carry you when you feel weak, for her infinite compassion is the sea of our liberation.

Raziel (Ratziel)

Is the Archangel of the secret mysteries, who gives Divine information by allowing us to understand the enigma of God. This knowledge is absolute and perfect...when we receive it we need no confirmation of our 'understanding' from others. Our crown chakra is opened, the flames of enlightenment descend, we transcend normal reality, we just are. In this moment we experience our own immortality and Divinity, we literally gaze upon the 'countenance of God'. These encounters with Raziel can seem extreme to our friends and family, but once you have sure and certain knowledge of the Divine, nothing will ever be the same again! Raziel awakens the prophets and religious reformers...use the power wisely!

Chamuel (Khamael)

Is the Archangel of Angelic Love (God's Love). His name means 'He who sees God'. His essence ignites and expands the flame of pure unconditional love within your heart. Its warmth melts and dissolves all resistance you may have to allowing the full manifestation of unconditional beneficial love into the heart and chakra system. True love conquers all! His temple of light is over St. Louis, Missouri, USA.

Zadkiel (Tzadkiel)

Is the Archangel of Divine Joy. Zadkiel's name means the 'Righteousness of God'. He is the guardian of the violet flame of transmutation, transformation, joy and freedom. This transforms lower energies into positive life-affirming energy. Zadkiel is the Archangel of mercy, who teaches trust in God and the benevolence of God. He brings comfort in our hour of need. His temple of light is over Cuba.

Raphael

Is the physician of the Angelic realm, for healing ourselves and helping find the inner guidance and inspiration to heal others. Raphael's name means 'God has healed'. His temple of light is over

Fatima in Portugal. Raphael is frequently associated with the balance colour of green. He carries a cup of healing balm. Raphael's energy is very peaceful and healing, but he has the power to cast out demons! He is also known as the chief of the guardian angels.

Michael

Is the protector of humanity, for strength and Angelic empowerment. He is chief commander of the celestial army. Archangel Michael's name means 'Who can stand against God' or 'Who looks like God' or 'Who is as God'. His main colour is yellow, in fact the fire of the solar plexus is his domain…but because he carries a sword made of a blue flame he is often associated with the throat chakra and the colour blue. His temple is at Banff, near Lake Louise, in Canada. Michael is commander-in-chief of the Archangels and he leads the heavenly forces against evil (the human vices of anger, hatred, negativity, cruelty, hostility and conflict). Michael can appear simultaneously in three of the seven heavens.

Jophiel

Is the Archangel of Wisdom. His name means 'Beauty of God'. He connects you to your higher self, bringing wisdom, intuition, perception, joy, bliss and soul illumination. Invoke Archangel Jophiel when you feel blocked or your creativity needs a boost. If you ask him, he will heal, cleanse, activate, balance and align your mental body, which stops feelings of low self-esteem and mental fog. He will also give you practical assistance by helping to absorb information. His temple of light is over Lanchow in China.

Haniel

Is the Archangel of Divine communication. His name means the 'Glory of God'. He is a *warrior* angel; his authority assists you to fulfil your 'Divine heroic mission'. He gives strength and perseverance when you feel weak, through Divine communication and revelations. Archangel Haniel is the protector of your soul. He gives the virtue of determination and provides the energy required for you to fulfil your Dharma. He is, in fact, the protector of the Dharma. Call on him when you feel life is difficult and you are beset by obstacles (even dark forces of negativity)…he will provide the spiritual armour necessary for your salvation. His temple of light is over the sacred mountain of Tibet.

Gabriel

Is the Archangel for dissolving fear and guiding us through change. He also awakens us by igniting the Divine flame that dwells in each and every one of us. Gabriel's name means 'God is my strength' or 'Hero of God'. His temple of light is over Mount Shasta in California. Gabriel's colours are white and orange. He carries a trumpet to awaken your inner Angel and bring good news. He is the Angel of revelation. He helps you to interpret your dreams and visions. His energy is joyful, light and bubbly. He is the 'Lord of the Dance' – as such, he is the Angel of annunciation, resurrection, vengeance, destruction, mercy and death. He guides the soul on its journey to paradise.

Uriel (Auriel)

Is the Archangel for emotional and mental clarity. He saves us from confusion and bestows wisdom and inner peace. Uriel's name means the 'Fire of God' or 'Light of God' – he brings the light of the knowledge of God to men. He helps us to interpret prophecies and our own prophetic dreams. His temple of light is over the Tatra mountains of Poland. Uriel is associated with the colour red, but this red can be the deep purple-red of fine rubies and Uriel's energy signature often has golden or silver glints contained within it. He carries a staff to use as support…he always gives us unconditional support on all levels. He teaches world service. **Auriel** represents the feminine aspect of the moon and helps us to reflect on our issues of living on the physical plane of human existence. Auriel teaches us that all humanity is just a mirror of the self.

Sandalphon

Archangel of the Earth, is in charge of Earth healing and planetary group work…a very 'big' Angel and Archangel Metatron's twin. His presence is always in the Kingdom (the Earth plane) and he does not move between the planes of existence, for he is so vast or tall that his energy spans all levels of the Tree of Life. He therefore unites heaven and earth…holding the Divine presence on planet Earth. In the Talmud it states 'Sandalphon's head reaches heaven'. Moses described him as being the 'tall Angel'. His temple of light is over Southern Spain. Sandalphon teaches us to have a grounded reality and balanced spirituality.

Part Two

Angels of the Rays

Angels of the Rays – Light and Colour

The physical world that human beings see is simply reflections of electromagnetic waves springing off objects into the retina of our eyes, generating the perception of light and colour. The universe is a magnetic field of positive and negative charges, resonating constantly to manifest electromagnetic waves. Each of these has a distinct wavelength and speed of vibration: this forms the electromagnetic spectrum. Sunlight is composed of 66% heat-emitting infrared light, 32% visible light – that allows us to see different colours – and 2% ultraviolet light. Humans can only see about 32% of the colours contained in sunlight. So although white light looks colourless it is made up of assorted definite colour vibrations which have not only wavelengths but also structure.

The radiant energy of pure sunlight is a vital component in nourishing us on every level. This includes our bodies, minds, spirits, souls, chakras, aura and meridians. Each colour vibration has its own unique energetic signature or bioinformation. The three primary colours generated by this visible light are red, yellow and blue. Every imaginable colour, shade and hue are created from these basic primary colours of light. As shown by Newton, white light is composed of all the colours of the rainbow intermingled. By passing a narrow beam of white light through a glass prism it can be spread out into a whole series of spectrum colours according to their wavelength. There are only six main colour names (or seven if one includes indigo). Red is the longest wavelength we can see and has the slowest frequency vibration. It is magnetic, warm and stimulating. Violet has the shortest wavelength and the quickest vibration. It is calm, cool and purifying. Green is the balance colour.

At either end of the visible spectrum of light are a multitude of wavelengths we, as humans, cannot see. Ultraviolet light is just beyond violet and further beyond this are electromagnetic rays with increasing frequencies as the wavelengths get progressively shorter: these include X-rays and gamma rays. At the other end, infrared light is found just beyond red light. Just as red has warming qualities, although it gives off more concentrated heat (these qualities are utilized in infrared lamps), beyond this are electromagnetic rays with increasing wavelengths and decreasing frequencies: these include radio waves. The ancient Yogic mystics have long been able to see colours outside the 'normal' – third dimensional 32% range during meditation.

Light therapy, chromotherapy (colour therapy) and hydrochromatic therapy (colour tinctures) are ancient methods of natural healing. Colour surrounds and affects everyone, but few people realise how colour can be used in a therapeutic fashion. Colour plays an integral function in our lives and whether we are aware of the effects or not it is a extremely potent force. Basically the colours that surround you affect you every moment of the day or night, making you happy or sad, healthy or sick, tense or relaxed. There is no doubt that our bodies are aroused and energized by some colour signatures or calmed and relaxed by others. Colours can be restorative – and they can make you over-excited, lethargic or dis-eased. The health of all our internal organs, the circulation of the blood, the nervous, lymphatic, skin and endocrine systems, basically all the workings of the body are constantly altered by the colours to which we expose ourselves. Physically, mentally, emotionally and spiritually, colour manipulates us all on a deep soul level, transforming our mood and our sense of well-being, as well as others' perception of us. We frequently betray ourselves with colour. Nature has furnished us with colour to support and nourish our whole system, supplying a vital energy that is an essential part of life. We respond to colour actively or passively in all that we do. Light waves affect us every minute of our lives and penetrate our energetic system, whether we are awake or asleep, sighted or blind. Our development, blood pressure, body temperature, muscular activity, sleep patterns and immune system function are all affected by light rays. The coloured rays affect not only our physical bodies, but our emotions, moods, mental faculties and our spiritual nature. We all have an intimate relationship with colour. Sometimes we give ourselves a subconscious colour treatment by choosing jewellery or clothes of a certain colour, or by surrounding ourselves with specific colour vibrations in our homes, offices and gardens. Mostly our reactions are unconscious and it is only when we start to use the magical signatures of colour in an informed enlightened way that we harness this wonderful vital force to improve the quality of our lives and our overall sense of harmony, balance and total well-being.

The human eye consists essentially of a flexible lens of changeable focal length, limited by the iris through which light is focused to form an inverted image as the retina, which lines the back wall of the eye. The retina is connected with the brain (where all messages of light and colour are translated into sensations) by the optic nerve. Impulses from the right eye travel to the left side of the brain, while those from the left side travel to the right half of the brain. This action of the nerve fibres means that they actually cross over, in part of the brain called the optic chiasma. The sensory layer of the retina consists of small rod-like structures interspersed with shorter conical bodies, which are known respectively as rods and cones. Only the cones are thought to be sensitive to colours and only the cones are capable of acute vision. A small central area known as the yellow spot near the emergence of the optic nerve contains cones only and it is here that the image of an object is focused for the clearest possible vision. The cones that are sensitive to green light are situated directly in the middle of the retina, allowing light to fall in the centre of the eye. This will make the green colour the most relaxing on the eyes and, in turn, the mind. The rods, on the other hand, are the structures which enable us to see to some extent in a dim light: for this reason they are the chief feature in the retina of a nocturnal animal. Rods therefore are more light sensitive, allowing us to see in dim light, but do not record colour. About 10 per cent of men and less than 1 per cent of women are in some measure colour-defective, or are colour-blind. In such persons it is supposed that one or more of the red, green or violet-sensitive colour receptors is not functioning, thus limiting and distorting to a lesser or greater degree the perception of hue.

However, not all the light impulses received through our physical eyes are used solely for the purpose of sight. Nervous impulses from the eyes travel not only to the visual cortex of the brain but also via the hypothalamus to the pituitary and pineal glands. We find, therefore, that many body functions are stimulated or retarded by light and different colours of light have specific effects on the brain and central nervous system. The pituitary gland, known as the 'master gland' of the endocrine system, is first affected by coloured light. It produces substances that regulate the hormones produced by the endocrine glands. These hormones regulate our body functions, which include growth patterns, sleep, our temperature control, our sex drive, our energy levels, our metabolic rate and appetite.

The pineal gland, located deep within our brain, is also light sensitive. It governs our internal body clock by producing melatonin: this controls our sleep cycles and also inhibits sexual maturation. Daylight suppresses the production of melatonin and at night the lack of sunlight increases its production. The quality and amount of the light reaching the pineal gland will also alter with the changing seasons. Therefore the proportions of the colours within sunlight, according to the season, cause our body functions, like those of plants and animals, to mimic the energy of the seasons. In summer we are full of vitality and life and very active, whilst in the winter months we feel sluggish, depressed and inactive. Colour affects us even when our eyes are closed. Light is required for our cells to function normally and individual colours affect them by causing changes in growth and behaviour patterns.

Each major visible colour or ray has a particular quality or resonance linked to the chakra with which it vibrates in the third dimension. An understanding of the nature of the chakras and their energetic links to the body's physiology is all that is needed for using a particular colour essence to ameliorate specific dis-ease or emotional states or even for spiritual development when the colours are used as fourth dimensional transmuting rays.

It is the 'Angels of the Rays' that direct the vital life-force of God into the healing rays. Invoking and becoming one with these Archangelically-directed energies will cohere, amplify, focus and direct the full potential of each colour signature, bringing about profound shifts in awareness which remove blockages that may have formed within the human energy system.

Ruby Red Ray brings Passion – ruled by Archangel Uriel – Root Chakra

The ruby red ray brings spiritual devotion through selfless service to others. It teaches us about the universal law of cause and effect known as karma. Archangel **Uriel** (Auriel) is the Archangel for emotional and mental clarity. He saves us from confusion and bestows wisdom and inner peace. Uriel's name means the 'Fire of God'. He carries a staff to use as support...he always gives us unconditional support on all levels.

Archangel Auriel

Represents the feminine aspect of the moon and helps us to reflect on our issues of living on the physical plane of human existence. Auriel teaches us that all humanity is just a mirror of the self.

Auriel's ray is pearly white, the transmuting ray of the root chakra which gives access to the fourth dimension.

The ruby red ray is also the transmuting fourth dimensional ray for the solar plexus chakra.

Physical Assimilation: Slowest vibration of the spectrum: infrared. Parts of the body: genitals and reproductive organs; gonads, ovaries; regulates adrenalin release into the bloodstream; blood; circulation; eases stiff muscles; feet; legs, knees, hips. Avoid red for all angry conditions, agitation, hyperactivity, fever, ulcers, high blood pressure, swellings, inflammation and nervous disorders. Also never place red or a red crystal anywhere near the third eye, or shine a red light anywhere near the eyes or top of the head. Activates, vitalizes, signifies and arouses lust, desire, armour, intensity. Releases energy blocks deep within the system. Brings action, life-force, courage, stamina...gives a new boost to processes that have been sluggish or stagnant. Survival issues reduced, restores the will to live. Dynamic, removes fear. Detoxification by removing inertia. Warms the body, stops chills. Increases physical energy and can be used if you are feeling tired.

Orange Ray brings Creativity – ruled by Archangel Gabriel – Sacral Chakra

Gabriel is the Archangel for dissolving fear and guiding us through change. He also awakens us by igniting the Divine flame that dwells in each and every one of us. Gabriel's name means 'God is my strength'. He carries a trumpet to awaken your inner Angel and bring good news. He helps you to interpret your dreams and visions. His energy is joyful, light and bubbly. The feminine aspect brings the energy of hope. Archangel Gabriel is the 'Lord of the Dance' – as such, he is the angel of annunciation, resurrection, vengeance, destruction, mercy, revelation, death and ascension. He guides the soul on its journey to paradise.

Gabriel's colour is white when used as the transmuting fourth dimensional ray of the root chakra.

Physical Assimilation: A mixture of red and yellow in perfect balance. Parts of the body: lower back, lower intestines; abdomen and kidneys; governs the adrenal function; aids digestion. Never place orange or an orange-coloured crystal (carnelian) anywhere near the third eye, or shine an orange light into the eyes. Ameliorates grief, bereavement and loss (trauma). Enhances creativity, optimism and a positive view of life. Ameliorates bronchitis and asthma. Useful during the menopause. Balances hormones and aids fertility. Helps ease fears and phobias. Very motivating, balances body energy levels, increases vitality…works more gently than red by building up energy step by step. Unlocks deadlocked processes. Eases constipation.

Golden Yellow Ray brings Wisdom – ruled by Archangel Jophiel – Solar Chakra

Jophiel is the Archangel of Wisdom. This solar ray is often called the sunshine ray. His name means 'Beauty of God'. He connects you to your higher self, bringing wisdom, intuition, perception, joy, bliss and soul illumination. Invoke Archangel Jophiel when you feel blocked or your creativity needs a boost. If you ask him he will heal, cleanse, activate, balance and align your mental body, which stops feelings of low self-esteem and mental fog. He will also give you practical assistance by helping to absorb information.

Pale golden yellow is the transmuting fourth dimensional ray for the crown chakra.

Physical Assimilation: Brightest colour of the spectrum. Parts of the body: pancreas; solar plexus; liver; gall-bladder; spleen; middle stomach; nervous system; digestive system; skin. Mental agility and learning enhancement. Fortifies, brightens, tones, stimulates, reinforces energy. Strengthens weak body processes. Sunshine. Wisdom and intellect stimulation. Concentration aid. Brings stable upliftment, freedom, laughter and joy. Brings weight loss for body and mind, increases self-control. Breaks down cellulite. Cleanses the body of toxins. Raises self-esteem and brings feelings of total well-being. Enhances communication. Helps to stimulate conversation, prevents shyness and gives courage. Prevents mental confusion.

Emerald Green Ray brings Balance – ruled by Archangel Raphael – Heart Chakra

Raphael is the physician of the Angelic realm, for healing ourselves and helping find the inner guidance and inspiration to heal others. Raphael's name means 'God has healed'. He carries a cup of healing unguent. Raphael's energy is very peaceful and healing, but he also has the power to cast out demons!

The emerald green ray is also the fourth dimensional transmuting ray for the third eye chakra, which then helps your visualisations and your manifesting powers of perfect health.

Physical Assimilation: Yellow and blue in perfect harmony. Parts of the body: thymus; heart; lungs; shoulders and chest. Equalizes, calms and relaxes. Encourages personal growth by bringing harmony and balance in all areas. Keeps mental and physical energy dynamically balanced. Releases painful tensed-up processes (especially in the chest and shoulders). Attunement to nature and the devic kingdoms. Eases claustrophobia. Helps to balance hyperactivity in children. Balances and stabilizes the nervous system. The ray of great healers and healing. Soothes emotions and reduces mental confusion.

Sapphire Blue Ray brings Communication – ruled by Archangel Michael – Throat Chakra

Michael is the protector of humanity, for strength and Angelic empowerment. Archangel Michael's name means 'Who is like God'. His main colour is yellow, in fact the fire of the solar plexus is his first domain…but because he carries a sword made of a blue flame he is often associated with the throat chakra and the colour blue. Michael is commander-in-chief of the Archangels and he leads the heavenly forces against demons (the human evils, the vices of anger, hatred, negativity, cruelty, hostility and conflict). The sapphire blue ray represents the power and will of God, as well as the powers of faith, protection and truth.

Electric blue is the fourth dimensional transmuting ray for the throat chakra.

Physical Assimilation: Parts of the body: thyroid and parathyroid; upper lungs; jaw; arms; base of the skull; and body weight. Soothes, restrains, inhibits – calms hot conditions where there is too much heat in the body. Seeker of truth and knowledge. Combats fear of speaking the truth. Reduces fevers and re-regulates hyperactivity, inflammatory and derailing processes; brings clarity and serenity. Eases stiff necks and stiff-necked attitudes. Heals ear and throat infections. Natural pain reliever. Aids weight loss by encouraging communication, thereby releasing stored words. Blue can help bring down high blood pressure. Good for the sickroom and for those terminally ill. Eases menstrual cramps and haemorrhoids. Royal colour of integrity. Calms the mind and helps you to think more clearly. The intellectual and mind colour. Will soothe your soul.

Indigo Ray brings Devotion – ruled by Archangel Raziel – Third Eye Chakra

Raziel is the Archangel of the secret mysteries, who gives Divine information by allowing us to understand the enigma of God. This knowledge is absolute and perfect…when we receive it we need no confirmation of our 'understanding' from others. Our crown chakra is opened, the flames of enlightenment descend, we transcend normal reality, we just are. In this moment we experience our own immortality and Divinity, we literally gaze upon the 'countenance of God'. These encounters with Raziel can seem extreme to our friends and family, but once you have sure and certain knowledge of the Divine, nothing will ever be the same again! Raziel awakens the prophets and religious reformers…use the power wisely!

Physical Assimilation: Indigo is a perfect balance of dark blue and dark violet. Parts of the body: the pituitary gland; the skeleton; lower brain; eyes and sinuses. Aids intuition and spiritual knowledge. Strongest painkiller of the rainbow spectrum. Releases negativity from the skeletal structure. Astral antiseptic and astral toxin release (clears negative thought forms). Kills bacteria in food, water or air. Clears pollution on all levels. Ameliorates chronic sinus complaints (unshed tears). Eases insomnia. Releases migraine headaches and pain. Ameliorates overactive thyroid conditions. Breaks up tumours and growths. Helps ease kidney complaints. Indigo helps to control diarrhoea. Eases bronchitis, asthma, lung conditions. Lowers high blood pressure. Ameliorates back problems, especially sciatica, lumbago, any spinal complaint. Transmutes and purifies negativity. Good for spiritual teachers and writers. Indigo can be addictive. Indigo is the domain of mystery and psychic understanding. The ray of artists and the acting profession.

Violet Ray brings Spirituality – ruled by Archangel Zadkiel – Crown Chakra

Zadkiel is the Archangel of Divine Joy. Zadkiel's name means the 'Righteousness of God'. He is the guardian of the violet flame of transmutation, transformation, forgiveness, joy and freedom. This transforms lower energies into positive life-affirming energy. Zadkiel is the Archangel of mercy, who teaches trust in God and the benevolence of God. He brings comfort in our hour of need.

The violet ray is also the fourth dimensional transmuting ray when used on the sacral chakra.

Physical Assimilation: Balance of blue and red: highest and fastest vibration in the rainbow. As Sir Isaac Newton discovered, translucent violet is the ray with the shortest length of wave. It is also the fastest: as such, it symbolizes a transition point between the visible and the invisible to the normal human vision – therefore it has always represented Divine alchemy and transmutation of energy from the gross physical into the unmanifested Divine. Amethyst rings have always been associated with spirituality and have been prized for their transformational properties. Parts of the body: the pineal gland; top of the head; the crown; brain; scalp. Inspires – aids psychic abilities and intuition. Brings spiritual dedication. Ameliorates internal inflammation. Eases heart palpitations. Aids the correct function of the immune system. Ameliorates bruises, swellings and black eyes. Calms emotional turbulence. Eases eye problems and eye strain. Used for past life regression. Allows for full soul development. Clears karmic debris, opens the gateway to the soul. Allows psychic protection. Enables you to 'see' visions. Can stop addiction and addictive traits within the personality. Cleanses and purifies anywhere it touches. Soothes irritations, relieves pain.

Pink Ray brings Divine Love – ruled by Chamuel – Hearth Chakra, Fourth Dimension

Chamuel (Khamael) is the Archangel of Angelic Love (God's Love) and Adoration. His name means 'He who sees God'. His essence ignites and expands the flame of pure unconditional love within your heart. Its warmth melts and dissolves all resistance you may have to allowing the full manifestation of unconditional beneficial love into the heart and chakra system. True love conquers all! Rose quartz crystal is the physical manifestation of this ray: as such it is gentle, soothing and excellent for balancing the emotional level of the aura by gently nourishing the emotional body. Rose quartz is revitalising and stimulates healing by helping to maintain energy levels to protect against unwanted influences from the outside world, which many sensitive souls find overwhelming.

The pink ray is also the fourth dimensional transmuting ray for the heart chakra.

Physical Assimilation: White and red in perfect balance. Parts of the body: aids digestion; any part of the body that you dislike or feel is un-lovely. Spiritual love, universal love, compassion. Forgiveness. Affection, romance, comforting and nurturing. Use after an operation or dentistry. This is the colour of love. Ideal for developing a loving attitude, for yourself and others. Gives emotional balance.

Brilliant White Light, the Supreme Ray – ruled over by Archangel Metatron

Metatron brings enlightenment and spiritual growth. He is the Angel of Ascension, known as the Prince of the Angels. Archangel Metatron is the guardian of the threshold. Behind him stands the void; under him are all the other Archangels. The void contains all possibilities and when we traverse this 'space', the void…we come face to face with the 'Godhead'. This is the ultimate goal of human existence. On our path 'home' to the 'one heart', Metatron is our most important guide to initiation. Metatron is keeper of the Akashic records. He is said to have taken human form as the prophet Enoch. He works with Lord Melchizedek (also known as Archangel Melchizedek). Melchizedek also took human form as a priest and king of Salem (present day Jerusalem) to form the order of Melchizedek…this was to co-ordinate the work of the Christ energy on Earth. Archangel Metatron's colours are brilliant white 'light' that contains and reflects all colours.

White is the transmuting ray for the root chakra.

Physical Assimilation: Cosmic Light: Brilliance. Parts of the body: affects all areas of the body and aura; multidimensional. Restores a person's vibrancy. Used for positive change. Used as a 'cure all' by colour therapists. Clears rooms of negativity. Clears the aura of negativity. New beginnings.

Part Three

Archangel Essences

Guardian Angels

For he shall give his angels charge over thee, to keep thee in all thy ways. Psalm 91:11

Your holy guardian angel is your personal helper who has sustained your soul through all your incarnations and faithfully records all your actions. Your celestial guardian angel loves you unconditionally and wishes to consciously assist you in raising your vibration to full enlightenment. This means your guardian angel is your first route to the Godhead and is your bridge to all the higher angelic realms. Your guardian angel will help you through all your trials and tribulations, comfort you, console you and encourage you in all your positive endeavours by helping you fulfil your life plan and learn all your individual karmic lessons. Your guardian angel is a very powerful member of the angelic realm: once you discover your soul connection with your angel it will give you faith in yourself and the confidence to move ahead with grace and ease.

Most children are very aware of their guardian angel, but as they grow up and go out into the world they tend to lose their deep connection and soon fall into the 'sleeping' energy of those who dwell in normal acceptable everyday reality. In the Koran it is Archangel Gabriel appearing as a brilliant white angel, shining like the light of the moon, who speaks to an Arab merchant with the question "Sleeper, how long do you sleep?" The Arab merchant is then transformed, through his spiritual awakening, into the prophet of God, Mohammed.

Your guardian angel can never interfere with your free will, although you may have heard a gentle voice encouraging you in times of personal crisis or despair. In fact most people only become aware of their guardian in times of disaster. It is these intense turning points that have transformed many lives and opened them to the angelic realm. Contact with your guardian angel is always positive, bringing feelings of peace and emotional well-being.

The following attunement will empower you by opening you to your angelic guardian; this relationship will place your feet very firmly on the upward spiral towards enlightenment. Contact with your guardian angel will help you to formulate a plan to improve your life and recreate your future with ease, learning new perspectives and reaching your highest potential. This attunement is a unique initiation and by following the simple formula you will activate your angelic chakra.

Most people do not realise they have an angelic chakra! It is not some 'new age' concept, but has been known about for thousands of years. This chakra is located just above your third and fourth eye chakras. We will look at the human chakra system later in this book, but here I will give a brief overview of the third, fourth and fifth eye chakras. The third eye or brow chakra is known in Sanskrit as *Ajna*, which means 'to command'. It is located right between and just above the physical eyes; it corresponds to the space between the eyebrows, the *trikuta*. There are two major conduits through which energy rises up the spine. These are the female *Ida* and the male *Pingala*, the yin and yang. Energy enters through the left side, Ida, and exits through the right side, Pingala. These female and male opposites intertwine as they twist their way up through the first five chakras. Then they merge to generate the third eye, which lies within the brain, just behind the centre of the brow. It is here that the earthly duality ends; yin and yang unify to become whole, causing the manifest and unmanifest to merge. The third eye, the sixth chakra, is feminine, intuitive, mysterious and yin. Its symbol is the pure white lotus flower which has two large pure white petals. They are on each side of a pure white circle, within which is a downward-pointing white triangle containing the *bija* seed letter *Om*. The white triangle represents the light of the soul, in its downward path. The fourth eye chakra is known in Sanskrit as *Soma*, which means 'water'. It is located just above the third eye chakra and controls the body temperature and balances the power chakra in the solar plexus, bringing the male-female balance to the whole body system.

The fifth eye or Angelic chakra is known in Sanskrit as *Lalata*, which translates as 'forehead'. It is located at the very top of the forehead. Its full activation brings Angelic attunement, ending the illusion of pain, suffering and duality. It kindles the light of truth – into the light of the soul, where all illusion vanishes and all suffering ends. The colours violet, white and gold are associated with this chakra.

The following attunement will activate your angelic chakra – we will use crystals that resonate very strongly with the angelic realm and create a unique energetic web of light; this will be activated by your guardian angel and the aura essence especially created for this purpose.

Guardian Angel Initiation – Attune to Your Guardian Angel

Guardian Angel aura essence
Angelite, placed on the throat chakra
Rose quartz (faceted) placed on the heart chakra
Danburite, placed on the third eye chakra
Seraphinite with pyrite inclusions, placed on the fourth eye chakra
Celestite point (bi-coloured) placed on the fifth eye chakra (Angel chakra)
Selenite, placed above the head, just above the crown chakra
Finally place 12 clear quartz crystals evenly around the body, terminations pointing inwards.

Dedicated to and overshadowed by 'Your Guardian Angel'

Uses: This unique web of light invokes the presence of your holy guardian angel by activating your angelic chakra. This attunement brings love, warmth and an overwhelming sense of peace and well-being. Angelic communion is enhanced. It will adjust your perception to the angelic realms.

Invocation: I now invoke my guardian angel to activate my angelic chakra for my conscious connection to the angelic realms of love, light and healing.

Physical integration: Revitalises and stimulates healing by helping to maintain energy levels to protect against unwanted influences from the outside world, which many sensitive souls find overwhelming.

Emotional consolidation: Soothing and excellent for balancing the emotional level of the aura by gently nourishing the emotional body with love. Once you discover your soul connection with your guardian angel it will give you faith in yourself and the confidence to move ahead with grace and ease.

Etheric assimilation: Perception is adjusted via attunement and activation of the angelic chakra to the angelic realms.

Process: See the therapy section – **Process** (page 185).

Meditation to Connect with Your Guardian Angel

When you first start the exercise you may want to pre-record the following instructions on tape.

You may wish to light a violet, white or gold candle.

You must purify your energy space – see the section **Purification – Creating A Sacred Space** (page 158).

Soothing angelic music is also useful…if it does not distract you too much.

Flowers are also very acceptable as energy offerings (gifts of love) to the angels.

You could hold a crystal, such as rose quartz, seraphinite, danburite, angelite, celestite or selenite.

Purifying your physical body by taking a shower or bath and putting on clean clothes can also make you feel more receptive and in tune…after all, you are going to invite your guardian angel into your life to be a co-creator in your healing, spiritual and vibrational work. Your guardian angel will be delighted to work with you and very often you will feel emotions of excitement and happiness even before you begin the meditation.

1.   Mist your aura with *Guardian Angel* essence *Attune to Your Guardian Angel*.

2.   Sit in a comfortable steady posture, with the spine and neck held erect but not tense. This helps steady the mind and aids concentration. The psychic current must be able to travel freely from the base of the spine to the top of the head. If you cannot sit cross-legged, sit on a straight-backed chair with your feet flat on the floor, your knees level with your hips and your spine upright. You can also lie on your back, on the floor sometimes, and it will give you a different meditation experience – usually sensory ventures into other states are heightened when lying down in a sleep posture. These trance-like dream meditations can be very intense. I would suggest you try both methods, which will lead to balance in your guardian angel meditation practice. Many people prefer to sit upright to begin the day in meditation and to lie down to finish the day with a more dream-like meditation.

3.   Place your hands on your thighs, palms upward, and join your thumbs to your index fingers. Now pull the shoulders back ever so slightly and the chin in a little, so that there is a small pull on the back of the neck; this will ease the blood flow to the brain. Close your eyes and, with the mouth ever so slightly open, rest the tip of the tongue on the roof of the mouth just behind the teeth. This placement of the tongue is vital because it naturally maintains the flow of energy to the head whilst keeping the jaw relaxed. There are two major energy channels (acupuncture meridians): the Yin channel (the conception vessel) begins at the perineum and flows up the front centre of the body, ending at the tip of the tongue; the Yang channel (the governing vessel) begins at the perineum and flows up the back centre of the body, over the top of the head and back down to the roof of the mouth. The tongue connects these two important currents when touched to the highest point in the roof of the mouth.

An easy way to open this energy channel is to sit in a relaxed posture. Allow your energy to complete the loop by letting your mind flow along with it. Start in the mouth and mentally circulate your attention with the energy. Eventually the current will begin to feel warm in some places as it loops around. Relax, try to bring your mind directly into the part of the loop being focused on. Experience the actual feeling of the flow of chi in that part of your body.

4.   Once the circuit is going smoothly, inhale as you go up the spine and over to the third eye, and exhale as you go down from the third eye to the perineum. Complete seven of these circuits (seven is a mystical number and it will serve to clear your chakras).

5. Bring the energy up your spine as you inhale and send it up to heaven. With it send gratitude for all the good things and blessings in your life.

6. Imagine an overcast day. See the clouds part, as a ray of cosmic white/gold/violet light comes through and bathes the top of your head. Absorb this brilliant cosmic angelic light into your being through the top of your head. This is your first link with your guardian angel…it allows the attunement process to start…

7. Allow this angelic light to pour in through your body…nurturing every cell, every fibre of your being…with pure consciousness, pure unconditional love. With every inhalation, breathe in the blessings, healing and empowerment that are meant for you. Feel this pure energy coursing through your body…as you receive your Divine blessings, sit with that energy. Bask in it. Allow it to bathe your body internally and externally.

8. Now focus on your crown chakra and feel your Divine connection…the aura essence *Guardian Angel* will make this connection very easy for you. Stay with this energy for at least five minutes…allow this consciousness that transcends normal thought and the ordinary senses to begin to take you…beyond space and time… into a state of deeper awareness. This is your link with an unlimited realm of understanding and knowing…you are becoming enlightened…the process of unlocking your enlightenment code has started.

9. It is now time to make full contact with your guardian angel…this initiates the attunement process…your guardian angel is about to activate your angelic chakra.

10. You can feel your guardian angel drawing closer to you…standing before you…from the deepest centre of your beautiful heart chakra send out your longing for your guardian angel to help you in your healing and spiritual development work…really feel your longing going out into the angelic realms of love, light, joy, healing and Divine understanding.

11. Feel your guardian angel drawing closer to you…really feel the change in your energy signature as your guardian approaches…imagine or feel your guardian standing before you…first feel the energy movement…in your third eye chakra…then the fourth eye chakra and then finally in your fifth eye chakra…allow your angelic chakra to be fully activated.

12. You may wish to ask for guidance…or even your angel's name…be still and wait for an answer…if necessary, tell your conscious mind to step aside. Breathe deeply…and allow yourself to relax completely…be aware of any feelings of love…maybe you will see your guardian angel…or experience beautiful colours…or delightful aromas…sacred symbols…you may even feel your guardian's wings as they enfold and cherish you…perhaps you will feel your own wings beginning to grow…you may hear angelic music…or your guardian's name…just be open to the attunement process.

13. When all energy movement has ceased…and the attunement process is complete…give thanks. Always give thanks. Focus on your gratitude towards your guardian angel…do not get caught up in thinking about how wonderful you are because you can do such a thing.

14. Now it is time to come back to everyday waking reality, but before you do…make an appointment to meet your guardian angel again.

15. Allow yourself plenty of time to come back to everyday reality…centre and earth yourself.

16. Keep a written record of the initiation experience. Write it in your angelic journal. Essential knowledge and personal experiences can dissipate like a dream unless they are immediately written down. Include all your experiences, however fragmented, vague or nebulous they

may have seemed to you. Enter fully into the experience with all your faculties: how did it make you feel? What was the most salient, prominent or striking feature of the initiation session? Do not be overly concerned if you cannot fully understand the experience right away; fragmentary information is often referenced again in subsequent meditations with your guardian angel. Some experiences make no sense to you for weeks, months or even years, and so your journal becomes a special way of assimilating understanding. You must record the messages exactly as they were given to you, no editing! If you are more of a pictorial person, you might decide to draw pictures of your experiences, or if you are verbal to record them in spoken form. Never be concerned with your spelling or writing style; allow yourself literary freedom.

17.   Keep your appointment to meet your guardian angel. The more you practise this attunement meditation, the stronger your links will become.

Angel of Light – Archangel Seraphiel – Healing and Angelic Protection

'Angel of Light' aura essence
Angelite, placed on the throat chakra
Aquamarine, placed on the heart chakra
Morganite, placed on the heart chakra
Azeztulite, placed on the third eye chakra
Danburite, placed above the crown chakra
Seraphinite, placed on the witness point (thymus)
Finally 12 clear quartz crystals placed evenly around the body, terminations pointing inwards.

Dedicated to and overshadowed by 'The Angel of Light' (Seraphiel)

Uses: Creates a harmonious, sacred, safe, angelic healing environment. Dynamically clears and releases spaces with built-up negative emotional, psychic and mental energies. Use for healing, angelic attunement, meditation practice and clearing karmic debris or miasms. The essence has also been successfully used for clearing crystals of stagnant energy and clearing homes of geopathic stress and lower astral entities. Lightbearers (those who are on the ascension path) can use it to increase their 'light' quota, thereby raising their vibratory rate. The *Angels of Light* are also known as the **Seraphim**. They are ruled by Archangel Seraphiel, who is dazzling and sometimes called the Prince of Peace, and Archangel Metatron, who presides over Kether on the tree of life.

The Angels of Light bring forward a healing energy known as 'brilliance'…it is pure 'Cosmic Iridescent Rainbow Light' and contains all the colours and 'rays'. The Seraphim, whose essence is perfect love, direct the 'Divine' energy which emanates from the first creative source. Seraphim means 'the inflamer', from the Hebraic root word *saraph*, which means burning. They are the angels of 'Divine' fire. In the Bible they bring a glowing coal to cleanse Isaiah, by placing it on his lips. In that moment he is cleansed of all karma. Seraphim have six wings: two cover their face, two cover their feet and they fly with the other two. It says in Revelation 4.8 that if we call on their power, our being is flooded with infinite love, light, joy and peace. In fact working with the Seraphim is like becoming pure iridescent cosmic light. Enoch, a Hebrew prophet, reported that Seraphiel is the most brilliant of all the angelic beings. We cannot invoke Seraphiel, but we can petition him through quiet contemplation to assist us in finding perfect peace.

The Seraphim assist the Ascended Master Serapis Bey, whose colour is white. His ascension temple of light is Luxor, in Egypt. His specialities are miracles, joy and the path of ascension, by purifying the root chakra with the sacred white crystal light ready for the raising of the sacred mother light which is sealed coiled up at the base of the spine, known as the kundalini. The mother light will, when raised, form the crown. Serapis Bey teaches self-discipline and intense devotion to the presence of God within our everyday lives. Until we feel the presence of God within us, we cannot raise the mother light with safety or ascend.

'Angel of Light' is a combination gemstone essence made for the Angel seminars I have been running since 1990. Very early on I devised a gemstone energy web that would adjust the human energy field to the angelic frequencies. The crystal web allows for easier contact with your guardian angel and other beings from the angelic realm of love, light, wisdom, truth, compassion, discernment and healing. The seminars have always been a huge success and many people have attended and gained insight, protection and healing from the angelic realm. But I still felt something was missing. When people attended the angel seminars they very quickly would adjust their perception to the angelic realms by raising their vibrational rate, but on returning home they would find it more and more difficult to maintain the energy shifts into the higher octaves required for conscious contact with the angelic realm. Slowly their vibrations would return to their previous state. After meditating on this problem I was guided by the *Angel of Light* (Seraphiel) to make a gemstone essence using the crystals from the *'Angel of Light'* energy web. The results have been not only dramatic, but very positive. Initially I just made a gem essence, then the *'Angel of Light'* aura essence was created. Each method brought immediate positive results. These varied from dramatic spontaneous healings to space clearing of negative energies to easily attainable meditative states. The Angel seminars and *'Angel of Light'* essence and aura spray have been featured on television and in the national press, as well as in women's magazines.

Invocation: I invoke the mighty *Angels of Light* to assist me in releasing all negative karma as I now allow angelic healing to manifest in my life.

Physical integration: The purification process is activated, which quickly causes old blocks and stagnant energy to simply dissolve, so that new pristine energy is quickly integrated.

Emotional consolidation: It allows for the joyful release and expression of emotions, which brings balance and stability to the heart chakra: this aligns it with the crown chakra. It therefore aids discrimination of the heart. A flowing healing grace descends, as we truly commit to our highest spiritual purpose this lifetime.

Etheric assimilation: This peaceful, gentle, powerful combination brings in the energies of angels and celestial guardians for healing and purification of the physical, mental, emotional and spiritual bodies.

Process: See the therapy section – **Process** (page 185).

The Seraphim Meditation

The 'Temple of Light' you wish to visit is the retreat centre overseen by the Ascended Master Serapis Bey, whose colour is white. His ascension temple of light is over Luxor in Egypt. His gift is the working of miracles through intense devotion to God. He directs the energy of the Seraphim (the Angels of Light). When you first start the exercise you may want to pre-record the following instructions on tape and hold a crystal, such as seraphinite or danburite.

Mist your aura with *'Angel of Light'* essence – Healing and Angelic Protection.

Get into your chosen position, close your eyes and begin to focus on your breathing: see the section – Breathing, Meditation and Relaxation section on page 129 for preparation details.

Once you are suitably relaxed, call on the Ascended Master Serapis Bey, Archangel Seraphiel and the Seraphim. You can use the word *Namaste* (a greeting of Divine love in *Sanskrit*). So it could be "Namaste Serapis Bey, Archangel Seraphiel and the Seraphim, please fill my body with the cleansing light of God to clear my lower bodies and increase my light quota for healing and spiritual upliftment."

Just relax and let yourself be enveloped in the power and energy of the Seraphim. You can stay basking in this energy as long as you like; when you are ready, allow yourself to be raised upwards on a spiral of light. Slowly the white light spiral raises you higher and higher and you feel yourself held perfectly safely in angelic arms. You feel yourself transported very safely to the temple of light.

You will find yourself in the ascension temple of light at Luxor, eastern Thebes, in Egypt…here you will find the etheric retreat as it is superimposed etherically over the physical temple…you will be guided along sparkling crystalline corridors until you reach the room of immortality…you will see a circle of diamond white crystal light in front of you…in the centre of this is a white lily of purity…in the very centre of this is a white pearl of utmost purity and perfection…the pearl's soft glow is impeccable, reminding you of the purpose of this lifetime…to become as clear as crystal and pure as a pearl. You will be approached by Archangel Seraphiel or one of the Seraphim or another angelic helper or even by Serapis Bey or one of his 144 master tutors…you will be asked what is the purpose of this visit…you will then state your purpose…you may wish for healing, or a raising of your vibrational rate, or you may wish to start the initiation process of the thirty-three initiations, which activates the nine gifts (siddhis), the highest of which is ascension…you may even witness another initiate, who has fulfilled all the initiations, ascending…as the twin flames of Alpha and Omega transform the initiate's being into an ascended master. The Alpha flame is white and descends from above…the Omega flame is crystal white and rises from below. Whatever happens to you…just allow the process to happen…you have chosen to visit the Seraphim for whatever purpose from a higher level of your being…enjoy the experience…

The Seraphim will let you know when it is time to leave and bring you safely back into your body, to the here and now. Give thanks and write down your experiences.

Archangel Sandalphon's Presence – Guardian of the Earth

'Archangel Sandalphon' aura essence
Black Druzy Quartz, placed at the earth star chakra
Ruby (faceted), placed between the feet
Red Beryl, placed between the knees for the root chakra
Vanadinite, placed on the sacral chakra
Spanish Red Quartz, placed on the hara point
Yellow Sapphire (faceted), placed on the solar plexus chakra
Cinnabar, placed on the heart chakra
Rainbow-coated Golden Labradorite (faceted), placed on the throat chakra
Goethite in Amethyst, placed on the third eye chakra
El Chorro Azeztulite, placed on the crown chakra
12 clear quartz crystals placed evenly around the body, terminations pointing inwards.

Dedicated to and overshadowed by Archangel Sandalphon

Uses: Archangel Sandalphon is the guardian of the Earth. On the Tree of Life configuration he rules over *Malkuth*, the Kingdom. Sandalphon is in charge of earth healing and planetary group work, by uniting heaven and earth. By way of holding the Divine presence on planet earth, Sandalphon teaches us to have a grounded reality and balanced spirituality. He is considered a very 'big' Angel and Archangel Metatron's twin reflection of the Divine. As twins they are the Alpha and Omega, the beginning and the end: their presence also reminds us of the esoteric expression "as above so below". There is an ancient tradition that Sandalphon once took human form as the prophet Elijah, just as Metatron was once the prophet Enoch. Sandalphon's presence is always in the Kingdom (the Earth plane) and he does not move between the planes of existence, for he is so vast or tall that his energy spans all levels of the Tree of Life. In the Talmud it states 'Sandalphon's head reaches heaven'. Moses described him as being the 'tall Angel'. His temple of light is over Southern Spain. Sandalphon resonates with all colours: when you think of the fabulous gemstones and crystals, Sandalphon is there; when you think of the vast variety of flowers and trees, he is there; in fact he is in every molecule and atom. His presence reminds us that everything is sacred, everything is God. We are not separate from God, it is only an illusion of our small egos that makes us feel separate from God.

My personal experiences of Sandalphon have been awe-inspiring as I encountered this Divine manifestation of the messenger of the God force. I remember the first time I was approached directly by Sandalphon in his Archangelic form it was surrealistic: all I could see were his sandalled feet and the brown sandals had sunflowers on! His presence towered above me, beyond anything I could fully see…I just experienced the most amazing energy which has remained with me ever since. One detail I did sense was that his presence felt feminine, which at the time fascinated me, as I was aware of who 'he' was. I think I was captured by the sheer beauty, love and pure rapture of Sandalphon and his flowery sandals, for he has led me a joyful dance around this planet and all planes of existence. Sandalphon fascinates me every hour of the day, every step of the way; he has taught me the beauty in everything and everyone.

His essence also balances the male aspect of the personality. It brings warmth and self-confidence leading to unprecedented spiritual growth. Sandalphon helps you to develop compassion, which can then be radiated outwards to others. On a deeper level the essence helps you to understand your aversion to authority figures and those who try to control and manipulate your personal energy field. For planetary healing it helps you to understand and combat the ego-centred male-dominated aggression which is rampant on the planet at the moment. It teaches the correct integration of the solar plexus chakra with the heart chakra to soften the emotions.

At present humanity is undergoing an intense spiritual transformation; we are about to make an evolutionary leap. This mass mystical awakening is unprecedented in the history of the earth. We are each required to align all our bodies, from the gross physical to the highest spiritual levels, as we ignite the Divine flame in our hearts. We are each required to birth ourselves into light – this means we must anchor our Light Bodies on planet earth. This process is being initiated by Archangel Sandalphon, in his female aspect of Earth Mother, and his twin Archangel Metatron. As we anchor our Light Bodies on the earth plane we will allow millions of others to awaken and align too. The following web of light and the Archangel Sandalphon essence, plus his temple meditation, will activate the process of igniting the Divine flame in your heart. This allows the birth of your light body, which – when fully activated and eventually grounded – will allow you full access to all levels and planes of existence.

Invocation: Archangel Sandalphon, guardian of planet Earth and holder of the sacred presence, please activate and support the pranic life force available to me. Help me to reclaim my soul mandala and original genetic blueprint and to activate latent DNA strands. Teach me through conscious evolution to be able to reclaim and balance my personal and sexual power through the integration of karmic lessons and clearing miasms that may have lodged in my root and sacral chakras. Help me to view and remove curses, psychic hooks, negative entities, negative entity thought forms, misqualified human projection, misqualified astral projection, implants and ghost prints. Begin the process of activating, birthing and anchoring my Light Body on to planet earth. Ignite the Divine flame in my heart to facilitate the descent of Divine grace into my heart chakra.

Physical integration: Instantly increases prana, which aids vitality and brings mental clarity. Overall personal creativity is greatly enhanced. Clears blocks in the meridian system and helps the full integration of prana: this ensures the correction has not only been fully assimilated into the meridian system, but the body has stabilized to a balanced sustainable level.

Emotional consolidation: Helps instill emotional maturity by assisting you to rise above the mundane world and see through the veils of illusion into the heart of the matter. It strengthens the heart chakra and allows for the downflow of energy known as Divine grace.

Etheric assimilation: Activates the process of igniting the Divine flame in your heart. This allows the birth of your light body, which, when fully activated and eventually grounded, will allow you full access to all levels and planes of existence.

Process: See the therapy section – **Process** (page 185).

Archangel Sandalphon's Temple of Light Meditation

The 'Temple of Light' you wish to visit is the retreat centre of Archangel Sandalphon. His ascension temple of light is over El Chorro National Park in Southern Spain. When you first start the exercise you may want to pre-record the following instructions on tape and hold a crystal, such as El Chorro azeztulite. Mist your aura with *'Archangel Sandalphon's Presence – Guardian of the Earth'* essence.

Get into your chosen position, close your eyes and begin to focus on your breathing: see the section – Breathing, Meditation and Relaxation section on page 129 for preparation details.

Once you are suitably relaxed, call on *Archangel Sandalphon* – use the invocation. "Archangel Sandalphon, guardian of planet Earth and holder of the sacred presence, please activate and support the pranic life force available to me. Help me to reclaim my original soul mandala and original genetic blueprint and to activate latent DNA strands. Teach me through conscious evolution to be able to reclaim and balance my personal and sexual power through the integration of karmic lessons and clearing miasms that may have lodged in my root and sacral chakras. Help me to view and remove curses, psychic hooks, negative entities, negative entity thought forms, misqualified human projection, misqualified astral projection, implants and ghost prints. Begin the process of activating, birthing and anchoring my Light Body on to planet earth. Ignite the Divine flame in my heart to facilitate the descent of Divine grace into my heart chakra.

Just relax and let yourself be enveloped in the power and energy of the Archangel Sandalphon. You can stay basking in this energy as long as you like; when you are ready, allow yourself to be raised upwards on a spiral of rainbow light. Slowly the light spiral raises you higher and higher, you feel yourself held perfectly safely in Angelic arms and you feel yourself transported very gently to the temple of light.

You will find yourself in the ascension temple of light at El Chorro, Southern Spain…here you will find the etheric retreat as it is superimposed etherically over the physical mountain of El Chorro…you will be guided along sparkling crystalline corridors until you reach the room of Purity…you will see a circle of ruby crystal-light in front of you…in the centre of this is a white lily of perfection…in the very centre of this is a faceted ruby crystal of flame red. In the ancient language of Sanskrit, ruby is called ratnaraj – king of precious stones – for they ascribed magical powers to these 'inner fires' that burned eternally… this clean, pure, pristine form of ruby will spiritually transfigure devotion into Divine love…the Cosmic Christ energy. You will be approached by Archangel Sandalphon or another angelic helper or even by one of his 144 master tutors…you will be asked what is the purpose of this visit…you will then state your purpose…you could ask for prana activation…or to reclaim your original soul mandala, your original genetic blueprint and to activate latent DNA strands…or help in removing curses, psychic hooks, negative entities, negative entity thought forms, misqualified human projection, misqualified astral projection, implants and ghost prints…or activation, birthing and anchoring your Light Body on to planet earth. Whatever happens to you…just allow the process to happen…you have chosen to visit the Archangel Sandalphon for whatever purpose from a higher level of your being…enjoy the experience…Archangel Sandalphon will let you know when it is time to leave and bring you safely back into your body, to the here and now.

Archangel Uriel's Initiation – Angelic Peace

'Archangel Uriel's Initiation' aura essence
Black Kyanite, placed beneath the feet in the earth star chakra
Rainbow-coated Golden Labradorite, placed on the third eye chakra
Malachite, placed on the solar plexus chakra
Opal, placed in the soul star chakra
Phenacite, placed in the crown chakra
Ruby in Zoisite, placed on the heart chakra
12 clear quartz crystals placed evenly around the body, terminations pointing inwards

Dedicated to and overshadowed by Archangel Uriel

Uses: Uriel is the Archangel for emotional harmony and mental clarity. He saves us from confusion and bestows infinite inner peace. Uriel's name means the 'Fire of God' or 'Light of God'. Archangel Uriel is the light of God that never fails. His task is to bring the light of the knowledge of God to men. In our personal search for angelic help, Archangel Uriel is our salvation: he reconnects us to the Divine and this gives us hope. He carries a staff to use as support. This gives us an indication as to how his energy works: he always gives us unconditional support on all levels. The staff also represents our spinal column, which reflects on our personal issues of support and feelings of not being supported in family, work, society, etc. The staff symbolically represents structure and balance and our ability to live harmoniously on the planet in the physical form. If our spinal column is not balanced and all the chakra centres embedded in it – our 'I AM' column (the spiritual spine) – are not functioning harmoniously together, we will not be able to support ourselves (or anyone else). He teaches world service: in fact one of his main themes is how we can, as individualised aspects of the Divine God-force, be of service (or support) to all the other aspects of the God-force living on the planet. Before we can truly support others unconditionally we have to clear ourselves of all ego-centred fear and anger, otherwise we will be judgemental of others and their own particular path. We must never judge others, as each soul incarnate has its own personal karmic lessons to undergo. Therefore Archangel Uriel brings peace and wisdom to our 'Earth walk' and illuminates our 'path through life'. This is because Archangel Uriel has an intense connection to the Earth and consequently our root chakra.

The light of God, transmitted by Uriel, gives us illumination. This crystal web is vital for those who feel they have lost their 'way', so it should be used whenever we feel lost, abandoned, fearful, forsaken, rejected, dissipated or even suicidal. Once we have found our 'way', our life is peaceful and filled with harmony. It can also be used to find our true path in life... our *Dharma*. We are all born with a special 'gift'...this is our reason for incarnating. Each being on the planet has a special 'place' in the scheme of the world and the Earth's evolution, as well as the whole of the human race's evolution. Very often we do not find our 'gift' or special purpose; this is because we may have blocked it in early childhood, due to parental influences or social conditioning.

Archangel Uriel urges us to listen to the wisdom of the body; this will integrate our body, mind, heart and soul. This integration always brings healing on all levels. He helps us to interpret prophecies, visions and our own prophetic dreams. His temple of light is over the Tatra mountains of Poland. Uriel is associated with the colour red, but this red can be the deep purple-red of fine rubies and Uriel's energy signature often has golden or silver glints contained within it. On the Tree of Life configuration he is located in *Malkuth*, the Kingdom.

Archangel Auriel represents the feminine aspect of Archangel Uriel – the moon – helping us to reflect on our issues of living on the physical plane of human existence. Auriel teaches us that all humanity is just a mirror of the self. She helps us to understand the deep subconscious, the hidden, the lost or forbidden. In traditional Hindu folklore, the kundalini energy is always portrayed as a feminine goddess and to awaken this latent power of the kundalini is definitely to awaken a feminine force. If you find that you are afraid of the mysterious, feminine, yin dimension of your personal energy system, then you will need to spend a lot of time learning to 'surrender' to your higher spiritual nature. In the Christian terminology it can be thought of as "Thy will be done", not my will. So to find your true path in life and your special gift for humanity you need to surrender to the God-force and allow this Divine power to flow through you. Only then can you truly know peace and work with the Angels of Peace...these are the legions of angels that Archangel Uriel commands. When you work with the peace vibration and allow this energy to flow through you with compassion, you will become a force for good, a force that can stop wars, end hunger and facilitate the birth of the age of enlightenment.

My personal visions of Archangel Uriel have always been supportive, especially when I have been beset by a multitude of obstacles and the tasks I have been given seem overwhelming and I cannot, with my logical mind, find a solution. He appears...vast white feather wings, dark hair, dark eyes aflame with the light of God. He commands respect by his very presence and peaceful disposition (although he often has a playful smile very much like the His Holiness the Dalai Lama). He always reminds me to 'let go and let God'... as soon as I surrender, all obstacles vanish as the mere illusion they are and I am able once more to fulfil my Dharma.

Invocation: Archangel Uriel, bring peace to my troubled mind and spirit. Reveal to me that which is true. Dissolve all obstacles on my spiritual path. Resolve all my hidden issues. Cleanse my body and mind to allow the power of peace to flow through me. Make me a pure channel of God's infinite peace. Show me my true path in life so I can fulfil my *Dharma*.

Physical integration: Aligns all the chakras of the central 'I AM' column (the spiritual spine) to bring harmony and balance on all levels.

Emotional consolidation: Harmony and peace are restored as all ego-centred fear and anger are released. Unconditional acceptance of other sentient beings is activated, as well as the ability to show compassion. Dream recall and interpretation are greatly enhanced.

Etheric assimilation: The soul star chakra is especially energised into full alignment with the higher self. Contact with Ascended Masters and Angelic guides is initiated. The light body is activated and assistance is given to consciously experience one's existence in higher dimensions.

Process: See the therapy section – **Process** (page 185).

Archangel Uriel Temple Meditation

The 'Temple of Light' you wish to visit is the retreat centre of Archangel Uriel. His ascension temple of light is over the Tatra mountains of Poland. When you first start the exercise you may want to pre-record the following instructions on tape and hold a crystal, such as phenacite or opal.

Mist your aura with *'Archangel Uriel's Initiation – Angelic Peace'* essence.

Get into your chosen position, close your eyes and begin to focus on your breathing: see the section – Breathing, Meditation and Relaxation section on page 129 for preparation details.

Once you are suitably relaxed, call on *Archangel Uriel* – use the invocation. "Archangel Uriel bring peace to my troubled mind and spirit. Reveal to me that which is true. Dissolve all obstacles on my spiritual path. Resolve all my hidden issues. Cleanse my body and mind to allow the power of peace to flow through me. Make me a pure channel of God's infinite peace. Show me my true path in life so I can fulfil my *Dharma*".

Just relax and let yourself be enveloped in the power and energy of the Archangel Uriel and his legions of angels of peace. You can stay basking in this energy as long as you like; when you are ready, allow yourself to be raised upwards on a spiral of ruby-gold light.

Slowly the light spiral raises you higher and higher, you feel yourself held perfectly safely in Angelic arms. You feel yourself transported very gently to the temple of light.

You will find yourself in the temple of light that is over the Tatra mountains of Poland. Here you will find the etheric retreat as it is superimposed etherically over the physical Tatra mountains…you will be guided along sparkling crystalline corridors until you reach the room of Peace…you will see a circle of ruby-gold crystal light in front of you…in the centre of this is a white lily of infinite peace…in the very centre of this is a beautiful rainbow opal, flashing the fire of fine rubies, brilliant amethyst, sea green emerald and sky blue sapphire, all shining together in incredible dazzling union.

A vision arises from the opal…it is a tree…around it are wound the coils of anger, hatred, misqualified desire and illusion that you have allowed to coil around you…these coils are bound very tightly around your being…they stop you from finding peace and blossoming into the infinite being of light and compassion you truly are…you know these coils must be released…your energy must be freed, you must expand your being…your soul is being stifled…as you watch the vision you begin to see the coils loosen, spring forth and fall away…you see the tree burst into a golden flame…as you gaze a little longer you see it is really blossom…ready to bear fruit. Now you will be approached by Archangel Uriel or one of his angels of peace or even by one of his 144 master tutors…you will be asked if you wish to visit the 'Scroll room'…here are stored billions of scrolls, one for each person incarnate on the planet…your scroll is here in this room…it is written in the language of light…it contains your *Dharma*…your soul agreement…your 'gift' to humanity. This agreement was made before you were born…at a higher level of your being…this is your true path in life. If you choose to see your scroll it will be handed to you with great reverence…it is up to you if you choose to open it or read it…whatever happens to you…just allow the process to happen…you have chosen to visit the Archangel Uriel for whatever purpose from a higher level of your being…enjoy the experience.

The Archangel Uriel will let you know when it is time to leave and bring you safely back into your body to the here and now.

Give thanks and write down your experiences.

Please note: Often when I use this meditation on my angel seminars to visit the scroll room of Archangel Uriel the following happens:

Some people who visit the scroll room are overawed by the experience and cannot open the scroll.

Sometimes they are not ready to read the scroll and it appears blank.

Sometimes they are not ready to understand the Angel script, the *'language of light'*, and can make no sense of the symbols as they appear on the scroll…you can only read the Angel script with your heart.

Sometimes they only get the first line – although on subsequent meditations more lines are revealed. This usually means that their task would appear too big for them and they are not quite ready to undertake it…yet.

The very fact that the participants on the Angel seminars have been in the presence of Archangel Uriel and actually visited the scroll room will cause major shifts in their awareness. I always tell them not to worry overmuch and to just try again later. I also instruct these people to work with clearing themselves of stagnant energy and with going deeper into the energy of surrendering themselves to God. In the Christian terminology it can be thought of as "Thy will be done", not my will. So to find your true path in life and your special gift for humanity, you need to surrender to the God-force and allow this Divine power to flow through you; only then can you truly know peace and work with the Angels of Peace…these are the legions of angels that Archangel Uriel commands.

Archangel Gabriel's Call – Angelic Guidance

'Archangel Gabriel's Call – Angelic Guidance' essence
Alexandrite, placed on the third eye chakra
Amethyst, placed in both palm chakras
Danburite, placed above the head in the crown chakra
Moldavite, placed on the heart chakra
Phenacite, placed in the soul star chakra
Ruby, placed in the earth star chakra
12 clear quartz crystals placed evenly around the body, terminations pointing inwards.

Dedicated to and overshadowed by Archangel Gabriel

Uses: Awaken your 'Inner Angel' and transform your mind to receive Archangel Gabriel's gifts of hope, happiness, love, angelic guidance and etheric celestial wings. When Gabriel sounds his call you will hear it. This crystal web of light and companion aura essence are specifically designed by beloved Archangel Gabriel to create a vortex of energy that will transform your life into a joyful Angelic experience. Gabriel is the Archangel for dissolving fear and guiding us through life changes. He also awakens us by igniting the Divine flame that dwells in each and every one of us. Gabriel's name means 'God is my strength'. Muslims say Archangel Gabriel dictated the Koran to the prophets of God. Gabriel is very well-known in Christianity too: he announced the forthcoming birth of Jesus, the Christ child, to Mary his mother and Gabriel was there at Jesus's death as the

Angel who watched over the tomb and gave the good news of his resurrection to the disciples (although he is not specifically mentioned by name). It is said Joan of Arc was also inspired by Gabriel. His beautiful temple of light is over Mount Shasta in California; you may have visited it often in your dream state, I know I have.

Gabriel's colour is white, so if you suddenly feel yourself guided to wearing white and purifying your life on all levels it is his Divine inspiration. He carries a golden trumpet to awaken your inner Angel and bring good news. *Yesod* or Foundation is ruled over by Archangel Gabriel. He is sometimes known as the angel of the moon and in this female watery reflective aspect he helps you to interpret your dreams and visions. His energy is intense, however it is also joyful, jubilant, optimistic, light and bubbly. He is the 'Lord of the Dance' – the cosmic dance of creation. He teaches us the virtue of wakefulness. Before we can move into the energy of enlightened love, we must let go of the energy of fear. Before we can start to ascend towards enlightenment we must let go of negative thought-forms and unfulfilled wishes that will have dragged our energy down. Archangel Gabriel will help you clear old karmic debris, stagnation and fear-based blocks within your energy system. Do you dread change, are you fearful, does the thought of death or the death of a loved one fill you with terror? Would you like someone to always be there with you, someone who is always on your side, someone who is always positive and optimistic – then involve Archangel Gabriel consciously in your life. I can guarantee from direct personal experience that your life will never be the same again…Gabriel will comfort and inspire you. He will fill your life with intense wonder and creative joy…each day will be a positive enjoyable experience, he will give your heart wings. You have only your own ignorance to blame if you choose not to work with this mighty Archangel. But it does not matter if you choose to ignore this message…Gabriel will wait…he will always be there for you…whenever you are ready…even at the moment of your death…and beyond…because to him eternity is but the mere blink of an eye.

Invocation: Beloved Archangel Gabriel, it is my true heartfelt desire to become more than human. Please raise my vibration by awakening my inner angel and guide me on my journey home on wings of infinite love, light and Divine joy.

Physical integration: Healing and alignment of the whole body systems, including the skeletal structure. The internal organs are cleansed, toned and given a 'spring clean'.

Emotional consolidation: Integration of the emotional, mental and spiritual bodies, bringing Divine creativity. The aura is cleansed and purified of old negative emotional debris and unfulfilled wishes that no longer serve your higher soul purpose.

Etheric assimilation: A vortex of energy is created within, above and around the body, bodies and aura…which allows for a massive shift in vibrational alignment. This alignment to the Angelic domain instigates unprecedented joy and spiritual growth. It truly is a wake-up call!

Process: See the therapy section – **Process** (page 185).

Archangel Gabriel Temple Meditation

The 'Temple of Light' you wish to visit is the retreat centre of Archangel Gabriel. His ascension temple of light is over Mount Shasta in California. When you first start the exercise you may want to pre-record the following instructions on tape and hold a crystal, such as amethyst, ruby or danburite.

Mist your aura with *'Archangel Gabriel's Call – Angelic Guidance'* essence.

Get into your chosen position, close your eyes and begin to focus on your breathing: see the section – Breathing, Meditation and Relaxation section on page 129 for preparation details.

Once you are suitably relaxed, call on Gabriel – use the invocation "Beloved Archangel Gabriel, it is my true heartfelt desire to become more than human. Please raise my vibration by awakening my inner angel and guide me on my journey home on wings of infinite love, light and Divine joy".

Just relax and let yourself be enveloped in the power and energy of the Archangel Gabriel and his legions of angels of refinement. You can stay basking in this energy as long as you like; when you are ready, allow yourself to be raised upwards on a spiral of pure white light. Slowly the light spiral raises you higher and higher; you feel yourself held perfectly safely in Angelic arms. You feel yourself transported very gently to the temple of light.

You will find yourself in the ascension temple of light that is over Mount Shasta in California. You will be guided along sparkling danburite crystalline corridors until you reach the room of activation of angelic wings…you will see a circle of white crystal light in front of you…in the centre of this is a lily carved out of pure crystal…in the very centre of this is an alexandrite…its vortex energy will awaken your inner angel which resides within your heart…by igniting the Divine flame.

You will be approached by beloved Archangel Gabriel…you will be asked what is the purpose of this visit…you will then state your purpose…you will ask for purification so you can have the Divine flame in your heart chakra ignited…this activation will allow your etheric angelic wings to manifest…you will be instructed to gaze at the faceted alexandrite vortex crystal…as you do so, a vision of the most wonderful angelic wings appears…they are amazing…they are the most exquisite wings you have ever seen…they are everything you find beautiful…as you gaze at them you are aware of a sensation on your spine…just between your physical shoulder-blades…you realise the wings you have just seen are in reality your wings…you feel them anchored on to your etheric body…just allow the wings to spread out fully…feel how well they fit you…allow your body time to adjust to the sensation of having wings.

Two angels approach you…they take hold of your hands…and you begin to fly with them…you fly out into the blue sky…then higher and higher…until you no longer need their support…allow yourself to fly free…fly up towards the stars…out into the universe…feel the freedom that is yours when you allow yourself to become angelic…enjoy the experience…you will eventually be approached once more by Archangel Gabriel, who will gently guide you back into your physical body, to the here and now. Give thanks and write down your experiences.

Use this meditation often…allow Archangel Gabriel to guide you on your journey home on wings of infinite love, light and Divine joy.

Archangel Michael's Empowerment – Angelic Protection

'Archangel Michael's Empowerment – Angelic Protection' essence
Blue Kyanite, placed in the crown chakra
Lapis, placed one in each hand, one on the throat chakra, and one in the earth star chakra
Phenacite, placed in the soul star chakra
Pyrite, placed in the earth star chakra, above the lapis
Rutile Quartz, placed on the hara
Blue Topaz, placed on the third eye chakra
12 clear quartz crystals placed evenly around the body, terminations pointing inwards.

Dedicated to and overshadowed by Archangel Michael

Uses: Mighty Archangel Michael is the protector of humanity: call on him for protection, strength, fearlessness, cutting cords that bind your soul, and Angelic empowerment. Archangel Michael's name means 'Who can stand against God'. Michael is the supreme incorruptible commander-in-chief of all the Archangels and he leads the heavenly forces, his 'legions of light', against evil (the human vices of anger, hatred, negativity, cruelty, hostility and conflict). Michael can appear simultaneously in three of the seven heavens. *Hod* – or, as it is sometimes interpreted in English, Splendour or Glory or Majesty or Honour – is Archangel Michael's domain on the Tree of Life. Islamic, Jewish and Christian holy scriptures all venerate Archangel Michael. His etheric temple is anchored over Banff, near Lake Louise, in Canada. His main colour is yellow, in fact the fiery power of the solar plexus is his domain, but because he carries a sword made of a sapphire blue flame he is often associated with the empowerment and development of the throat chakra and the colour blue. The sapphire blue ray represents the power and will of God, as well as the powers of faith, protection and truth. Electric blue is the transmuting ray for the throat chakra.

Archangel Michael says…you all have free will, you can choose a life-path of fear and restriction or a life-path of joy and freedom. Many people on the earth plane have the restriction of multiple fears, some founded and some unfounded. Fear is almost always used as a controlling 'tool' by those who want to have authority over you. You even choose sometimes to bind yourself with fears and phobias. This web of light helps you to confront your fears, phobias and terrors. This is accomplished lovingly with the help and Angelic protection of Archangel Michael and his 'legions of light'. It gives you freedom from the nagging fear of self-doubt; it strengthens your faith, brings inner strength and courage. It strengthens the immune and meridian systems and activates the *Hara* centre.

The Hara is not a traditional chakra centre in the Hindu system; in fact the word comes from the Japanese language and relates to a very powerful important centre. The Hara is located three finger-widths below the navel. You may have heard of the word Hara before, as in the Japanese ritual suicide hara kiri! When the Hara centre is damaged or breached, the life force is released very quickly. The Hara is vitally important in both men and women It deals with issues of stability, stamina, personal life force and healthy boundaries. It also plays a very direct role in creativity, joy and abundance.

This web of light will also bring immediate practical assistance, giving you a mantle of protection from physical and spiritual dangers. This web of light will bring you Archangel Michael's empowerment, if you should choose to be a sword-bearer of the legion of light. Since 1991, I have been teaching the meditation you will find at the end of this chapter. You can ask for this empowerment whilst you are in the web specifically created by Archangel Michael.

Archangel Michael has played a major role in my life so many times that to recount all the stories would take a book in itself. I suppose you could say I live dangerously! When you imagine all the tasks I have undertaken to facilitate the empowerment of others to 'heal' themselves by opening up to the infinite power of the God-force and releasing those souls who have attracted negative situations to themselves in the form of illness, negative energy, negative entities, psychic attack, physical attack or even full-blown possession by entities created by those who seek to control and manipulate others for their own selfish purposes and gain, these tasks I have been given have sometimes seemed beyond belief. And I might add I did not choose this work, but in my daily practice as a qualified vibrational therapist I attracted those souls who needed help. One of my 'Archangel Michael experiences' has been featured in Glennyce Eckersley's best-selling book 'Angel at my Shoulder'.

The story I would like to share with you about Archangel Michael and his 'legions of light' shows how they work constantly to give protection in the most intensely dangerous life-threatening situations. Early in 1996 I was in my metaphysical centre called Gaia, in the Corn Exchange in Manchester, when I was given the message by Archangel Michael "something BIG was about to go down" (these words were very specific). I could also feel an energy surrounding the BIG that I could only describe as pure malevolence. I was not the only one to feel this energy, in fact one of my staff also got the same message. As we spoke about it we could not actually discern what 'it' was, other than it was very BIG. As the months went by I could feel the tentacles of evil reaching closer, but still I was not sure what it was. I was told, though, to relocate my shop to another part of Manchester, which seemed ridiculous considering it had taken me seven years to build up a wonderful centre and loyal customer base. On Saturday the 9th of June I was told by Archangel Michael to put protection around Manchester, especially the Corn Exchange building and all the surrounding area. The instructions were very specific and so were the words I had to use and the visualisation I had to hold in my mind. I had to put my hands on to the buildings and say "walls protect me", then put my hands on the windows and say "glass protect me". I then had to put my hands in the air and feel the element of air and say "air protect me"…all the time visualising I was 'everyone'…the 'me' was the All, in fact everyone who would be there…but there for what? On the evening of the 15th of June I was given another message "You are not karmically obliged to be there and we cannot guarantee your physical safety…your physical body may die. You may choose to cancel the crystal therapy course this weekend and keep the metaphysical centre closed, but if you are there it will allow Archangel Michael and his 'legions of light' to bring about a better result". I was at a loss what to do. It seemed impossible that anything that bad could happen and it was the students' final first-year exam weekend. I could just imagine phoning everyone and telling them it was cancelled, especially after all the revision they had all undertaken, not to mention pre-exam nerves. I wondered if I should phone the 'authorities' and tell them…but tell who what? That something BIG was about to go down? I could just imagine them taking me seriously, or anyone else for that matter; in the mid-nineties, being a vibrational therapist had no credibility.

The next morning, Saturday the 16th of June, I set off for the Mitre Hotel, which was near the Corn Exchange. This is where I operated the crystal course. With great foreboding, but drawing on my total faith in God, I found the words from the 23rd Psalm brought peace to my troubled heart and my mind "Yea, though I walk through the valley of the shadow of death, I will fear no evil: for thou art with me; thy rod and thy staff they comfort me". As I arrived at the Mitre Hotel the malevolent energy was tangible; I could see a thick, grey entity fog settled over the area. It was full of hatred, of entity souls twisting and writhing in pure hatred and spitting venom. I started to unload my car and get all the crystal resources into the Mitre. Some of the students started arriving and we were setting up the room when a policeman arrived and said there was a bomb scare, we must leave everything and immediately evacuate the building. We quickly left the building, telling everyone in our path that there was a bomb scare and to turn around, to go back. It was a very hot sunny day and I went towards the train station, which had not been evacuated, to buy some water for myself and the students. While I was in Victoria train station (which had a glass ceiling) the bomb went off and one and a half tons of explosives were unleashed on Manchester, near the Corn Exchange…80,000 lives were put at risk, 200 people injured, £700 million pounds worth of damage done. But no-one was killed, which was a miracle! The blast threw me out of my body, as my physical body was lifted up in the air and thrown about. Glass rained down on me (and everyone else who was in the train station)…the tiled floor was covered in a thick layer of black bomb dust, which made it as slippy as ice. Everyone was in shock, but the amazing thing was that I did not have a scratch on me. Of course my metaphysical centre was destroyed, as was the heart of Manchester…it was literally down. The room in the Mitre Hotel was destroyed too. If we had been in that room we would all have been killed. Did Archangel Michael and his 'legions of light' make a difference to the outcome? Considering the miracle that no-one was killed, I personally know he did.

Invocation One: Mighty Archangel Michael empower me. I acknowledge I have free will, so I now choose a life-path of joy and freedom. I ask that this is done lovingly with the help and protection of your 'legions of light'. I call on you now in my hour of need for total protection, strength, fearlessness and cutting the cords that bind my soul in ignorance. Give me freedom from the fear of self-doubt, reinforce my faith, bring inner strength and outer courage. Energize and support my immune and meridian systems and activate my *Hara* centre to give me radiant health.

Invocation Two: Mighty Archangel Michael empower me. I acknowledge I have free will, so I now choose a life-path of joy and freedom. If it is appropriate to my spiritual path, allow me to join your legions of light and become one of the family of light bearers. Give me my sword of freedom. I promise to use it only for the highest good of all and never to infringe on others' free will knowingly.

Physical integration: The immune and meridian systems are strengthened for general healing of the physical body. Protection of the physical body is instantly activated. Psychic aggression and projection is stopped from interfering with your personal energy field.

Emotional consolidation: Upliftment! Personal power is activated, so it helps you feel empowered and truly guided. This helps you make up your mind and heart. It clears the mind and mental body and this stabilizes the emotional body.

Etheric assimilation: What is your greatest fear? Name it…call it…you can face it. You are an eternal being of infinite love and light…you have nothing to fear but fear itself and you have gifted yourself your fear…only you can now empower yourself to release it…with the loving support of Archangel Michael and his legions of light.

Process: See the therapy section – **Process** (page 185).

Archangel Michael Temple Meditation

The 'Temple of Light' you wish to visit is the retreat centre of Archangel Michael. His ascension temple of light is at Banff, near Lake Louise, in Canada. When you first start the exercise you may want to pre-record the following instructions on tape and hold a crystal, such as blue topaz, kyanite or lapis.

Mist your aura with *'Archangel Michael's Empowerment – Angelic Protection'* essence.

Get into your chosen position, close your eyes and begin to focus on your breathing: see the section – Breathing, Meditation and Relaxation section on page 129 for preparation details.

Once you are suitably relaxed, call on Michael – use the invocation "Mighty Archangel Michael empower me. I acknowledge I have free will, so I now choose a life-path of joy and freedom. If it is appropriate to my spiritual path, allow me to join your legions of light and become one of the family of light bearers. Give me my sword of freedom. I promise to use it only for the highest good of all and never to infringe on others' free will knowingly".

Just relax and let yourself be enveloped in the power and energy of the Archangel Michael and his legions of light. You can stay basking in this energy as long as you like; when you are ready, allow yourself to be raised upwards on a spiral of pure white light. Slowly the light spiral raises you higher and higher; you feel yourself held perfectly safely in Angelic arms. You feel yourself transported very gently to the temple of light.

You will find yourself in the ascension temple of light that is over Banff, near Lake Louise, in Canada. You will be guided along glittering blue topaz corridors with lapis floors until you reach the door of the sword room. Here you will be approached by mighty Archangel Michael and you will be asked what is the purpose of this visit…you will then state your purpose…you wish your sword of freedom. Archangel Michael will take you inside the sword room; there you will see rows and rows of swords; each is already assigned to one of those who are meant to be light sword bearers. These are the ones who agreed to carry the sapphire blue flame of freedom. Each sword is very different in appearance, just as each being on the planet is an individual. But each sword is identical too in respect of the authority it carries, in bringing freedom and protection. Archangel Michael will hand you your sword: on it will be written in the 'language of light' the name of your sword. He will also give you the authority to use it. You will be given also a special secret symbol that will be placed within your energy field; this 'crystalline' symbol has to be always in balance in your energy field, otherwise your sword will be rendered useless. This is a 'fail safe' device that stops you harming others and incurring a karmic debt when you go out of balance. This is not a judgement on you, it is for your own safety and the safety of all that lives. When you are in balance you are a force for good and will be able to have the full weight of the legions of light behind you in all your positive endeavours. You will become invincible and one day gain enlightenment to join all the other enlightened souls who are here to help all sentient life return home to the one heart of God.

Archangel Michael will let you stay in the sword room as long as you need to. It is a very special moment on your evolutionary path. When you are ready, Archangel Michael will gently guide you back into your physical body, to the here and now. Give thanks and write down your experiences.

Use this meditation often…allow Archangel Michael to instruct you on your path home as you meet more and more of the other 'light bearers'. You will also be able to instantly recognise the others of Michael's legions of light on not only the earth plane but all those who dwell in other dimensions and worlds too. You will see the crystalline symbol within their aura. You will also be able to recognise when they are in balance, too, by the appearance of the symbol within the aura.

Please note: Often when I use this meditation on my angel seminars to visit the sword room of Archangel Michael the following happens:

Some people who visit the sword room are overawed by the experience and cannot be given a sword…are you ready for your sword or do you need to perform some more 'clearing' work on yourself?

You cannot read what is written on your sword.

Sometimes you are not *ready* to understand the Angel script, the *'language of light'*, and can make no sense of the symbols as they appear on the sword…you can only read the Angel script with your heart. You will have to develop faith in God.

You do not have the crystalline symbol placed within your auric shell…you are not ready, then, to use your sword. Have faith and practise this meditation again.

Or you are uncertain of the secret crystalline symbol. Have faith and practise this meditation again.

You practise this meditation and are given two swords. That is your choice and will have been agreed at a higher level of your awareness, possibly even before you were born.

Your sword is taken away from you and another is given in its place. This is just part of your spiritual evolution. Just accept the new sword.

The very fact that the participants on the Angel seminars have been in the presence of Archangel Michael and actually visited the sword room will cause significant changes in their spiritual evolution and raise their vibration. I always tell them not to worry overmuch and to just try again later. I also instruct these people to work with clearing themselves of stagnant energy and with going deeper into the energy of surrendering themselves to God. In the Christian terminology it can be thought of as "Thy will be done", not my will. So to become a light bearer you need to surrender to the God-force and allow this Divine power to flow through you; only then can you truly become the light (light worker).

Archangel Haniel's Glory – Angelic Communication

'Archangel Haniel's Glory – Angelic Communication' aura essence
Aquamarine placed on the heart chakra
Blue Danburite placed in the soul star chakra
Gem Silica placed on the witness point (thymus)
Indicolite placed on the sacral chakra
Larimar placed in the earth star chakra
Bi-coloured Celestite placed in the crown chakra
Blue Topaz placed on the third eye chakra
12 clear quartz crystals placed evenly around the body, terminations pointing inwards

Dedicated to and overshadowed by Archangel Haniel

Uses: Haniel is the Archangel of Divine communication through clear perception. His name means the 'Glory of God'. He is a *warrior* angel; his authority assists you to fulfil your 'Divine heroic mission' which is to praise honour, love and reunite with God by using and trusting in your own great God-connectedness which will inspires others too. He gives strength and perseverance when you feel weak, through Divine communication and personal revelations, visions and steadfast faith. Archangel Haniel is the protector of your soul. He gives the virtue of determination and provides the energy required for you to fulfil your Dharma. He is in fact a Dharmapala, a protector of the Dharma. Your personal Dharma is your truth, your own God reality which, when followed, is conducive to gaining enlightenment. Call on him when you feel life is difficult and you are beset by obstacles (even dark forces of negativity) and he will provide the spiritual armour necessary for your salvation.

His temple of light is over the sacred mountain of Tibet. *Netzach* or Victory is Archangel Haniel's domain on the Tree of Life. Netzach is normally translated as victory, but it can also translate as eternity or glory, hence the name of the essence 'Archangel Haniel's Glory' because the essence is definitely glorious, as it invokes the transcendent, sublime, celestial energy of God. Haniel's colour is pale turquoise blue. This colour invokes the essence of *shunyata*, the infinite blue emptiness, radiating in all directions, absolutely clear, pristine and glorious. By this blue sky stretching out to infinity we can gain an understanding, a comprehension of the expansiveness and true soul-freedom which could be ours if we did not allow our horizons to become narrow, dull, clouded and limited, if we did not permit our minds to become fixated and hypnotized by cravings and worries centred on what really are empty passing phenomena. In reality our little lifespan is but a nano-second in the scheme of eternity and we should not dull our minds with trivial concerns, but devote ourselves to spiritual pursuits, which would free us completely from the day-to-day manipulations of our lower small ego-self.

Haniel's glory is definitely a warrior energy, providing spiritual armour to protect your soul when faced with obstacles and negativity, assisting in the fulfilment of your life's mission through Divine communication. This web of light and essence is uplifting, as it aligns you with your own greatness.

It is a pillar of light which will sustain you through the 'dark night of the soul' when you doubt yourself or feel unworthy of God's infinite love. With use, this essence will transform you into a pillar of light, a beacon towards which others will be drawn. As each one of us connects and aligns to our own God-self we will raise the vibration of the Earth, allowing her peaceful transition into the 'Age of Aquarius'. This vibrational shift started with the 'Harmonic Convergence' in 1987 and will be fulfilled by the year 2012. This is an amazing time to be incarnate on planet Earth as she makes her transition into the higher dimensions of light.

We who hold the pillar of Light, live in the pillar of Light and will become the 'Family of Light' have each the clear intention and childlike humility to become more than we have ever thought possible, even the ones amongst us who have studied for years this lifetime and could be considered adepts! If we ever consider ourselves adepts we have failed because we have taken on a fixed horizon, a fixed persona which will limit our potential to become multi-dimensional beings of pure unconditional love and by becoming the living embodiment of unconditional love we will unite all the aspects of God. This is our purpose for living; we must never become blinded by our own light, our own self-importance. But by the same token we must never make ourselves smaller than we truly are or limit our potential to change the world. We must begin to explore, with the help of Archangel Haniel, the areas where we have chosen to restrict ourselves, the areas of our life where we have given away our freedom. We must look at the multitude of restrictions we have taken upon ourselves which have stifled our voice, our communication, our opinions and choices. We must never become compliant and choose the easy option, as this will restrict our growth and limit our fields of perception. As we each begin to experience this massive infusion of light and feel the changes which are upon us, we must remind ourselves of the exquisite possibilities that are placed before us and allow ourselves to choose wisely and for the highest good of all.

This essence and crystal web of light also offers us the superb potential for past life healing of deep hidden problems related to negative emotional states and deep fears associated with personal power and how we can misuse it or have allowed others to misuse our power through fear-based manipulation. Therefore Haniel is a most beneficial essence which, when used regularly with focused intent, will release karmic miasms – crystallized old patterns of dis-ease and decay which we may have carried over from previous lives.

Invocation: Archangel Haniel, warrior and protector of the dharma, keep my feet forever on the path towards full enlightenment of my soul. Encourage me when I feel weak, disillusioned or beset by obstacles. Reveal to me the glory of God and renew my spiritual armour so that my soul will find true salvation and enlightenment.

Physical integration: Releases karmic miasms from our neural pathways which we may have carried over from previous lives, which leaves us open and susceptible to attracting dis-ease caused by viruses, bacteria and parasites.

Emotional consolidation: Calming and soothing to the emotions. Bestows faith in yourself and confidence in your higher spiritual nature.

Etheric assimilation: Transmits pure spiritual substance into the transcendental chakras above the head to help you find original inspiration, inner joy and exquisite visions that will refresh your life.

Process: See the therapy section – **Process** (page 185).

Archangel Haniel Temple Meditation

The 'Temple of Light' you wish to visit is the retreat centre of Archangel Haniel. His ascension temple of light is over Tibet. When you first start the exercise you may want to pre-record the following instructions on tape and hold a crystal, such as blue danburite or celestite.

Mist your aura with *'Archangel Haniel's Glory – Angelic Communication'* essence.

Get into your chosen position, close your eyes and begin to focus on your breathing: see the section – Breathing, Meditation and Relaxation section on page 129 for preparation details.

Once you are suitably relaxed, call on Haniel – use the invocation 'Archangel Haniel, warrior and protector of the dharma, keep my feet forever on the path towards full enlightenment of my soul. Encourage me when I feel weak, disillusioned or beset by obstacles. Reveal to me the glory of God and renew my spiritual armour so that my soul will find true salvation'.

Relax and let yourself be enveloped in the potent energy of the Archangel Haniel and his legions of angels of clear perception through heartfelt communication. You can stay basking in this energy as long as you like; when you are ready, allow yourself to be raised upwards on a spiral of pure white light. Slowly the light spiral raises you higher and higher; you feel yourself held perfectly safely in angelic arms. You feel yourself transported very gently to the temple of light.

You will find yourself in the ascension temple of light that is over Tibet. You will be guided along sparkling crystalline corridors until you reach the room of Angelic communication…you will see a tube of white crystal light in front of you…in the centre of this is a huge blue lily carved out of indicolite…in the very centre of this is a pyramid of gem silica, Mediterranean sky blue in colour, with a cap-stone of pure pristine celestite.

You will be approached by beloved Archangel Haniel…you will be asked what is the purpose of this visit…you will then state your purpose…perhaps you will ask to see the glory of God that will help you overcome the obstacles in your path through life to give strength and perseverance when you feel weak, through Divine communication and personal revelations. Archangel Haniel will then place you inside the gem silica pyramid which is his chamber of spiritual protection…enjoy the experience as you feel your body and aura gently bathed in protective empowering energy…allow yourself to really absorb the light…eventually Archangel Haniel will let you know when it is time to return to your physical body; he will gently guide you back to the here and now. Give thanks and write down your experiences.

Use this meditation often to contact Archangel Haniel whenever you feel weak, disillusioned or beset by obstacles on your spiritual path. He will reveal to you the glory of God and renew your spiritual armour so that your soul will find true salvation.

Archangel Raphael's Dream – Angelic Healing

'Archangel Raphael's Dream – Angelic Healing' aura essence
Aphrodite placed on the heart chakra
Gem Silica placed on the witness point (thymus)
Herderite placed on the third eye chakra
Moldavite placed in the crown chakra
Phenacite placed in the soul star chakra
12 clear quartz crystals placed evenly around the body, terminations pointing inwards

Dedicated to and overshadowed by Archangel Raphael

Uses: Raphael is the physician of the Angelic realm, the Divine healer for healing ourselves and helping find the inner guidance, love, compassion, beauty and inspiration to heal others. Raphael's name means 'God has healed'. His temple of light is over Fatima in Portugal. Raphael is associated with the colour emerald green and he carries a cup of healing balm. *Tiphareth* or Beauty is

Archangel Raphael's domain on the tree of life. Raphael's energy is extremely peaceful and healing, but he has the power to cast out demons! He is also known as the chief of the guardian angels. The blessings, mercy and compassion of Archangel Raphael and his legions of healing Angels gently bring healing into wholeness for body, mind, spirit, soul and relationships. On our personal path to the enlightenment of the soul we have first to heal ourselves. This healing begins with our relationships to ourselves and 'others', the 'others' being everything in our small ego-centred awareness we view as 'not self'. This healing of the soul will include all our relationships, past, present and future, for it comes only when the full realisation 'dawns' on us that as we treat others so we treat ourselves. As the sleeping prophet said: 'karma is only the soul meeting itself'.

Archangel Raphael brings balance, stability and harmony to the heart chakra, the ability to experience wholeness, harmony and love. He is restorative and tunes you in to the plant kingdom, helping you understand environmental issues and giving you a social conscience and planetary awareness. Archangel Raphael gets to the root of the problem, the very heart of the matter; in fact he will leave no stone unturned in doing so. This makes him an extremely strong and powerful Archangel, an idealist, who can cause heart palpitations as he casts out your demons! Raphael does open doors, though, to intense emotional healing – and under his emerald green mantle you will eventually find a sanctuary of peace and nurturing. The act of nurturing is fed by the different emotional feelings generated by the heart chakra. Feelings of love, compassion and empathy are a direct outpouring of spiritual growth, therefore the heart chakra is important in developing higher levels of consciousness.

Raphael also heals through the realization of the body – mind connection, 'psycho-neuro-immunology' (this is a new science which attempts to understand the interactions between the nervous system, the immune system, the mind and the emotions), which has been proved to play a significant role in the origins and exacerbations of many illnesses. The emotions work at a subtle energy level through the influences of the astral body, which feeds into the etheric body. It has become clear that depression and other emotional disorders can cause a suppression of the body's natural defence against illness. This state of immuno-incompetence can later become translated into physical illness through an increased susceptibility to viral, fungal and bacterial agents, as well as through internal sources of disease like cancer. Distortions originating at the level of the astral body or aberrations in the mental body take time to work their way down through the etheric to the physical levels. This is why it may take weeks, months or even years before changes in the emotional/mental/astral constitution become manifest as physical illness. An aversion to Archangel Raphael's emerald green ray always indicates that we do not feel at ease with our emotions. If we are not at ease with our emotions we will have distortions in our emotional body. These distortions are usually due to childhood trauma and a dysfunctional early family background, where emotions had to be denied or hidden, as the trauma of showing emotion was forbidden… a crime, punishable by disapproval and rejection.

The emerald green ray of Archangel Raphael is also the transmuting ray for development of the third eye chakra and indeed Raphael does play a vital role in the development of this important chakra, as he is connected with science and knowledge as well as healing. You can ask Archangel Raphael to help you develop the third eye, which is about the surrendering of your dualistic concepts and feelings of separation from your source of Divine wisdom, inspiration and bliss. Before the third eye opens, you see through the two eyes; you experience a duality between your normal self (your conscious mind, intellect, ego) and your higher self (your intuitive mind or spirit). As you merge with the higher self and become one with the Divine, all the masks of the ego-self fall away, you no longer identify with what you thought you were, who you thought you ought to be, or who your parents, teachers and the mawkish tribal mentality of society said you should be. Suddenly you 'are', your true self shines through, there is no longer any need for pretence, guilt, illusion or being judgemental: you are flooded with compassion, love, wisdom and understanding for yourself and others. You view your past lives for what they are and you see yourself in everyone and everything. You no longer have any karmic debts…you move beyond dualism.

Invocation: Archangel Raphael, guide me as I release all limiting thought patterns that have blighted my soul. I now choose a healthy body, mind, spirit and soul. I am instantly transformed.

Physical integration: Healing of the physical level, including the energy we would call a miracle. For what is a miracle? Perhaps it is a 'happening' or event we would not have believed possible with our 'ordinary' mind and awareness!

Emotional consolidation: Universal love and acceptance are activated. This brings healing of body, mind, spirit and soul.

Etheric assimilation: Transformation on all levels of the body and aura, including past, present and future lives and relationships.

Process: See the therapy section – **Process** (page 185).

Archangel Raphael Temple Meditation

The 'Temple of Light' you wish to visit is the retreat centre of Archangel Raphael. His ascension temple of light is over Fatima, Portugal. When you first start the exercise you may want to pre-record the following instructions on tape and hold a crystal, such as aphrodite, herderite or moldavite.

Mist your aura with *'Archangel Raphael's Dream – Angelic Healing'* essence.

Get into your chosen position, close your eyes and begin to focus on your breathing: see the section – Breathing, Meditation and Relaxation section on page 129 for preparation details.

Once you are suitably relaxed, call on Raphael – use the invocation 'Archangel Raphael, guide me as I release all limiting thought patterns that have blighted my soul. I now choose a healthy body, mind, spirit and soul. I am instantly transformed'.

Just relax and let yourself be enveloped in the power and energy of the Archangel Raphael and his legions of angels of healing. You can stay basking in this energy as long as you like; when you are ready, allow yourself to be raised upwards on a spiral of pure white light. Slowly the light spiral raises you higher and higher; you feel yourself held perfectly safely in angelic arms. You feel yourself transported very gently to the temple of light.

You will find yourself in the ascension temple of light that is over Fatima, Portugal. You will be guided along sparkling crystalline corridors until you reach the room of angelic healing…you will see a circle of white crystal light in front of you…in the centre of this is a huge lily carved out of pure emerald…in the very centre of this is a pyramid of gem silica, Mediterranean sky blue in colour, with a cap-stone of deep pink aphrodite.

You will be approached by beloved Archangel Raphael…you will be asked what is the purpose of this visit…you will then state your purpose…you will ask for healing. Archangel Raphael will then place you inside the gem silica pyramid which is his healing chamber…enjoy the experience as you feel your body and aura gently bathed in healing energy…allow yourself to really absorb the healing…eventually Archangel Raphael will let you know when it is time to return to your physical body; he will gently guide you back to the here and now. Give thanks and write down your experiences.

Use this meditation often to contact Archangel Raphael, the Divine healer, for healing yourself and helping you find the inner guidance, love, compassion, beauty and inspiration to heal others.

Archangel Chamuel's Embrace – Angelic Love (God's Love)

'Archangel Chamuel's Embrace – Angelic Love (God's Love)' aura essence
Aphrodite placed on the heart chakra
Kunzite held in the right hand
Morganite held in the left hand
Pink Calcite placed on the solar plexus chakra
Pink Danburite placed in the crown chakra
Pink Petalite placed on the third eye chakra
Rose Quartz placed on the heart chakra
Rubellite placed on the heart chakra
Phenacite placed in the soul star chakra
12 clear quartz crystals placed evenly around the body, terminations pointing inwards

Dedicated to and overshadowed by Archangel Chamuel

Uses: Chamuel (Khamael) is the Archangel of Angelic love. He is the messenger that directs God's love towards those who need a strong immediate infusion of pure love energy. His name means 'He who sees God'. His amazing essence ignites and expands the flame of pure unconditional love within your heart. Its warmth melts and dissolves all fear and resistance you may have to allowing the full manifestation of unconditional beneficial love into the heart and chakra system. *Geburah* or judgement is the sphere of Archangel Chamuel *(Khamael)* on the kabalistic Tree of Life. True love (God's love) releases all fear-based judgemental attitudes which de-humanise and demonize others who have chosen a different belief system or way of life. Therefore Archangel Chamuel and the millions of angels of love he directs can be used against the negative forces of anti-love. Use his essence often to banish the fear-based energy of cruelty, hatred and war which many of us feel powerless to overcome at these turbulent times as planet earth makes her transition into the fourth dimension. Archangel Chamuel has his ascension temple of light over St. Louis, Missouri, USA. You can visit it often during your dream state to have your heart chakra transformed by love while you dream. You will wake up feeling joyful and positive: perhaps you will even remember your dreams. This is especially potent if you have people or situations you need to forgive and release.

The pink ray of Archangel Chamuel is the transmuting ray for the heart chakra, which is normally represented as the beautiful balance colour of green, but the pink ray is also a balance colour of the red ray of Mother earth with the pure white ray of the cosmic Father. Whilst the green ray is found in the centre of the colour spectrum, which means it is completely neutral, it is not magnetic, warm and expansive as the reds, oranges and yellows are, nor is it cool as the blue – violet spectrums are; it therefore brings balance, harmony and healing, allowing emotional stability, maturity and interconnectedness with others and the earth plane. But it is a very physical balance for the third dimension. If we need to move beyond the physical plane and into the higher chakras and dimensions, we must transmute the physical heart and the heart chakra, allowing us to take on the 'cosmic human form' of the fourth dimension. Therefore this cosmic expansion demands the higher vibration balance colour of the pink ray. The paler the pink, the higher the vibration as we infuse more cosmic Father white ray into the red of the Mother earth ray.

The heart chakra administers our ability to love and nurture others, to give and receive love, unconditionally free from all self-interest. There are no conditions attached to this giving. It is a love that transcends and transforms the self and moves us through compassion towards the Divine state of emotional maturity. Many people are afraid of opening their heart chakra. Those who have been able to overcome this fear have a charismatic warmth which others find reassuring, soothing and uplifting. Archangel Chamuel essence is useful for birth and rebirth situations within our lives; it is also useful in helping us cope with bereavement, loss, change, mid-life crisis or relationship problems personal and planetary. The realisation of the pink ray of Archangel Chamuel and his millions of Angels of love is that it is only the love energy within any given purpose that gives lasting value and benefit to all creation. Only love can free you from the ego-directed bonds of self-limiting beliefs. Open your heart to love and find that yes, it is true, love is the only answer. And *yes*, LOVE is all you need. If you work with no other ray, pink will bring enlightenment.

The following simple meditation will assist you in working with Archangel Chamuel and the Angels of love. It is designed to open and develop your heart chakra from the third dimensional physical level into the higher fourth dimensional aspect. This is accomplished through the expansion of the flame of pure unconditional love within your heart. The warmth of Archangel Chamuel's pink ray melts and dissolves all resistance and fear you may have to allowing the full manifestation of unconditional beneficial love into the heart and chakra system. It also allows you to evolve and develop compassion for others by radiating the unconditional love outwards to the world.

Pushpaputa Mudra

1.   Spray the Archangel Chamuel essence above your head.

2.   Invoke Archangel Chamuel and the angels of love.

3.   Place your hands on your lap.

4.   Visualise your hands as beautiful lotus flowers.

5.   Visualise a third lotus flower on the top of your head.

6.   While inhaling, allow the pink rays which flow from Archangel Chamuel and the Angels of love, embodying unconditional love, to flow through the open flowers into your innermost self, your heart chakra. Hold your breath and absorb them. As you exhale, radiate this unconditional love energy through your heart out to the world.

Invocation: Archangel Chamuel, ignite and expand the flame of pure unconditional love within my heart. Dissolve all resistance and fear I may have to allowing the full manifestation of unconditional beneficial love into my heart and chakra system. Guide me and help me to evolve and develop compassion for others by radiating this unconditional love outwards to the world.

Physical integration: Revitalising. Stimulates healing by helping to maintain energy levels.

Emotional consolidation: Balances and expands the heart chakra, which increases our ability to love and nurture others and also to give and receive love unconditionally, free from all self-interest.

Etheric assimilation: Powerful realisations occur in the true vibration of unconditional love. Only by treating others with unconditional love and compassion can we ever hope to heal ourselves into wholeness. Fills the heart with the love that transcends and transforms the self and moves us through compassion towards the Divine state of emotional maturity.

Process: See the therapy section – **Process** (page 185).

Archangel Chamuel Temple Meditation

The 'Temple of Light' you wish to visit is the retreat centre of Archangel Chamuel. His ascension temple of light is over St. Louis, Missouri, USA. When you first start the exercise you may want to pre-record the following instructions on tape and hold a crystal, such as morganite or kunzite.

Mist your aura with *'Archangel Chamuel's Embrace – Angelic Love'* essence.

Get into your chosen position, close your eyes and begin to focus on your breathing: see the section – Breathing, Meditation and Relaxation section on page 129 for preparation details.

Once you are suitably relaxed, call on Chamuel – use the invocation 'Archangel Chamuel, ignite and expand the flame of pure unconditional love within my heart. Dissolve all resistance and fear I may have to allowing the full manifestation of unconditional beneficial love into my heart and chakra system. Guide me and help me to evolve and develop compassion for others by radiating this unconditional love outwards to the world'.

Just relax and let yourself be enveloped in the potent energy of the Archangel Chamuel and his legions of angels of Love. You can stay basking in this energy as long as you like; when you are ready, allow yourself to be raised upwards on a spiral of pure pale pink light. Slowly the light spiral raises you higher and higher; you feel yourself held perfectly safely and surrounded by love in strong angelic arms. You feel yourself transported very gently to the temple of light.

You will find yourself in the ascension temple of light that is over St. Louis, Missouri, USA. You will be guided along sparkling crystalline corridors until you reach the room of Angelic Love. This is an amazing room, as the walls and ceiling are made of millions of faceted crystals of pure morganite, sparkling kunzite and dazzling pink danburite. Just being in this room is a beautiful experience. You will be approached by beloved Archangel Chamuel who will ask you the purpose of your visit. Perhaps you will ask to have your heart chakra transformed by God's love. Archangel Chamuel will ask you to lie down on a raised plinth made of deep pink rose quartz. Twelve angels of love will then enter the room and position themselves around you, forming a circle. They will then beam the energy of pure unconditional love towards you. You will feel your body relax as you allow the beneficial energy to bathe your body and aura. Eventually Archangel Chamuel will let you know when it is time to return to your physical body; he will gently guide you back to the here and now. Give thanks and write down your experiences. Use this meditation often to contact Archangel Chamuel whenever you feel you need the infusion of God's love.

Archangel Jophiel's Illumination – Angelic Wisdom

'Archangel Jophiel's Illumination – Angelic Wisdom' aura essence
Amblygonite placed in the soul star chakra
Fine Gold placed in the soul star chakra
Golden Topaz placed in the crown chakra
Yellow Apatite placed on the solar plexus chakra
Yellow Calcite placed in the soul star chakra
Yellow Sapphire placed on the third eye chakra
Sunshine Aura Quartz in the soul star chakra
Sunstone placed on the sacral chakra
12 clear quartz crystals placed evenly around the body, terminations pointing inwards

Dedicated to and overshadowed by Archangel Jophiel

Uses: Jophiel is the Archangel of Wisdom: he works with the Angels from the Halls of Wisdom. His yellow-gold solar ray is often called the sunshine ray, bringing illumination, expansion and energy mostly through the honesty of self-reflection. He helps you to develop a fresh approach and eternal child-like delight, bringing back enchantment and pleasure to your everyday life. Jophiel's name means 'Beauty of God'. He builds connections to align you to your higher self through the multitude of dimensions; he can be thought of as a cosmic ladder or bridge. He can instantly help you recover 'soul' fragments and 'soul loss' which may have been caused by shock, fright, severe illness or any other time you lost your personal 'power' or joy in life. Jophiel's gifts for you include the wisdom flame, inspiration, intuition, perception, joy, bliss and soul illumination. Invoke Archangel Jophiel when you feel blocked or your creativity needs a boost. If you ask him he will cleanse, activate, heal, balance and align your mental body, which stops feelings of low self-esteem, inertia and mental fog. He will also give you practical assistance by helping you to absorb new information and learn from the rich patterns life has bestowed on you in the schoolroom of earth. His wisdom flame can be invoked to help you in any situation that needs clear mental perception and inspiration.

His temple of light is over Lanchow in China. *Hod* or Majesty is Archangel Jophiel's sphere of influence on the Tree of Life. Pale yellow-gold is the transmuting ray for the crown chakra which, when balanced and transmuted into its highest vibration, gives soul illumination and direct contact with your higher self and access to all the transcendental chakras above your head. Archangel Jophiel strengthens your connection to your higher self, bringing wisdom, intuition, perception, mental clarity, joy, bliss, soul illumination and boundless energy and enthusiasm for life and your spiritual evolution.

Archangel Jophiel's essence will help you understand the logical functioning of the human mind. This means it improves intellectual prowess, thought processes and personal will-power. By understanding your personal power as you evolve spiritually, you will begin to bring your will-power (ego) more into line with the Divine will and the evolutionary plan of the Divine; this will immediately quicken your spiritual evolution. It also helps you understand energy and energy manipulation on all levels. This includes astral energy and cold-hearted wilful aggression, which may have been directed at you. Archangel Jophiel's essence will also help you understand any negative emotions you may have, such as oversensitivity to criticism, a need to be in control, low self-esteem or the addictive personality, as well as sluggishness, negative thinking, boredom, cowardice, being judgemental, sarcastic, acidic and impatient. Jophiel's essence is strengthening, comforting and uplifting.

On a higher level, it will aid intuition and telepathy, bringing spiritual wisdom and the manifestation of your dreams. As we evolve spiritually and take control of our personal power and personal responsibility, we step outside the limiting rigid mental strait-jacket of late twentieth-century analytical thought patterns – moving into the abundance of personal responsibility and global abundance.

Invocation: Archangel Jophiel, align and strengthen my connectedness to my higher self. Allow wisdom and soul illumination to flow through me. Guide and encourage me to go towards the infinite, dazzling, incomparably brilliant light of the void and find the connectedness with God/Goddess that is my true spiritual evolution.

Physical integration: Can help release toxins and promote the flow of gastric juices, as well as stimulating the lymphatic system and energising the nervous system.

Emotional consolidation: Can help clear low self-esteem and issues of low self-worth and the fear of responsibility. On a mental level clears and stimulates the mind, activating the intellect and intuition.

Etheric assimilation: Expansive, increasing the capacity for laughter and joy. Rids the energy field of parasites and astral entities, as well as recovering soul fragments and soul loss.

Process: See the therapy section – **Process** (page 185).

Archangel Jophiel Temple Meditation

The 'Temple of Light' you wish to visit is the retreat centre of Archangel Jophiel. His ascension temple of light is over Lanchow in China. When you first start the exercise you may want to pre-record the following instructions on tape and hold a crystal, such as topaz or amblygonite.

Mist your aura with *'Archangel Jophiel's Illumination – Angelic Wisdom'* essence.

Get into your chosen position, close your eyes and begin to focus on your breathing: see the section – Breathing, Meditation and Relaxation section on page 129 for preparation details.

Once you are suitably relaxed, call on Jophiel – use the invocation 'Archangel Jophiel, align and strengthen my connectedness to my higher self. Allow wisdom and soul illumination to flow through me. Guide and encourage me to go towards the infinite, dazzling, incomparably brilliant light of the void and find the connectedness with God/Goddess that is my true spiritual evolution'.

Just relax and let yourself be enveloped in the potent energy of the Archangel Jophiel and his legions of angels of wisdom. You can stay basking in this energy as long as you like; when you are ready, allow yourself to be raised upwards on a spiral of pure golden-white light. Slowly the light spiral raises you higher and higher; you feel yourself held perfectly safely in angelic arms. You feel yourself transported very gently to the temple of light.

You will find yourself in the ascension temple of light that is over Lanchow in China. You will be guided along sparkling crystalline corridors until you reach the room of Angelic illumination...you will see the wisdom flame of white-gold crystal light in front of you...in the centre of this is a huge pale golden-yellow lily carved out of sapphire.

You will be approached by beloved Archangel Jophiel...you will be asked what is the purpose of this visit...you will then state your purpose...perhaps you will ask for soul illumination and to bathe in the wisdom-illumination flame...whatever happens...enjoy the experience as you feel your body and aura gently bathed in the wisdom flame...allow yourself to be cleansed and purified...then really absorb the light...eventually Archangel Jophiel will let you know when it is time to return to your physical body; he will gently guide you back to the here and now. Give thanks and write down your experiences.

Use this meditation often to contact Archangel Jophiel and the Angels from the 'Halls of Wisdom'.

Archangel Zadkiel's Joy – Angelic Violet Flame of Freedom

'Archangel Zadkiel's Joy – Angelic Violet Flame of Freedom' aura essence
Amethyst placed on the heart chakra
Iolite placed on the third eye chakra
Lithium Quartz placed on the solar plexus chakra
Phenacite placed in the soul star chakra
Sugilite placed on the throat chakra
Tanzanite placed in the crown chakra
12 clear quartz crystals placed evenly around the body, terminations pointing inwards

Dedicated to and overshadowed by Archangel Zadkiel

Uses: Zadkiel (Tzadkiel) is the Archangel of Divine joy. Zadkiel's name means the 'Righteousness of God'. He is the Angelic guardian of the violet flame of transmutation, transformation, joy and freedom. This high frequency spiritual energy known as the 'violet flame' instantly transforms lower energies into positive life-affirming energy. This miracle flame was brought down for us by Saint Germain, who is an Ascended Master and Chohan of the seventh ray.

Zadkiel is the Archangel of mercy, who teaches trust in God and the benevolence of God. He brings comfort in our hour of need and helps us release negative karma and negative karmic miasms. His temple of light is anchored over Cuba in the Caribbean. *Chesed* or mercy is the sphere of Archangel Zadkiel on the kabalistic Tree of Life.

Archangel Zadkiel's violet flame of cosmic freedom can be invoked and used in numerous ways. This God flame has the highest vibrational frequency which, when summoned, brings soul freedom and joy by releasing you from your own limiting behaviour, concepts and karmic miasms, including past life memories that may have been carried over to this lifetime. Use it often to cleanse all areas of your mind, body and aura. It instantly purifies all the chakra centres, giving relief from addictions and addictive traits within the personality. It works as an amplifier of healing and spiritual energies. When consciously directed by Archangel Zadkiel it will break down and transform blocked or stuck energies, such as those which have been caused by anger, hatred, resentment, bitterness, jealousy, intolerance, blame, fear and guilt. It also helps protect from over-indulgences which have lodged in the emotional body, it calms the mind and touches the Divine spark within you, thereby aiding spiritual and personal growth, giving understanding into the cause of the indulgence. Using the Archangel Zadkiel essence before meditation practice instantly purifies your body and aura, which will enhance the meditation experience, helping to calm the mind and bring the necessary stillness which is most desirable for enhanced spiritual growth. The essence can also be used for clearing planetary miasms and planetary or group karma.

Invocation: Archangel Zadkiel and the Angels of joy, direct the energy of the violet flame of freedom into all areas of my body, bodies and aura until I am purified of all negativity and I stand in my mighty I AM presence, shining like a jewel in the crown of the Creator.

Physical integration: Purifies all the chakra centres and can be used anywhere on the body and on all levels of the aura, giving relief from addictions and addictive traits within the personality. It works as an amplifier of healing and spiritual energies.

Emotional consolidation: Brings emotional peace, dignity, humanitarianism and creativity. Enhances psychic abilities, allowing for mystical experiences. It can develop faith and inner strength.

Etheric assimilation: Raises personal vibratory rate and facilitates a thinning of the veil between the various planes of consciousness, allowing for clear communication with Ascended Masters, Angels, spirit guides and other enlightened beings from other dimensions. Facilitates deep meditation, astral journeys, materialisation and alchemy. It can activate and integrate the energies of the base, sacral, solar plexus, heart, throat, third eye, fourth eye, fifth eye and crown chakras, as well as the chakras eight to fourteen above the head.

Process: See the therapy section – **Process** (page 185).

Archangel Zadkiel and the Violet Flame Temple Meditation

The 'Temple of Light' you wish to visit is the retreat centre of Archangel Zadkiel. His ascension temple of light is over Cuba. When you first start the exercise you may want to pre-record the following instructions on tape and hold a crystal, such as iolite, tanzanite or amethyst.

Mist your aura with *'Archangel Zadkiel's Joy – Angelic Violet Flame of Freedom'* essence.

Get into your chosen position, close your eyes and begin to focus on your breathing: see the section – Breathing, Meditation and Relaxation section on page 129 for preparation details.

Once you are suitably relaxed, call on Zadkiel – use the invocation 'Archangel Zadkiel and the Angels of joy, direct the energy of the violet flame of freedom into all areas of my body, bodies and aura until I am purified of all negativity and I stand in my mighty I AM presence, shining like a jewel in the crown of the Creator'.

Just relax and let yourself be enveloped in the potent energy of the Archangel Zadkiel and his legions of Angels of joy. You can stay basking in this energy as long as you like; when you are ready, allow yourself to be raised upwards on a spiral of violet light. Slowly the violet light raises you higher and higher; you feel yourself held perfectly safely in angelic arms. You feel yourself transported very gently to the temple of the violet flame.

You will find yourself in the ascension temple of the violet flame that is over Cuba. The temple is fashioned from pure white marble shot through with veins of deep violet and majestic purple. You are led through many corridors by the Angels of joy; these exquisite beings are vast white Angels with golden hair and violet-flame-coloured wings. You follow them until you reach the heart of the temple. This is a magnificent round vast hall several storeys in height. The floor is made of deep purple amethyst crystal and the walls are made of tanzanite, which changes colour from lilac, purple, deep blue and ultra-violet as the light of the violet flame plays upon it. In the very centre of the room is an opening which is surrounded by a low golden wall which is studded with amethyst, tanzanite and iolite.

The cosmic violet flame burns in the very centre. All around you are others who have come to bathe in the energy of the flame. You stand in a long line and await your turn. Eventually you will be approached by beloved Archangel Zadkiel...you will be asked what is the purpose of this visit...you will then state your purpose...purification in the violet flame of freedom. Archangel Zadkiel will then place you inside the violet flame...enjoy the magnificent experience as you feel your body and aura gently bathed and purified as the violet flame transmutes all that is negative and cleanses all areas of your mind, body and aura. Feel it instantly purifying all the chakra centres, giving relief from addictions and addictive traits. Feel it breaking down and transforming blocks, stagnant or stuck energies, such as those which have been caused by anger, hatred, resentment, bitterness, jealousy, intolerance, blame, fear and guilt. Allow it to calm your mind and activate the Divine spark within you, thereby aiding spiritual growth and transmuting negative karma...eventually Archangel Zadkiel will let you know when it is time to return to your physical body; he will gently guide you back to the here and now.

Give thanks and write down your experiences.

Use this meditation often to contact Archangel Zadkiel whenever you need to free your mind and raise your vibratory rate through the transformational energies of the violet flame of ultimate joy and soul freedom.

Archangel Tzaphkiel – Cosmic Contemplation

'Archangel Tzaphkiel' aura essence
Alexandrite, placed on the throat chakra
Ajoite, placed on the heart chakra
Papagoite, placed on the heart chakra
Amethyst, placed in the soul star chakra
Pink Lazurine TM, placed on the heart chakra
Charoite, placed on the fifth eye chakra (also known as the Angel chakra)
Tanzanite, placed on the third eye chakra
Sugilite, placed on the fourth eye chakra
Danburite, placed just above the crown chakra
Pink Sapphire, placed on the heart chakra
12 clear quartz crystals placed evenly around the body, terminations pointing inwards

Dedicated to and overshadowed by Archangel Tzaphkiel

Uses: Tzaphkiel (Zaphkiel) is the Archangel of deep contemplation of God, representing the Divine feminine watery aspect of creation, the Shakti of Shiva. Tzaphkiel has the power to nurture all things and gives us glimpses of other realities to which, through our own ignorance or arrogance, we have become blind. Tzaphkiel will catch us if we fall or falter – for the feminine aspect of God's infinite love is unconditional and non-judgemental. Allow Tzaphkiel to carry you when you feel weak, for her infinite compassion is the sea of your liberation.

On the Kabalistic Tree of Life Archangel Tzaphkiel *(Zaphkiel)* is the 'Cosmic Mother' who rules over Binah or Understanding. Binah is the third sphere of the holy trinity at the top of the tree. It is here that conception takes place when the seed of life enters from *Kether* (The Divine), passes through *Chokmah* (Cosmic Father) and into Binah. This cosmic conception within the womb of Binah is, as the Zohar depicts, 'an explosion of light'. It is here that all other sparks of life are generated, which then flow outwards into all worlds and dimensions. Binah is receptive and feminine – it is the Divine loving female aspect of God – the Great Mother or *Imma* to whom we will all one day return. Archangel Tzaphkiel as the Cosmic Mother is personified as the 'Great Mother' Mary and Kwan Yin, the Bodhisattva of Compassion. She is also personified by Pistis Sophia (Faith and Wisdom) of the Coptic Gnostics documents, who portray her as "Queen of the Stars" and in her lesser form Sophia, the 'Divine' spark 'trapped' within each soul incarnate.

Archangel Tzaphkiel, who rules over Binah, by her very nature bestows blessings that are designed through faith to increase your understanding by imparting wisdom which increases your spiritual growth. In fact Archangel Tzaphkiel casts out *all* that is superficial to your spiritual development. She increases your insight, mysticism, intelligence and discernment by helping you to fully develop the feminine side of your nature, but she will do this only if you ask to be re-born into a new level of consciousness which allows your heart to fully open and your soul's purity to be made manifest on Earth for the freedom and salvation of all.

Her temple of light is situated etherically over a vortex area of the Atlantic ocean where the ancient island civilization of Atlantis once flourished. Atlantis actually sank through several stages between 12,000BC and up to 5,000BC through a series of catastrophes which were caused by various geological impulses, such as volcanic eruption, earthquakes, meteor impact, tidal waves, etc. This area is still very unstable, as it is situated on the mid-Atlantic ridge; this fracture line encircles planet earth and it is where four vast tectonic plates all meet and collide. Some people also believe high technical warfare also played a large part in the destruction of Atlantis. This was brought about as the original population slowly turned away from the 'Divine' feminine matriarchal principle and became increasingly more patriarchal and war-like.

Invocation: Archangel Tzaphkiel, nurture me, be my salvation. Redeem me, shower me with your blessings as you teach me to love myself and others unconditionally. Let my words be full of wisdom and the flame of understanding and discernment burn in my heart.

Physical integration: Strengthens and nurtures the physical body.

Emotional consolidation: Releases emotional turmoil.

Etheric assimilation: Raises the vibratory rate, bringing peace, tranquillity, wisdom, discernment, understanding and eloquence.

Process: See the therapy section – **Process** (page 185).

Archangel Tzaphkiel's Temple of Light Meditation

The 'Temple of Light' you wish to visit is the retreat centre of Archangel Tzaphkiel. Her temple of light is situated etherically over a vortex area of the Atlantic ocean where the ancient island civilization of Atlantis once flourished. When you first start the exercise you may want to pre-record the following instructions on tape and hold a crystal, such as amethyst.

Mist your aura with *'Archangel Tzaphkiel – Cosmic Contemplation'* essence.

Get into your chosen position, close your eyes and begin to focus on your breathing: see the section – Breathing, Meditation and Relaxation section on page 129 for preparation details.

Once you are suitably relaxed, call on *Archangel Tzaphkiel* – use the invocation "Archangel Tzaphkiel, nurture me, be my salvation. Redeem me, shower me with your blessings as you teach me to love myself and others unconditionally. Let my words be full of wisdom and the flame of understanding and discernment burn in my heart".

Just relax and let yourself be enveloped in the vibration of the Archangel Tzaphkiel. You can stay basking in this energy as long as you like; when you are ready, allow yourself to be raised upwards on a spiral of light. Slowly the light spiral raises you higher and higher; you feel yourself held perfectly safely in Angelic arms and you feel yourself transported very gently to the temple of light.

You will find yourself in the ascension temple of the Cosmic Mother that is over the Atlantic Ocean. The ancient temple is fashioned from etheric pure white quartz crystal shot through with veins of pale to deep pink and turquoise blue. It almost seems transparent and appears to float in front of you. You are led through many corridors by the Angels of the Mother-light; these exquisite beings are vast white Angels with flowing golden hair and pink-turquoise coloured wings.

You follow them until you reach the centre of the temple. This is a magnificent round vast hall several storeys in height. The floor is made of pink sapphire and the walls are made of danburite, which is perfectly clear and throws out brilliant white illumination as the light of the mother-flame plays upon it. In the very centre of the structure is a star-shaped opening which is surrounded by a low wall. The blessed mother-flame burns in the very centre. All around you are others who have come to bathe in the energy of the flame. You stand in a very long line and peacefully await your turn. Eventually you will be approached by beloved Archangel Tzaphkiel…you will be asked what is the purpose of this visit…you will then state your purpose… 'nurturing, salvation, redemption and blessings which will allow me to love myself and others unconditionally'. Archangel Tzaphkiel will then place you inside the flame. You feel your body and aura gently bathed in the Cosmic Mother flame…eventually Archangel Tzaphkiel will let you know when it is time to return to your physical body; she will gently guide you back to the here and now.

Give thanks and write down your experiences.

Archangel Raziel – Secret Mysteries

'Archangel Raziel' aura essence:
Ajoite, placed on the heart chakra
Papagoite, placed on the heart chakra
Iolite, placed on the fifth eye chakra (also known as the Angel chakra)
Tanzanite, placed on the third eye chakra
Rainbow aura quartz, placed on the witness point
Phenacite, placed in the soul star chakra
Aquamarine, placed in the soul star chakra
Fluorite, placed in the soul star chakra
Indicolite, placed on the throat chakra
Lapis lazuli, placed in the earth star chakra beneath the feet
Lilac herderite, placed just above the crown chakra
12 clear quartz crystals placed evenly around the body, terminations pointing inwards

Dedicated to and overshadowed by Archangel Raziel

Uses: Raziel (Ratziel) is the Archangel of the secret mysteries, who gives Divine information by allowing us to glimpse the enigma that is God. This experience is bestowed as knowledge and it is total, absolute, unequivocal and perfect…when we receive these amazing 'insights' we need no confirmation of our 'understanding' from others. Our crown chakra is opened, the flames of enlightenment descend, we transcend normal reality, we just are. In this moment we experience our own immortality and Divinity, we literally gaze upon the 'countenance of God'. These encounters with Raziel can seem extreme to our friends, family, work colleagues and society in general…but once you have sure and certain knowledge of the Divine, nothing will ever be the same again!

On the Kabalistic Tree of Life Archangel Raziel is the 'Cosmic Father' or *Abba*, who rules over *Chokmah*, which is the second sphere of the holy trinity at the top of the tree. The seed of life enters from *Kether* (The Divine), passes through *Chokmah* (Cosmic Father) and into *Binah* (Cosmic Mother). Archangel Raziel as the 'Cosmic Father' is the Chief Angel of the Supreme Mysteries which includes the legendary book of Raziel, which holds all terrestrial and heavenly knowledge. This secret knowledge was bestowed on King Solomon, imparting him with celestial wisdom. The prophets Enoch and Noah also benefited from encounters with Raziel.

When you work with Archangel Raziel you will experience a metamorphosis, in fact your life and the way you view the world will never be the same again! These 'mind blowing' encounters with Archangel Raziel need time to be fully integrated into all levels of your being, otherwise you can find yourself completely unbalanced. These 'full blown' encounters usually only occur after many years of meditation, prayer, purification and total dedication to leading a 'spiritual' life. Once this knowledge has been assimilated, most people who receive Raziel's transcendence become teachers and writers, sharing their abundance, wisdom and understanding with the world. Raziel awakens the prophets and religious reformers…use the power wisely and become a father to all!

Archangel Raziel's temple of light is situated etherically over a primary vortex in the Pacific ocean. This is where the spiritually advanced island empire of Lemuria or Mu once flourished some 70,000 years ago. Lemurian society was in complete harmony with nature and followed God's law – 'The Law of One'. This law sees everything as inter-connected. Lemuria sank to the ocean bed leaving only a few islands visible some 12,000 years ago.

The ray Archangel Raziel works through is indigo, which is a perfect balance of dark blue and dark violet. The parts of the body the indigo ray influences are the pituitary gland; the skeleton; lower brain; eyes and sinuses. Indigo aids intuition and spiritual knowledge. It is the strongest painkiller of the rainbow spectrum. It can release negativity from the skeletal structure. It is an astral antiseptic which transmutes and purifies negativity. Indigo is good for spiritual teachers and writers to instill in them humility, mercy and wisdom. Indigo can be addictive though, as it holds the domain of mystery, miracles and psychic understanding.

Invocation: Archangel Raziel, grant me mercy by allowing my sins to be cleansed in the purification of your lightning flash. Restore the Divine blueprint of not only my soul but all creation, so all souls are restored to their original perfect design. In the dark night when my soul is sorely tested, send your light to illuminate my path so I can ascend swiftly to your Divine grace. Hallelujah.

Physical integration: Cleansing and rejuvenating.

Emotional consolidation: Gives understanding to the process known as the 'dark night of the soul' and the soul's life path and need to reincarnate again and again until the soul finally cleaves to God.

Etheric assimilation: With conscious repeated use will restore the original 'Divine' blueprint of the soul.

Process: See the therapy section – **Process** (page 185).

Archangel Raziel Temple Meditation

The 'Temple of Light' you wish to visit is the retreat centre of Archangel Raziel. His ascension temple of light is over the Pacific ocean vortex where Lemuria once flourished. When you first start the exercise you may want to pre-record the following instructions on tape and hold a crystal, such as tanzanite or iolite.

Mist your aura with *'Archangel Raziel – Secret Mysteries'* essence.

Get into your chosen position, close your eyes and begin to focus on your breathing: see the section – Breathing, Meditation and Relaxation section on page 129 for preparation details.

Once you are suitably relaxed, call on Raziel – use the invocation 'Archangel Raziel, grant me mercy by allowing my sins to be cleansed in the purification of your lightning flash. Restore the Divine blueprint of not only my soul but all creation, so all souls are restored to their original perfect design. In the dark night when my soul is sorely tested, send your light to illuminate my path so I can ascend swiftly to your Divine grace. Hallelujah'.

Just relax and let yourself be enveloped in the potent energy of the Archangel Raziel. You can stay basking in this energy as long as you like; when you are ready, allow yourself to be raised upwards on a spiral of pure indigo light. Slowly the light spiral raises you higher and higher; you feel yourself held perfectly safely and surrounded by mercy in strong angelic arms. You feel yourself transported very gently to the temple of light.

You will find yourself in the ascension temple of light that is over the Pacific Ocean. The temple is fashioned from pure white marble which is shot through with veins of deep iridescent indigo. You are led through many beautiful corridors by the Angels of mercy and miracles; these exquisite beings are vast white Angels with golden hair and indigo-coloured wings. You follow them until you reach the centre of the temple. This is a magnificent round vast hall several storeys in height. The floor is made of deep indigo tanzanite and the walls are made of phenacite, which is perfectly clear and throws out brilliant indigo light as the light of the miracle flame plays upon it. In the very centre of the room is an opening which is surrounded by a low golden wall which is studded with iolite, tanzanite, lapis, phenacite and aquamarine. The flame of miracles burns in the very centre.

All around you are others who have come to be cleansed in the energy of the flame. You stand in a very long line and humbly await your turn. Eventually you will be approached by beloved Archangel Raziel…you will be asked what is the purpose of this visit…you will then state your purpose…cleansing in the flame of 'that which will cleanse my soul of my sins, unkindnesses and transgressions of spiritual law that I have committed through my actions and inactions. Bestow on me miracles, especially in the following petitions which are close to my heart…'.

Archangel Raziel will then place you inside the flame. This will bring mercy as you are cleansed of your transgressions…your soul's Divine blueprint will be restored to the amount that is perfect for your spiritual progress at this time and your understanding of Divine laws. You feel your body and aura gently bathed and purified as the miracle flame transforms your sins…eventually Archangel Raziel will let you know when it is time to return to your physical body; he will gently guide you back to the here and now. Give thanks and write down your experiences.

Use this meditation often to contact Archangel Raziel whenever you need to raise your vibratory rate and transcend your 'lower self' and renew your relationship to God.

Archangel Metatron – Angel of Ascension

'Archangel Metatron – Angel of Ascension' aura essence
Phenacite placed in the soul star chakra (optional)
12 clear quartz crystals placed evenly around the body, terminations pointing inwards

Dedicated to and overshadowed by Archangel Metatron

Uses: Archangel Metatron brings enlightenment and spiritual growth.

He *is* the Angel of Ascension and ascension is the path of love.

He is known as the Prince of the Angels. Archangel Metatron is the guardian of the threshold. Behind him stands the void; under him are all the other Archangels. The void contains all possibilities and when we traverse this 'space', the void, we come face to face with the 'Godhead'. This is the ultimate goal of human existence. On our path 'home' to the 'one heart', Metatron is our most important guide to initiation. Metatron is keeper of the Akashic records and he holds the keys to understanding sacred geometry. He is said to have taken human form as the prophet Enoch. He works with Lord Melchizedek (also known as Archangel Melchizedek). Melchizedek also took human form as a priest and king of Salem (present day Jerusalem) to form the order of Melchizedek; this was to co-ordinate the work of the Christ energy on Earth.

Archangel Metatron is the guardian of the Tree of Life – the journey of love; he is also known as the angel of the presence. His vortex of light is so luminous and vast that we often perceive him as a pillar of fire more dazzling than the sun. He is the light Moses saw as the burning bush. He is the light St. Paul encountered on the road to Damascus. In fact he is the light often seen by those who have experienced life-changing 'near death experiences'.

Metatron is considered a vast Angel and Archangel Sandalphon's twin reflection of the Divine. As twins they are the Alpha and Omega, the beginning and the end: their presence also reminds us of the esoteric expression "as above, so below".

Archangel Metatron's colours are brilliant white 'light' which contains all colours and pure dazzling incorruptible gold. Archangel Melchizedek's colour is gold. Archangel Metatron's retreat centre/temple of light is over Luxor, Egypt. Melchizedek has his temple of light over Jerusalem. On the kabalistic Tree of Life, Metatron is in Kether, the crown, representing the highest energy of the Divine. Kether is eternal, it has no beginning, as it contains the Divine presence, the first cause.

'Archangel Metatron – Angel of Ascension' aura essence creates a vortex of white light energy which purifies and aligns all the master chakras on the physical body. It also activates the 8th to 14th transcendental chakras above the head. This causes a download of information and understanding of the energy we call God. This is not a passive understanding of God, but an active, dynamic flow of information which emerges ever greater through the continued use of this essence. This essence is in one sense "royal", meaning it carries with it great power and great responsibility. The essence is an access key to multiple inner dimensions and realities, able to open doors for communication with the highest vibrational beings and also to precipitate etheric patterns into this material world. We know already that those things we hold in thought are brought into manifestation. This essence can be used to greatly magnify and hasten that process. Therefore the user is advised to hold the highest thoughts while communing with the energies brought through this essence, so as to manifest that which will best serve the individual and humanity. There are no limitations here.

It is used for meditation, light body activation, spiritual evolution and Divine inspiration. When working with this essence you need to make sure to ground yourself very well afterwards as it is extremely powerful, bringing deep altered states of consciousness (many people report that they are instantly transported out of the body). Using it for meditation is suggested (you would never use this essence if you were going to drive a car, operate machinery, go up scaffolding or climb ladders).

Some people are in awe of this essence or they find the vibration too strong for their light body level, so I suggest they combine it with the Archangel Sandalphon essence. Others find it releases blocks in their energy field too quickly, so they need to use it only when they are ready to really relinquish all their fears. Still others have found it is like having Archangel Metatron 'on their back' so to speak and they feel that all their 'faults' are visible to him and they are being shaken out of their comfort zone. A comfort zone is really a cage erected by the 'little ego', full of self-limiting beliefs which are caused by fear. All fear is caused by a lack of love and this essence is definitely an essence of love. It brings you to the greatest love, the unconditional love of God, but to really be comfortable in the presence of God you have to relinquish all fear and accept yourself and others just as you and they are. You must truly relinquish egotism, pride and arrogance, replacing them with humility and goodwill to all.

The phenacite used in this essence by Archangel Metatron was a six-pointed star: this faceted gem, a hexagonal cut with a six-pointed star geometrically cut into the top and concentric ones also visible below, weighs 49 carats and measures 25 x 25 x17 mm. It was cut from the natural phenacite crystal known as 'Clear Light' and it is indeed a manifestation of its name. There are almost no inclusions in this gem and it throws back a great deal of pure light when one gazes upon it.

When I first started showing this phenacite, named 'White Light', to other 'light workers' in 1993, I found the energy of the gem was just too powerful for most people: it accelerated their spiritual path too fast. It initiated karmic clearing at a speed most people could not integrate or tolerate. In fact the more the 'light worker' thought that they could 'handle' the energy, the faster was the clearing. So I asked the Ascended Masters, who had etherically engineered this stone, for guidance. They said I should work with it myself and keep it on my personal Angel altar, only bringing it out on the second year of the two-year professional crystal course I was teaching at the time – usually on the final weekend. This use proved perfect. The groups were very advanced after two years' continual study of vibrational healing energies and 'White Light' learned to adjust itself to accommodate the energy fields of the users. Over the years many groups have worked with 'White Light', as the Ascended Masters suggested this was to raise the vibrational rate of the planet and its inhabitants ready for mass 'Ascension'. This will occur in the next decade of the 'New Millennium'.

In November of 2000 I was in Bournemouth, giving an Ascension seminar. I had made an aura essence of 'White Light' as I had many times before, but this time it was different: everyone seemed ready to use it, no one held back or seemed fazed by it. In fact everyone who used it was transfixed by the essence and wanted it. So I asked the Ascended Masters who had etherically engineered the stone what was my best course of action. They said I must make it into a 'commercial' aura essence. It would be called 'Archangel Metatron – The Angel of Ascension', as that was the true purpose of this stone – Ascension.

This essence has the predisposition to accelerate the energy field of all who come into contact with it, including the activation of the light-body-ship. It teaches the use of inner space to access the 'Star Gates' within and without the physical and etheric bodies. With regard to the communication aspects of this stone, it will readily open the doors to the highest levels of Angelic light. The essence will be used by millions of 'light workers' who will be consciously choosing to accelerate their growth ready for the full manifestation and integration of the Ascension process. As an aura essence, this vortex of energy within and without will suffuse with light the one who is experiencing it. This will align the user into a column of light – immaculate pristine light – and the auric field will take on the brilliance and purity of the stone's vortex of light, but this must be done without attachment to previous limitations and ego fixations. Because this stone (and therefore its essence) is in constant communication with the Ascended Masters' energies, it will facilitate communion with the Masters' energies; with it, one may more readily transmit one's atom of identity into these rarefied realms. The Masters with their 'light' servants will be awaiting this contact, but it is advisable that, in making it, the one who is experiencing should ask either for teaching or assistance in the Ascension process.

The other use of the essence would be for the user to project their atom of awareness into the Ascended Master realms and offer their services to the Light and for the good of all and to aid the Ascension process. These realms are not to be entered for curiosity or idle conversation.

Healers who desire to make use of this essence are counselled to use it daily for refreshing and purifying their own energies and to use it on their clients only with their allowance and full assent and only when fully guided to do so. 'Archangel Metatron – Angel of Ascension essence' and the crystal it was made from have the ability to swiftly sweep away myriad disharmonies and imbalances but, as always, free will must dictate that permission is fully given or the practitioner may incur karmic debt.

Invocation: Archangel Metatron, angel of the presence and all-seeing one, transform me with the sacred fire of the phoenix, so that I can rise from the ashes of my former illusory self as the veils of ignorance and separation are removed from my eyes. May I become worthy of my crown of glory and unite my sacred I AM presence with I AM THAT I AM, so that I can shine like a diadem of beauty in the hand of God. Seal me with your perfect white light. Guide me every step of the way, so that I can fulfil my mission and allow the light of God to shine through me to fill the earth with Divine Light so that peace can descend on earth.

Physical integration: Purifies and balances the energy centres, bringing perfect energy renewal.

Emotional consolidation: Releases fears and cleanses ego-centred energy blocks.

Etheric assimilation: Light body activation.

Process: See the therapy section – **Process** (page 185).

Archangel Metatron Temple Meditation

The 'Temple of Light' you wish to visit is the retreat centre of Archangel Metatron. His ascension temple of light is over Luxor. When you first start the exercise you may want to pre-record the following instructions on tape.

Mist your aura with *'Archangel Metatron – Angel of Ascension'* aura essence.

Get into your chosen position, close your eyes and begin to focus on your breathing: see the section – Breathing, Meditation and Relaxation section on page 129 for preparation details.

Once you are suitably relaxed, call on Metatron – use the invocation 'Archangel Metatron, angel of the presence and all-seeing one, transform me with the sacred fire of the phoenix, so that I can rise from the ashes of my former illusory self as the veils of ignorance and separation are removed from my eyes. May I become worthy of my crown of glory and unite my sacred I AM presence with I AM THAT I AM, so that I can shine like a diadem of beauty in the hand of God. Seal me with your perfect white light. Guide me every step of the way, so that I can fulfil my mission and allow the light of God to shine through me to fill the earth with Divine Light so that peace can descend on earth.'

Just relax and let yourself be enveloped in the transcendental energy of the Archangel Metatron. Feel yourself surrounded by a column of perfect brilliant white light. You can stay basking in this energy as long as you like; when you are ready, allow yourself to be raised upwards on a spiral of brilliant white light. Slowly the light raises you higher and higher; you feel yourself held perfectly safely in angelic arms. You feel yourself transported very gently to the temple of the phoenix flame.

You will find yourself in the ascension temple of the phoenix flame that is over Luxor, in Egypt. The temple is fashioned from pure white marble shot through with veins of deep brilliant gold. You are led through many corridors by the Angels of light; these exquisite beings are vast white Angels with golden hair and gold-flame-coloured wings. You follow them until you reach the heart of the temple. This is a magnificent round vast hall several storeys in height. The floor is made of gold and the walls are made of phenacite, which is perfectly clear and throws out brilliant white light as the light of the phoenix flame plays upon it. In the very centre of the room is an opening which is surrounded by a low golden wall which looks like a crown. It is studded with diamonds, clear sapphires, phenacite and quartz. The blessed phoenix flame burns in the very centre. All around you are others who have come to bathe in the energy of the flame. You stand in a very long line and peacefully await your turn.

Eventually you will be approached by beloved Archangel Metatron…you will be asked what is the purpose of this visit…you will then state your purpose…cleansing in the flame of 'that which will rescue me from egotism, pride and arrogance'. Archangel Metatron will then place you inside the flame. This will bring mercy as you are cleansed of your transgressions and weaknesses…you will feel humility flow through you, your spiritual vows will be renewed…from this day forward you will shine with the attributes of humility, joyfulness, goodwill, right speech, right seeing, right hearing and right thinking. You feel your body and aura gently bathed and purified as the phoenix flame transforms all that is negative into perfection…eventually Archangel Metatron will let you know when it is time to return to your physical body; he will gently guide you back to the here and now.

Give thanks and write down your experiences.

Use this meditation often to contact Archangel Metatron whenever you need to transcend your 'lower self' and renew your connection to God.

Archangel Shamael's Sacred Sound

'Archangel Shamael's Sacred Sound' aura essence
12 clear quartz crystals placed evenly around the body, terminations pointing inwards

Dedicated to and overshadowed by Archangel Shamael

Uses: Shamael *is* the Archangel of sacred sound; he utilizes the transformational healing energy of sound in its pure sacred aspect. His sonic 'Starseed' emanation is designed to initiate transformational soul journeys. Shamael carries the colour vibrations of indigo, violet and gold. He is depicted as an aspect of Archangel Metatron in Western Kabalistic spiritual mystical tradition. He represents the first impetus of creation. On the cosmic scale, sound is a universal unseen power, able to bring about profound changes on many levels: physical, emotional, mental and spiritual. This essence allows you to harness and focus the power of sound – as precise mathematical proportions which are directed by Archangel Shamael. The origins of healing by sound can be traced into prehistory and beyond, into the realm of the sages and mystics, into myth, religion and soul memory. Recent scientific advances have verified that we are all vibrating atomic and sub-atomic particles. Everything has a resonant frequency, the frequency at which it most naturally vibrates. The philosophers of the school of Pythagoras regarded all physical forms as manifestations of music; the relative proportions of musical sounds parallel the physical proportions of natural and architectural shapes. These ancient doctrines held that life, health, balance and harmony depended upon a continuum of ratios and harmonic relationships, from within the mind and through the body and into the natural world and cosmos. The same ratios and harmonics were manifested as sound and music. Correctly applied sound could bring about cures by restoring the vibratory integrity of the body and soul and their relationship to the environment. These ancient cures often included rhythmic singing, chanting or incantations, from a traditional selection of sacred melodic sequences.

Archangel Shamael's sacred sound essence can bypass the mind's logical and analytical filters to make direct contact with profound emotions buried deep in the cellular memory. This, in turn, produces physical, psychological and spiritual reactions. Sacred healing sounds such as mantras, chants and incantations, affirmations, prayers and decrees have very ancient obscure origins. The knowledge of sounds, rhythms and words of 'power' has survived for centuries and by using these you invoke the power of the 'Light of God' directly into the physical world. The acoustic principles of resonance apply not only to musical instruments, but also to the human body. As the sound waves enter the aura and physical body, sympathetic vibrations occur in the body's living cells, which help to restore and reinforce healthy organisation. The high water content of the body's tissue helps to conduct sound and the overall effect is likened to a deep massage at the atomic and molecular level. By using the Archangel Shamael essence you can raise your personal frequency or vibratory rate to align with your perfect body and mind, bringing in the energy of our higher God/Goddess nature. When used in meditation Archangel Shamael essence has caused profound vibratory shifts in consciousness which have resulted in amazing visions and mystical experiences. Those who use sound as a vibrational healing tool will find their healing practice amplified and refined when combined with this incredible Angelic essence.

Invocation: Archangel Shamael, I petition you to swiftly send the alchemical 'Light of God' known to us as sacred sound to profoundly change our world for the perfection of all. Let the Light of God surround me. Let the Light of God guide me. Let the Light of God shine through me. Allow the Light of God to descend on Earth.

Physical integration: Purification of the energy centres, bringing the harmonious flow of healing energy to the chakra system which will promote healing on all levels of the body and aura.

Emotional consolidation: Purification of the emotional and causal bodies.

Etheric assimilation: Peace, harmony and balance are activated on all levels by the direct action of the 'Light of God'.

Process: See the therapy section – **Process** (page 185).

Archangel Shamael's Temple Meditation

The 'Temple of Light' you wish to visit is the retreat centre of Archangel Metatron (Archangel Shamael is an aspect of Archangel Metatron). His temple of light is in Luxor, Egypt. When you first start the exercise you may want to pre-record the following instructions on tape.

Mist your aura with *'Archangel Shamael's Sacred Sound'*.

Get into your chosen position, close your eyes and begin to focus on your breathing: see the section – Breathing, Meditation and Relaxation section on page 129 for preparation details.

Once you are suitably relaxed, call on Shamael – 'Archangel Shamael, I petition you to swiftly send the alchemical 'Light of God' known to us as sacred sound to profoundly change our world for the harmony of all. Let the Light of God surround me. Let the Light of God guide me. Let the Light of God shine through me. May peace descend on Earth'.

Relax and let yourself be enveloped in the potent energy of Archangel Shamael. You will feel his perfect presence very powerfully behind you. You will quickly be transported to his temple of light for your initiation into the use of sacred sound. You will find yourself seated in a round high-domed room. The ceiling is made of pure quartz crystal which looks as clear as glass, so that above you is the cosmos. Many other souls who have asked for this 'Light of Sacred Sound', the pure 'Light of God' initiation, will be with you…all sitting in a circle…you will find yourself surrounded by the 'Light of God', which will purify your vibratory signature, bringing profound changes in your awareness into the use of sacred sound. Eventually Archangel Shamael will let you know when it is time to return to your physical body; he will gently guide you back to the here and now. Give thanks and write down your experiences.

Use this meditation often to contact Archangel Shamael whenever you need your subtle energy bodies to evolve and increase your 'light quota'.

Angel of the Animals – Animal Healing

'Angel of the Animals' aura essence contains:
Sea Jasper
Botswana Agate
Blue Lace Agate
Red Coral
Marcasite
Smoky Quartz Phantom

Dedicated to and overshadowed by The Angel of the Animals

The Assisting Patron Angels

Thuriel	– Wild Animals	Behemiel	– Tame Animals
Hariel	– Tame Creatures	Arael	– Birds
Tubiel	– Wild Birds	Muriel	– Angel of the Sea and her Creatures
Rahab	– Angel of the Sea	Nahariel	– Creatures of the Streams
Anpiel	– Birds	Manakel	– Angel of Aquatic Creatures

Uses: This Angelically-inspired essence provides a supportive and nurturing space for those working tirelessly to heal the Animal kingdom. Animals, just like humans, can suffer a wide range of age-related problems and dis-eases. They, too, are subject to environmental pollutants and toxins, as well as bad diets and the stress of city living. Many animals are also very aware of their owner's stress levels and because they are so empathic they can absorb their owner's emotional problems and stresses of modern living. If a pet is absorbing their owner's negativity you may need to treat the owner as well. Animals do not have the same rigid 'mind set' as humans and so they are very open and more willing to change. Animals respond very favourably to Angelic essences and quickly integrate the new behaviour patterns offered to them. Angel of the Animals essence has also been successfully used on animals which have been abused, abandoned or neglected by their owners. It has been successfully used on wild animals and birds, as well as planetary species healing.

My personal belief is that some animals are ancient souls; they come into our lives for only a brief time. This can often be when we need immediate emotional assistance to look at the larger picture of life's rich tapestry. Animals teach us so much about unconditional love, loyalty, humility, gratitude and support. But, because their life-span is much shorter than ours, we need to release them with love and gratitude when it is time for them to move on to the next person who needs their help or it is time for them to progress in their own soul's evolution. I have experienced both personally – and in related stories from my friends and students – that some animals become our 'guides' and 'power' animals after their death.

I also believe that in aiding us on the 'other' levels it also helps them in their own soul's evolution, as well as enriching our soul's experience of the interconnectedness of all life. One of my cats who was called Vincent (after Vincent Van Gogh) was my wonderful companion on the earth plane; he

86

was a large ginger cat who had the most enlightened energies I have ever felt. His heart chakra was very pale pink which meant he was in constant fourth and fifth dimensional awareness. Vincent radiated his beautiful heart chakra energies outwards and brought transformation through love. He sadly passed away in 1992; before his death he 'got very into crystals' and would open the drawer where I kept some of my crystals, 'fish out' his favourite and go to sleep with his head on it. His choice of crystals changed daily, but amethyst and smoky quartz phantoms were always a particular favourite of his. Soon after his earth death I encountered Vincent on the higher Angelic levels; he was walking by my side. He appeared totally transformed – he was now as big as a lion, but with the same ginger fur, only now it seemed much longer and fluffier – but the most amazing change were his 'new' large deep pink Angelic wings! I am not the only person to have encountered their earth animal companion on the Angelic levels. One lady I know meets up with her horse regularly, too. He was dark brown on the earth level, but transformed to white on the Angelic level.

Some people are very arrogant by believing humans are superior to animals or that animals are only aware of the third dimension, or that animals have only one chakra – these people always have a damaged heart chakra. Perhaps the quickest way to heal a wounded heart chakra is through the healing power of animals, which is the gift of expressing love unconditionally.

The Angel of the Animals essence was angelically inspired many years ago when several 'light-workers' all experienced the great loss of an animal companion. These companions had all been great teachers to their human guardians. They were mostly dogs and cats, but there was a horse, rabbit, hamster, fish and seagull too. Although each light-worker released their animal companion with unconditional love and gratitude, I was aware that they all needed support during this process. As I meditated on this theme I was contacted by Archangel Thuriel, who said there was a desperate need for an Angelic essence which would also support those who work in healing the animal kingdom. The artwork designed by my daughter Martyne which is used on the 'Angel of the Animals' label was also born at the same time and was, in fact, the first artwork of the Archangel label range.

Treating Animals

Animals really enjoy receiving Angelic healing just as much as we do and usually respond very quickly to the energies. You can safely treat all animals with our Angelic essences. Unfortunately it is not possible or appropriate to place the crystals on or around the body of your tame animals, as they might inadvertently ingest them! I have found over the years that dogs really like eating crystals, cats seem to like sleeping on large quartz, amethyst or smoky quartz clusters and it has been known for some dogs and cats to 'purloin' their owners' crystals and crystal jewellery, which they usually hide in their favourite sleeping spot.

The crystals used in the essence 'Angel of the Animals' have proved very beneficial to household pets when they have been worn on their collars as tumbled stone pendants or sewn into their bedding. Some owners also put their pet's favourite crystals into a small pouch, which is then attached securely to their pet's collar. I have found over the years that sea jasper, Botswana agate, blue lace agate, red coral, marcasite and smoky quartz are especially beneficial.

As the essence is designed to support you in your animal healing sessions, please do not spray the essence directly onto your pet. The essence is designed to be applied to your hands and aura before commencing a treatment. Of course some people have used the Angel spray directly in their pet's aura with very positive results; I can only caution you in doing so, as it can frighten some pets. I must also add that you must seek veterinary care for your pets for serious health or aggression problems.

Developing Empathy

You will need to develop both your observational skills and empathy to treat animals as clients successfully. I generally find animals communicate in 'pictures'. When I attune to an animal and make contact with them, I mentally or physically just ask them "What is wrong?" and I am always rewarded by them showing me in pictorial form what the problem is, although usually I feel their emotions or pain too. You will develop this sensitivity in time, as everyone has this ability.

Intuitive Sensing of your Pet's Subtle Bodies

Intuitive sensing of your pet's subtle bodies is something you might like to do before and after giving a treatment to see what changes have taken place. You can use either hand or both hands and begin at the head or the feet. Allow yourself to be drawn to any area where you are guided.

Angelic Essences – Reiki – Animals

You can use the Angelic essences on your animal clients in many different ways. If you are a Reiki practitioner you can easily incorporate the Archangel essences into your practice by using them on your hands during the Reiki energy transmission.

Transmission

A simple way of using the essences on your animal clients is to transmit the vibration through your palm chakras. You will have already cleansed your own aura before you start the therapy session. You can work in the aura, chakras, meridians or directly on the physical body. Allow your intuition to guide you.

Angelic Alignment

Align yourself with the source of healing energies you will be using by spraying 'Angel of the Animals' essence on your left hand, then spreading the essence over the palms of both hands. As you do so, establish contact with the energy. You will normally feel the energy pouring in through your crown chakra and downwards to your heart chakra, before flowing down your arms into your hands and flooding out of your palm chakras. Allow yourself to be completely surrounded and supported by this energy. You are now ready to transmit the Angelic vibration towards your animal client.

Establishing Contact

Establish contact with your animal client for the energy transmission to commence by positioning yourself about 30 cm away from them. Hold your hands out in front of you, palm chakras towards them. Allow their aura to be completely flooded by the energy. Spend some time observing how the energy is flowing around your animal client. Allow your hands to guide you. You may choose to go through the aura layer by layer. You may use gently slow sweeping movements in the aura – remember, this whole process is intuitive and can take as long as your client will allow it. You will generally know when it has had enough, as it will move away or become distracted. When you are ready, you may feel intuitively guided to work through the chakra centres. You may be guided to work on the chakras in any order or combination. To work on the physical body, allow yourself to be guided to either your animal client's head or feet. You can work directly over an injury or wound. The Angelic essence has also proved useful for emotional upsets too. The length of time you keep your hands in each position is entirely up to your intuition, but animals normally absorb energy very quickly, so usually less time in each hand position is needed.

Distant Healing

Sometimes you will be more successful if you give a distant healing session. You can also augment the 'hands on' session with distant healing: Please see the section – **Distant Healing** (page 190).

Angel of the Animals Temple Meditation

The inner sanctum of the Angels connected to animal healing is a garden. It appears very much like the 'Garden of Eden'; it is paradise. When you first start the exercise you may need to pre-record the instructions on tape. You may wish to light a white candle or hold a crystal, such as blue lace agate or sea jasper. You must purify your energy space. Please see the section **Purification – Creating A Sacred Space** (page 158). Soothing sounds of nature music are also useful if they do not distract you too much.

Mist your aura with *'Angel of the Animals'* essence.

Sit in a comfortable steady posture; if possible, sit cross-legged or lie on your back.

Without making any effort to alter your breathing, simply tune in to the actual physical sensations of your breathing. Be sure to relax your jaw and tongue. Feel the sensations in your chest as you breathe.

As you inhale slowly, consciously focus upon the sensation of energy flowing up from the earth into your root chakra and then on upwards in sequential order through each chakra. Now, as you exhale slowly, open up to receive a spontaneous flow of energy from above. Experience a downflow of pure light, insight and power into your body, moving through each chakra in turn until all seven chakras have been illuminated from above and you are empty of air. Then again, without effort, let your breath spontaneously come rushing into you; allow energy to flow up from the earth into your chakras all the way to the crown. Rather than just visualising this, see if you can actually feel this experience happening inside you.

Again, after the full inhale, reverse the experience…opening to the downflow of universal energy into your personal energy system. Continue with this pattern for seven breaths.

Now call on the Angels of animal healing – use the invocation 'I call on all the Assisting Patron Angels that watch over the animal kingdom in all its manifold forms to be with me now and teach me your ways, so that I may find harmony for myself within the cosmic web of life to use for the good of all that lives'.

Just relax and let yourself be enveloped in the potent energy of all the Angels of the animal kingdom. Feel their soft white wings around you, giving you protection, peace and serenity. You are allowed to bask in this energy as long as you like; when you are ready, allow yourself to be guided towards the 'Garden of Paradise'.

You will find yourself standing before a high-walled garden…you will walk around the wall until you find a beautiful wrought-iron gate which is the entrance…you can just see glimpses of the garden of paradise beyond…at the gate stand two tall Angelic guardians who will ask you what is the purpose of your visit…you will explain to them why you are wishing to visit paradise…the gates are then flung open to you and joyfully you enter the garden…before you is the most beautiful garden you can imagine…your senses are alerted by the aroma of the hundreds of different types of flower, herb and fruit tree...you hear the sound of bird song and the gentle humming of bees...the warm breeze gently ruffles your hair and you feel the warm sunshine caressing your skin...all your senses are engaged in the experience of pure beauty. The colours are unworldly and you are sure you can see colours you have never seen before... these colours quickly attune your inner vision to see the auras around the flowers and trees, in fact you can see the life force moving in everything...even the soil is alive with pulsating colour and you feel drawn to pick up a handful of it...it is moist and full of nutrients and minerals...everything is just so alive, you feel your 'soul cramp' leave you...all that has kept you small or cramped your energies simply melts away to be replaced by feelings of bliss.

In the distance you can hear someone calling your name...you feel compelled to find the Angelic guide who calls you. As you run swiftly towards them, you find yourself overwhelmed by the presence emanating from an avenue of statues...intricately carved statues of Angels and Ascended Masters, Saints and Buddhas. Even though you are in awe of this energy, you know you must walk between the pathways they create...as you start to walk through the statues you realise, to your overwhelming joy, that they are not only welcoming you with open arms but you can feel the pure unconditional love vibration emanating from them...you respectfully move between them and feel your body, mind, spirit and soul being cleansed by the unconditional love they exude.

You can still hear your Angelic guide calling your name...it is the sweetest sound you have ever heard...they say your name in such a tone as you have only heard it spoken by those you have loved and who truly loved you...you find your heart just expands with so much love...and to your great joy your Angelic wings suddenly unfurl and you find yourself gliding towards your guide, who is seated on a stone bench just in front of you...your guide motions for you to be seated alongside...you sit in silent communion with your guide...you feel their thoughts and they feel yours...there is no need for words...simply a melding of minds...then they silently take your two hands in theirs and you now feel comfortable in gazing deep into their eyes...nothing is hidden between you...all is perfect...they know you wish to heal the animal kingdom and all that lives...this includes your own healing...you feel empowered by your guide...you now know with all your heart that each time you give healing to your clients, both animal and human, you are also healing yourself. There is no separation...there never was, there never will be...all is one, all is perfect, all is well...

Your guide finally lets you know it is time to leave and gives you a gift...you feel almost reluctant to take it, as this experience has been the greatest gift you have ever had...but you feel compelled to take the gift, as you know it would seem churlish not to...and you also know that you must now leave...but you are also aware that you are a multi-dimensional being of pure light and love and are on several different levels of reality all at the same time...so that in future you can visit this sanctuary of paradise any time you choose...you have only to close your eyes and will your awareness-self here...

As you gently return to your body, allow yourself some quiet time for integrating the experience...and use your Angelic gift wisely...for now you fully understand you traverse through the mind of God.

Please note: The Angel of the Animals aura essence has been successfully used hundreds of times on 'humans' to ground their energies into the physical plane when they have become 'spaced out' due to emotional upset, fright, fear, releasing of negative emotions during a therapy session or meditation. I have found it will even ground the most reluctant 'space cadet'.

Part Four

Subtle Anatomy

Subtle Anatomy

Health can be viewed as the continuous harmonious flow of vital energy between the body, mind, spirit and soul. The communication currents and insights gained in the study of the subtle bodies are a wonderful journey into sacredness for the soul. While anatomically unrecognized by current Western medical science, the subtle energy systems are nevertheless metaphysically connected with all the different systems within the physical body. The subtle anatomy is composed of the chakras, aura and meridians. These subtle systems are invisible to most people, although this talent can be developed. As with all other systems and even the gross physical system, a tiny change in one area will create a larger overall effect, so care must be taken to become proficient at understanding subtle energy. If you are already a complementary therapist, the following chapter will be somewhat familiar to you and by studying the karmic lessons or *soul initiations* it will help you develop your awareness of the subtle bodies even more. If you are a member of the orthodox medical or caring professions, the following could validate and expand on what you may intuitively feel. I know from talking to doctors, nurses and midwives who attend my seminars that many who spend their lives looking after others are very sensitive souls, who through their work have had experiences which may need validating by acknowledging the sacred aspect of their clients.

Chakras

Chakra is a Sanskrit word. It literally means wheel; it can also be described as a disc, ring or circle. *Prana* (vital energy, qi, chi or ki) is said to flow through the human body along the three main *nadis* (channels), namely *susumna* (fire), *pingala* (male) and *ida* (female). Susumna is situated inside the physical spinal column. Pingala and ida start respectively from the right and left nostrils, move up past the temporal lobes to the crown of the head and course downwards to the base of the spine. These two major nadis intersect with each other and also with the susumna. These junctions of the nadis are known as chakras or wheels, which regulate the mechanism of the bodies. Even to think of a chakra as a wheel is merely not enough. It is, in metaphysical terminology, a vortex. Chakras pick up cosmic vibrations, or Universal Life Force, and distribute them throughout the body and aura via the *nadis*, *dhamanis* and *siras*.

The body is a replica of the universe, a microcosm of the macrocosm on the physical and spiritual levels. As you develop spiritually you will become aware of your own chakras spinning and you will observe many subtle changes in them as your vibratory rate raises and your light body (mystical ascension vehicle) is activated. Although there are literally hundreds of chakras within the human body, we are most familiar with the seven main ones, the first five of which are aligned or 'embedded' within the spinal column. These moderators of subtle energy are envisioned in classic lore as a 'lotus' flower. Each chakra's lotus has a different number of petals. The number of petals is related both to Sanskrit symbolism concerning the configuration of subtle nerves, called nadis (think of these as the roots of the lotus flowers) that emanate from the particular region of the spinal column where the chakra is located, and also to the meaning of particular vowels and consonants in the Sanskrit alphabet. When these vowels are sounded correctly it causes awakening and spiritual growth in the particular chakra being 'sounded'. The chakras must always be seen as a complete system. Each chakra is aware of all the other chakras through the etheric consciousness known as the aura.

Master Chakras

These seven main chakras are called 'master' chakras. They are also gateways between various dimensions, physical, emotional, spiritual, etc. On a physical level, chakras correspond to nerve ganglia, where there is a high degree of nervous activity, and to the glands in the endocrine system. Each person's chakras are unique, yet there are basic similarities among us all. You will find, though, that you instantly get on well with people with a chakra system similar to yours, but people with very dissimilar chakras may well take an instant dislike to each other.

When the master chakras are clear and free-flowing, vital optimum health results. When the energy centres are blocked, split, damaged, overloaded, distorted or inactive, we find ill-health, emotional turmoil or dis-ease occurs. The aim of all of us is to maintain the free-flowing energy within the body, keeping it as clear as possible to maintain a happier healthier life. In the ancient Yogic tradition it was important to conserve the energies generated within the body and prevent their dissipation, therefore *asanas* (postures) and *mudras* (hand positions), *pranayamas* (life-force-breath) and *bandhas* (seals or locks) were used. The heat so generated causes the *Kundalini Shakti* (Divine cosmic energy) to uncoil. The serpent lifts her head, enters the susumna and is forced up through the system of chakras one by one to the *sahasrara* (chakra at the top of the head). This journey upwards through the chakras is spoken of as 'Kundalini rising'. The Kundalini Goddess is represented as a coiled snake wrapped around a phallus, or *Lingam*, which represents male sexuality.

Endocrine System

While anatomically unrecognized by current medical science, the seven major chakras are nevertheless metaphysically connected with all the different systems within the physical body. In this section on the chakras we will begin to explore how the chakras bridge the visible, physical body – in the form of the spinal cord, the autonomic nervous system and the endocrine system – with our 'subtle' body, that envelope of vibrational energy known as the aura. While orthodox medicine describes our physical system in terms of chemistry, what is now understood is that, for any chemical action to happen, a change in the electromagnetic energy signature of the body must occur first. This energy emanates from the mind and explains the importance of the mind-body link to our physical, emotional, mental and spiritual health.

The endocrine system is central in controlling chemical messages, which include adrenalin, insulin, dehydroepiandrosterone (DHEA), progesterone, testosterone, oestrogen, serotonin etc. These are secreted into the bloodstream from specific organs in the body to stimulate or inhibit certain essential physical processes. In simple terms, hormones are chemical messengers which course through your bloodstream and enter tissues where they turn on switches to the genetic machinery that regulates everything from reproduction to emotions, general health and well-being. Hormones can be thought of as the life-giving force that animates you physically, mentally and emotionally.

The endocrine system, along with the autonomic nervous system, helps maintain the parameters needed for optimum health by adjusting levels of hormone secretion to suit special demands. In the same way that an imbalance in one chakra affects the others, the nervous and endocrine systems are functionally interconnected and any disturbance in one part can lead to a malfunction elsewhere. In order to enlighten ourselves and gain a greater understanding of how the endocrine system links with the master chakras we shall look at each pair in turn.

Root Chakra – Adrenals – Nerve Plexus Coccygeal

The adrenal glands cap the kidneys; they are triangular in shape. They are responsible for secreting a variety of hormones including those that regulate the body's metabolism of fats, proteins and carbohydrates and the ones that control the balance of salt in our body fluids. The adrenals also produce adrenalin, the hormone responsible for our basic primitive issues of survival, the fight or flight hormone.

Sacral Chakra – Ovaries/Testes – Nerve Plexus Sacral

The gonads, or male and female reproductive organs, are responsible for the secondary sexual characteristics, such as body hair and the depth of the voice. The testes in males control men's sexual development as well as their sperm production. In females, the ovaries produce the eggs. Oestrogens (estradiol, oestrone, oestriol) are predominantly female hormones and in adults they are important for maintaining the health of the reproductive tissues, breasts, skin and brain. Excessive oestrogens can cause fluid retention, weight gain, migraines and over-stimulation of the breasts, ovaries and uterus, leading to cancer. Other oestrogen problems are rapid skin ageing, urinary problems, excessive bone loss and possible acceleration of dementia. An excess of oestrogen, relative to testosterone, is thought to play a role in the development of prostate problems in men. Most scientists now agree that by-products of oestrogen metabolism are the cause of both breast and prostate cancers. Emotional balance, sexuality and relationships are also the sacral chakra's domain.

Solar Chakra – Pancreas – Nerve Plexus Solar

The pancreas produces insulin, which regulates the blood sugar levels. It is also responsible for producing other essential substances which work on the effective digestion of food. The pancreas (pan = all and creas = creation) is situated just behind the stomach. The solar plexus chakra has a direct influence on the adrenal glands, which are also responsible for producing glucocorticoids, primarily cortisol; these are produced in response to stressors such as emotional upheaval, exercise, surgery, illness or starvation. Cortisol plays an essential role in immune function, mobilising the body's defence against viral or bacterial infection and fighting inflammation; however, chronic elevated cortisol levels suppress the action of the immune system and predispose to frequent infections. The solar plexus chakra also rules the digestive system.

Heart Chakra – Thymus – Nerve Plexus Heart

Located just above the heart, the thymus produces hormones that stimulate growth in early life. It also has a purifying role in the body by stimulating the production of lymphocytes, which form part of the blood's white cells' defence system, attacking invading organisms and providing immunity. Recently science has recognised that the auto-immune diseases, whereby the immune system attacks its own proteins, mistaking them for a substance that is foreign, have an emotional link and are not simply due to environmental or physical causes.

Throat Chakra – Thyroid/Parathyroid - Nerve Plexus Cervical Ganglia Medulla

Situated on either side of the larynx and trachea in the neck, the thyroid gland manufactures thyroxine, which regulates the metabolic rate of the body. This controls the body's efficiency in converting food into energy. The parathyroid gland, which lies just behind the thyroid gland, controls the calcium levels in the bloodstream. In addition to physical growth, these glands are also believed to affect mental development. The throat chakra is the link between the body and the head: it corresponds with balance and communication.

Third Eye Chakra – Pituitary – Nerve Plexus Hypothalamus Pituitary

The pituitary gland is located within a structure at the base of the skull, close to the eyebrows. Once called 'the master gland' of the endocrine system, it has since been found to be only a 'puppet' controlled by hormonal substances released by the hypothalamus, part of the brain. This gland influences growth, metabolism and general body chemistry, which includes the hormone producing contractions during labour.

Crown Chakra – Pineal – Nerve Plexus Cerebral Cortex Pineal

Once, not so long ago, scientists and doctors thought the pineal gland served no useful purpose. It is tiny, about the size of a pea, and lies deep within the brain. The pineal gland produces melatonin (first discovered in 1958), which affects the pituitary, thyroid, adrenals, ovaries and testes. It is a master gland and is the subject of a lot of scientific research. Research scientist Professor Russell Reeiter's clinical studies in the early 1970s proved that melatonin is one of the most effective antioxidants ever discovered and is the only known compound which can diffuse into the body cells and savage free-radicals – a factor which may offer real benefits to those seeking long-term health and well-being. Melatonin is produced in the pineal gland and released in the body at night time. Its primary function is to regulate the body's sleep and wake cycle and control our 24-hour clock. As we age, the body produces less of this hormone. The pineal gland and crown chakra are the control centre of the whole body.

Chakras and Conscious Evolution of the Soul

Through the conscious evolution and integration of the three aspects of the soul you will be able to balance your master chakras. This means you will begin to understand and reclaim your unique God-given personal power through the integration of karmic lessons or soul initiations. God has given us freedom (free will) as an evolutionary experiment. We are each allowed to experience good and bad. These positive and negative experiences can be seen as a series of karmic lessons or soul initiations which are basically a process of spiritual self-discovery. As you identify more and more with the sacred aspect of your evolution you will become aware that all your experiences, good or bad, are actually Divine right action which is taking place in your life. True alchemy of the soul comes from understanding that only good will come from each experience. This allows you to bring light into darkness – changing negative into positive.

Soul Loss

All of us have had bad experiences in our lives; we can view these times as 'darkness'. This is when we feel without hope and no 'light' is entering into our lives. We may even have experienced soul-fragmentation, soul-loss, soul-shock or emotional trauma. It is the true alchemy of the soul which allows us to see the good within a bad situation. It is, in essence, an act of faith. The path of *recovery* on a soul level after soul-shock, emotional trauma etc has splintered the soul into fragmentation has been called 'soul retrieval'. It works very much with acknowledgement and acceptance, allowing healing through spiritual insight and emotional intelligence. Once we step into the energy of love – non-judgemental, unconditional love – we allow the light of the soul to flood through us, which releases the negative experience to be transmuted into the positive energy of soul evolution.

We create our belief system every day (whether we are conscious of doing so or not). By changing our limited beliefs we manifest a different reality for ourselves and the world at large – miracles can then manifest. Nothing is impossible. But the law of magnetism is the law of attraction. We attract into our lives our reality. By changing our signature to a positive vibration we begin to vibrate at a much more refined level and we can then attract energies of love, healing, peace, joy etc. When we become energy aware, we no longer have a victim consciousness and we can take responsibility for our thoughts, words and actions. We become aware of our past karma and can dissolve our past mis-takes; that is just what they are – just like making a movie, you keep doing the same scene over and over again until you get it right. Mis-takes need not be thought of as negative – they do hold a vast learning potential for the soul.

Soul Initiations

Soul initiations or karmic lessons are represented by the seven master chakras. When we fully balance and integrate the seven positive attributes of the master chakras into our daily life we initiate the restoration of our soul's original Divine blueprint and in so doing step on to the path of ascension – the journey of love. Total avoidance of a particular karmic lesson can result in blockage of the related chakra. This brings inadequate vital flow to the associated organs. When the subtle energy flow due to chakra underactivity becomes evident, it will manifest in the related organs associated with that particular chakra. Underactivity causes degenerative, destructive or cancerous lesions, while conversely, over-exaggeration or over-focusing on a particular emotional issue causes the chakra to become overloaded with energy. This overactivity will cause over-stimulation of the associated glands and over-production of cells in the form of tumour growth and inflammation.

We will look at the chakras and karmic lessons of the soul, as each of the three soul aspects needs to be fully integrated. Each chakra builds on the previous one, much as one would build any enduring structure. Unless the karmic lessons are learned and the chakras are balanced one by one, it is impossible to grow spiritually. For this reason, those who wish to grow to great spiritual heights must embrace the karmic lessons and balance their chakras. This is a cosmic connection to be established, which will allow your soul true authentic identity to fulfil its assignment within the structure of human evolution.

The Three Parts of the Soul

The soul has three soul parts and each resides in a different chakra. Just being aware of this information will raise your vibratory rate. Archangel Chamuel's essence is excellent for developing and integrating your awareness of the three soul aspects.

Nefesh is sourced from the root chakra and sustains the body, giving it life and allowing it to participate in the material world. This red drop of life energy is inherited from your mother at the time of conception. At the time of death, this red drop of life energy, *Nefesh*, leaves its earthly element in the root chakra and rises upwards through the spiritual spine; it moves through the sacral chakra's water element and through the fire element of the solar plexus chakra, moving into the element of air and merging completely with the white drop of life energy, *Neshamah*, in the heart chakra, ready for the Divine alchemy of death.

Ruah originates from the heart chakra and is the spirit. It is the aspect that allows us to transcend the lowly human condition by using our intellect, insight and reason. It is the aspect of your soul which stirs you into the deep contemplation of God. In the normal human, who is only aware of the third dimension and the resulting reality that brings to their outlook on life, it is green. As you develop spiritually, you have access to the fourth dimension and your heart chakra colour of pink – which is a mixture of the red of the mother with the white of the father – is established. You can think of pink as the transmuting ray of the balanced higher fourth dimensional heart chakra. As you move into the fifth dimensional awareness through extended meditation or devotional practice, which will develop unconditional love, the core colour changes to gold. This means your spirit is growing strong as you aim towards enlightenment.

Neshamah is an emanation of the third eye chakra. It is the super-soul, pure spirit, and can never die or be corrupted; it is the eternal aspect of God. It is pure white and is the drop of life energy inherited from your father at the time of conception. At death, *Neshamah* leaves the third eye or brow chakra and descends through the spiritual spine to the heart chakra, where it merges with *Nefesh*. This merger produces the brilliant light reported by those who practise deep meditation or by those who have had near-death experiences. Depending on your vibratory rate at the time of your death, you will leave by the appropriate chakra. Your death awareness will influence your rebirth circumstances and enlightenment potential. There are two higher aspects of the soul and these are stored in the transcendental chakras above your head, awaiting your mystical light body activation.

The karmic lesson of the root chakra is associated with strong masculine actions related to survival. Does your soul rejoice in the experience of being on the earth? This means self-preservation and self-acceptance…standing up for oneself by being 'earthed' and having a grounded reality, feeling good and taking care of the physical body. It also relates to letting go of fear and the past in order to move forward. It is the start of your journey on the earth plane. If you have not learned this karmic lesson, you will react in a childish manner to threatening situations, usually by blaming others instead of taking direct personal responsibility. You will be the perpetual victim of your circumstances. You will have feelings of separation from God, apathy, spaciness, an unfocused mind, be incapable of stillness and have difficulty achieving your goals.

The karmic lesson of the sacral chakra is self-nurturing within the associated challenging motivations based on sentimental tribal or social conditioning, as well as absorption, assimilation and reproduction. This feminine chakra teaches you to take care of yourself emotionally, not just physically. You need to develop emotional intelligence. Although prana flows throughout the entire body, the sacral chakra is considered to be the pivotal distributor of pranic intake. When the karmic lesson related to this chakra is fully understood it becomes evident that we must take responsibility for our emotions and our capacity to experience joy. We must be able to take the good with the bad. We realise that both are just illusion and in truth we are responsible for our own emotional happiness, regardless of outside influences or circumstances. We no longer blame others for our own emotional problems. Our lives are filled with originality, creativity, gratitude and joy. We realise every second is precious and life is to be enjoyed. We are born anew moment by moment as we nurture our inner child.

The karmic lesson of the masculine solar plexus chakra is associated with the mind – personal self-esteem and self-confidence, in other words learning to honour and respect ourselves. We must establish a sense of personal power in relation to self and our external relationships. This chakra teaches very firmly the lesson of being true to one's own beliefs, however unpopular or different from the 'current' acceptable tribal truth. Once you have learned to stand in your truth and accept personal responsibility, you will be able to overcome all obstacles in your spiritual path. You will also learn to be immaculate energy-wise and always behave in a pristine impeccable manner to all you meet on your life journey.

The karmic lesson of the feminine heart chakra is forgiveness and compassion through unconditional self-love. On our journey through the lessons our focus has been with the lower chakras and building a strong balance of self-acceptance, self-nurturing, self-honouring, self-esteem; this in turn has allowed us to love others and honour them too, for each one's uniqueness of being, allowing ourselves and others to follow our own unique path on our journey through life.

This is unity within diversity, for if we cannot accept others exactly as they are, in this present moment, we will not be able to accept ourselves exactly as we are, right now, in this present moment. This is our sacred test, our karmic lesson of the heart chakra: unconditional love. We are challenged on this on a daily basis, but in order to move to the higher centres we must have this balance, otherwise we cannot successfully make this movement upwards, and when we begin to focus on the higher chakras all our hatred, anger, resentment, bitterness and fear issues will come back to haunt us, only this time it will bring the full force of our focused mind with it. So before you move on, make sure you truly unconditionally love and have compassion for yourself and for all life, because when the mind looks at itself in the mirror of the soul, if you are not full of love, you will be full of fear. This fear will manifest as your own demons of darkness and if you have not learned the karmic lessons of the lower three chakras you will try to project them outwards and project them onto others, so seeking an escape route and someone else to blame. You and you alone are your only judge and jury; all illness and feelings of separation start with a lack of unconditional love. You need no-one else to validate you: you know who you are.

The karmic lesson of the masculine throat chakra is self-expression. This means being aware of your communication on all levels, not just in the spoken or written word, but being aware of your unspoken communication too, your mind chatter, your body language and your communication with God and your higher self. Your body language speaks volumes, not just to others but to yourself. If you constantly affirm that you are depressed, sad or angry, be aware that your body is listening to you with 100% concentration and will act on your communication. It will subconsciously give you exactly what you ask for. What you dwell on day after day attracts even more of the same; this is the universal law of resonance, like attracts like. Soon you will have lots of negativity to deal with. The universal law of resonance always gives you exactly what you ask for (even subconsciously) in ever greater abundance! Your personal communication with others should be clear, honest and precise too. You must integrate your mind with your heart before you speak, which will allow your soul to express itself.

The karmic lesson of the feminine third eye chakra is to develop soul-expression. Perhaps I should list how you can tell if you passed this soul initiation. You will have access to all knowledge; when I say access, I mean you know through prayer and meditation how to access your own source of wisdom and Divine personal communication direct from the Akashic records, the mind of God. You receive inner guidance on a daily basis and follow it without the rational mind (ego) sabotaging you. You will experience cosmic consciousness and are aware of the sacredness and interconnectedness of all life. You are not attached to material possessions, you know the transitory impermanence of these things; you know you are an eternal being of light, love, wisdom and truth and you are limitless, so why do you need to hold on to possessions, which are just illusions anyway? You have no fear of death or dying, you are not preoccupied with fame or fortune; you show the pathway to liberation to others by example. You experience astral travel, telepathy and all your past lives. At this level of development you perceive yourself as androgynous and you no longer require another person to complement you; you are complete in yourself. You can choose what, who or where you want to be; your life flows effortlessly. You can manifest your reality daily, as miracles occur naturally to you. Life is one 'big' miracle filled with joy, unconditional love and spiritual enchantment.

The karmic lesson of the crown chakra is to develop selflessness. This lesson is a natural progression of the last one; by the time you reach this level of development you are one with the Divine, you can work miracles and are ready to merge your consciousness at the time of death with God or maybe you will choose to be immortal, as transcending the laws of 'nature' is no mystery to you. You will probably be able to live without food or water because you know that it is the pranic life force that supports and nurtures you, not physical food and water.

Journey Through the Seven Levels of Consciousness

Root Chakra

The first master chakra is frequently referred to as the root chakra. It is our most powerful contact and reflects our personal soul relationship to this Earth, the beautiful planet we live on, whose energy field we interact constantly with from the moment of our conception via the force of gravity. In Sanskrit the word for this chakra is *muladhara*. The direct translation is *mula* – root, *adhara* – support. It is also known as the base or earth chakra. In fact, the physical nerve bundle at the base of the spine that is associated with the root chakra resembles a massive root system that leaves your spine and runs down both legs as the sciatic nerve. This is the largest peripheral nerve system in your body, about as thick as your thumb as it leaves the sacral plexus at the bottom of your spine and spreads just like a great root system down each leg, all the way to the very tips of your toes and the heel of each foot. The root chakra is physically located in the perineum, the base of the spine, halfway between anus and genitals. This chakra is associated with our gift of life, physical health, self-preservation, survival and being grounded. It is the energetic gateway between us and the earth, also energies of childhood and the past. When this chakra is developed, we are grounded, solid, stable, reliable and powerful at physical levels of survival. Knowledge of the past, present and future are also bestowed when this chakra is fully activated by being balanced with the crown chakra. The root chakra, even though some people think of it as lowly, is directly linked to the crown chakra. Without a strong foundation it will be impossible to fully activate the crown chakra. Each chakra is envisioned in classic lore as a lotus flower. Every chakra has a different number of petals. The number of petals is related both to Sanskrit symbolism concerning the configuration of subtle nerves, called nadis, that emanate from that particular region of the spinal column where the chakra is located, and also to the meaning of particular vowels and consonants in the ancient Sanskrit alphabet. Thus, the symbol of the root chakra is a four-petal crimson-red lotus flower, around a solid yellow square containing a downward-pointing white triangle containing the *Bija* symbol Lam. The natural name of the root chakra, according to ancient Yogis who learned to listen directly to the sound emanating from their awakened chakras, is LAM in the Hindu tradition and a slightly altered and even more powerful LANG in the Tantric Buddhist tradition of Nepal and Tibet.

The colours associated with this chakra are the bright shades of red, scarlet and crimson. As you begin to activate this chakra, you will first envisage the lotus flower opening from a bud, with the 'warmth' of your focused attention. Over a period of time you will become aware of the flower beginning to focus upwards; this is a good sign. It means you have stopped wasting your energy on basic survival mechanism and ordinary fear-based tribal mental pursuits. The root chakra, as its name suggests, connects you to your roots – your 'tribe', your birthplace, your culture, your foundation and your earliest relationships, which can influence you all your life. If these early relationships were unbalanced, due to a dysfunctional family life, it is very important to look at your roots, otherwise you may find problems with your physical health, overall vitality and enthusiasm to complete your goals. Strength, courage, endurance, perseverance and stamina are key words that relate to this primary energy centre.

The yellow square in the centre of the lotus flower represents the solid element of earth. In the centre of the square is a white triangle: this represents the power and purity of the trinity. In the centre of the triangle is the lingam, a symbol for male sexuality. Around the lingam is the location of the resting place of the *Kundalini* Goddess. She is said to lie coiled three-and-a-half times around this chakra. The three coils represent the three stages of *avastha* (mind), namely *jagrt* (awake), *svapna* (dreaming) and *susuptiin* (deep sleep). There is a fourth level, *turiya*, combining and transcending the others, which represents the last half-coil. It is attained in *samadhi* (enlightenment). Around the yellow square is a white circle, which in turn represents the ultimate circular unity of every dimension of the universe. There are four red lotus petals around the periphery of the circle, then there is a white space around the petals; this signifies the pure white light and void of the human consciousness.

The first chakra, with its earth element, is masculine. All the chakras have a polarity and as you move upwards through the master chakras, in sequential order, they alternate male, then female. It is vitally important to fully understand these dualistic polar opposites, as by their combined action we have the unifying manifesting power of the Universe, the One. All your chakras are interlinked, of course, and you need to memorise all the information on the chakras. To return to yin and yang, masculine and feminine, neither is better than the other, regardless of any cultural bias you may have been indoctrinated into – only by truly understanding manifestation can you rise above duality and dualistic concepts.

The first chakra (Earth) – root – is masculine; solid; earthy; yang; male sexuality – balanced and paired to the crown chakra.

The second chakra (Water) is feminine; liquid; flowing; female sexuality; yin – balanced and paired with the third eye chakra.

The third chakra (Fire) is masculine; power; wilful; yang – balanced and paired with the throat chakra.

The fourth chakra (Air) is feminine; loving; integrating; yin – balanced in the centre.

The fifth chakra (Ether) is masculine; manifesting; logical; yang – balanced and paired with the solar plexus chakra.

The sixth chakra (Spirit) is feminine; intuitive; mysterious; yin – balanced and paired with the sacral chakra.

The seventh chakra (Cosmic) is masculine; pure bright light; yang – balanced and paired to the root chakra.

The root chakra should always spin clockwise in a male body and anti-clockwise in a female body. The master chakras in sequential order follow clockwise, then anti-clockwise. So in a male body it goes – clockwise, anti-clockwise, alternating through the chakras to finish at the crown chakra with clockwise. In a female body it goes – anti-clockwise, clockwise, alternating through the chakras to finish with anti-clockwise at the crown.

If you have any physical dis-ease or chronic ill-health you must give extra special attention to this primary chakra. In order to grow to great spiritual heights and consummate the marriage of Heaven and Earth (crown and root chakras), you must have a strong physical body. Your physical body is your only vehicle with which to make this transition into enlightenment. The glands, organs and parts of the body directly influenced by the root chakra are the blood (by its colour association in haemoglobin), adrenal glands (by the adrenalin release mechanism in fight or flight), spinal column, nose (the root chakra rules the sense of smell), all the solid elements of the body – bones and teeth, your sciatic nerve, lower back, prostate, feet, ankles, legs, knees, thighs and large intestine. Physical malfunctions include osteoarthritis, obesity, haemorrhoids, constipation and problems associated with the hips, feet and legs. Mental lethargy, 'spaciness', incapability of inner stillness are also malfunctions of this chakra's unbalanced energy.

Sacral Chakra

The highest function of the second chakra is to manifest primal creative energy in the form of functional 'sexual' resonance, which the nervous system then transmutes by Divine alchemy into the higher spiritual force that powers enlightenment. The second chakra is thus an essential ingredient in the opening of the higher chakras; without the 'pressure' of this chakra's raw sexual power transmuted into spiritual energy, all hope of perfectly balanced higher chakra functioning is futile. The Sanskrit name of this chakra is *svadhisthana*; the direct translation is *sva* – vital force, soul; *adhisthana* – seat or abode. It is commonly known in the West as the creative sexual chakra. In Hindu scriptures the second chakra is located in the sexual organs and upwards towards the navel, although it is not easy to draw a line between where the root chakra finishes and the sacral chakra begins, due to the position of the genitals, which dwell in both chakras. The area on the spine where the sexual ganglia leave the spinal cord and move down and forward to the sexual organs is located very high and close to the navel.

The root chakra provides the basic energy for strong masculine actions related to survival; now, with the second chakra, we switch into its opposite polarity, as it brings us directly to the flowing, nurturing, emotional, feminine power needed to conceive and give birth to a new life. From the opposites we begin to explore manifestation. Chinese scriptures which examine yin and yang, male and female, black and white, night and day, teach us the constant of change, of the balance of opposites. Your breathing is a perfect example of yin and yang in perfect harmony, the in-breath and the out-breath. Through the movement of opposites manifestation takes place.

Without the in- and out-breath of life your physical body dies. This constant dance of energy, this interaction between the chakras, is vital for harmony. When we become overly fixated with any one of the chakras, we cause a disturbance in the integral essential balance of yin and yang in our bodies. We then end up either physically ill, emotionally distressed, mentally disturbed or spiritually unstable – or all of the above together. Your body has the innate ability to heal itself so, during the meditation I personally suggest, you will always be guided to give conscious attention to all your chakras in any one session.

Looking deeply within the second chakra we find it associated with water, joy, vitality, attraction, magnetism, desire, creativity, sexuality and the emotions of the inner child. The word emotion comes from the Latin *movere*, which means "to move" and e, which means "out". The second chakra, therefore, is wholly linked to our emotional movements and movement in all its forms. The bodily parts it rules are all fluid functions of the body, kidneys and bladder, lymphatic system, reproductive system, breasts, tongue, fat deposits, skin. It links the physical and mental energies. An unbalanced sex drive, emotional instability and feelings of isolation can also be healed through balancing this chakra. This energy centre also gives you your social awareness and relates to your partnerships. Other malfunctions are: frigidity; impotence; bladder, kidney and uterine disorders; some prostate problems; middle back pain; fertility; asthma; bronchitis; gout; gallstones and obesity. This chakra also deals with purification and removal of poisons from the intestines. Physical lethargy and apathy, also the emotions of fear, shock and guilt, are under the domain of this feminine chakra.

The symbol for this chakra is the six-petal orange-red lotus flower, containing a second lotus flower: this represents the various intensities of the emotions. By meditating on this chakra you learn to turn the tidal wave of your emotions upwards – to feel them flowing through your body, bringing spiritual surrender. An upward-pointing crescent moon in the centre is where the attention must be fixed when meditating on this chakra. This gives command over the water element and confers psychic powers, intuitional knowledge and knowledge of the astral plane. Because the moon is part hidden, portrayed as a crescent, it gives the feeling of the yin/yang balance needed to manifest cosmic awareness within the body. Within the moon lies the *'Makara'*, a fish-tailed alligator with a coiled tail. This water dragon of ancient Asian mythology is unable to live in captivity; it would rather die than lose its joyful freedom of liquid movement.

As you explore the second chakra, allow yourself to open to a liquid, feminine, emotional surrender of oneness. In traditional Hindu folklore, the kundalini energy is always portrayed as a feminine goddess and to awaken this latent power of the kundalini is definitely to awaken a feminine force. If you find that you are afraid of the mysterious, feminine, yin dimension of your personal energy system, then you will need to spend a lot of time learning to 'surrender' to your higher spiritual nature. In the Christian terminology it can be thought of as "Thy will be done" (not my will), or your entire spiritual development will be hindered.

Although each of the master chakras is envisaged in sacred lore as a lotus flower, this is only a representation. The lotuses are not the map, merely the signposts, which initially begin to help you make sense of these vast mysterious energy centres. The study of the chakras is a lifetime pursuit, as each chakra is a complete universe within itself. Perhaps an understanding of this can be gained by studying the 'sounds' of the chakras. Mantras are what are called essence-sounds. They have been heard deep in meditation both by the great Masters of ancient times and by contemporary Masters as well. The master chakras are swirling vortexes of energy: they resemble, when viewed from a particular distance, spiralling galaxies that we see through our telescopes; likewise, atoms are miniature galaxies with their own spinning vortexes and central fixation points – this gives us our major clue to the nature of not only the universe but also ourselves. As above, so below; we are a directed replication of the universe, the microcosm of the macrocosm. The swirling, spiralling vortex of energy creates a particular tone, just as a spinning top will make a particular humming sound, which is audible to our physical ears. The chakras, though, have an infinitely more intricate vibrational quality; in fact each chakra is an immense symphony and each person's chakras make a symphonic sound distinctive to that person. So we are on the brink of an extraordinary vast sphere of reality when we begin to tune in to the subtle vibratory realm of reality generated by the energy centres in both our own bodies and those of people around us. The traditional sound for the sacral chakra is the *bija* mantra VAM in the Hindu tradition and a slightly altered and more powerful VANG in the Tantric Buddhist tradition of Nepal and Tibet.

The orange ray is primarily associated with this chakra, as is the colour red. The first three chakras are all associated with red, but in the sacral chakra it is defined as the marriage of the physical red with the intellectual of the yellow. This gives the colour orange, which is for creativity, joy, activity, rejuvenation and benevolence. When this chakra is balanced you will 'flow'. When this chakra is activated fully you become healthy, full of vitality and originality. Your originality originates from validity – you no longer need outside forces to validate your existence; once your kundalini has been awakened your freedom is never in doubt; indeed the colour orange stands for freedom.

Solar Chakra

So far we have discovered that the root chakra is firmly fixed in the element of earth and the water chakra is concerned with the fluidity and movement of water; now we need to move upwards into the solar plexus chakra, which is aflame with the element of fire. If we move up the human torso a little further we discover the heart chakra, which is imbued with the magical quality of air. Thus, in the human body, within our own spinal column below the neck we have all the basic elements of earth, water, fire and air. They interact and complement each other when balanced. We are each unique as well and sometimes this balance is hard to achieve. As we explore the element of fire we must be aware that in order for fire to burn it must be fuelled from below and fanned by the air element of the heart chakra above, and this gives us a clue to major blockages in the solar plexus chakra. In order to balance the solar plexus chakra completely we need to engage the lightness and airiness of the heart whilst having a grounded reality. Remember, it is hard to think clearly when your stomach is too full or you are very hungry.

The traditional Sanskrit name for the solar plexus chakra is *manipuraka*, which means jewel of the navel. It is also known as the power chakra, navel chakra or lustrous gem. It is indeed located at the navel, but its effects are felt from just below the navel to just below the tip of the sternum. As with all the chakras we must always keep in mind that their locations are not static; they are located in slightly different places in different bodies. They also drift up and down the spine a little, depending on one's spiritual and emotional condition. It is interesting to note that the medical profession recognises this area as being related to the sun – hence everyone is familiar with the term solar plexus. In China and other Eastern countries this chakra has been held in high regard due to the attention over millennia to the tradition of the male-dominated martial arts. In the martial arts tradition it is located just below the umbilicus and is a potent point for the gathering of qi. This third chakra's polarity is masculine, explosive, wilful, powerful and yang.

Traditionally this chakra is associated with the logical functioning of the mind. This means it also rules our intellectual prowess, thought processes, will-power and energy manipulation on all levels, especially the astral and cold-hearted wilful aggression. It is also associated with the fire of anger and hatred, personal power, ambition, combustion, happiness, laughter and fun. It rules and assimilates energy for the pancreas and adrenals, also the central nervous system, stomach, liver, gall-bladder, spleen and eyesight. Malfunctions include stomach ulcers and other digestive and eating disorders, also diabetes, low vitality, depression, phobias, chronic fatigue and allergies, constipation, flatulence, headaches and poor skin conditions due to faulty elimination. Negative emotions such as oversensitivity to criticism, a need to be in control, low self-esteem or the addictive personality, as well as sluggishness, negative thinking, boredom, cowardice, being judgemental, sarcastic, acidic and impatient. The yellow ray is associated with this chakra. The colour yellow is for meditative analytical thought, intellectual activity, abundance and the manifestation of your dreams. The solar plexus is the junction that absorbs all the emotions. Emotional upset will register here first. Always remember this chakra is raw power which can lead to enlightenment or annihilation.

Just as all life on this planet needs the energies of the sun to survive, we too need our sun centre. This chakra will assist us when balanced to move beyond the polarities of the two lower chakras' wilful desires, which are selfish and ego-led, into the manifestation of personal and planetary joy. As we evolve spiritually and take control of our personal power and personal responsibility, we step outside the limiting rigid mental strait-jacket of late twentieth-century analytical thought patterns, moving into the abundance of personal responsibility and global abundance. It is also said "If you meditate on this chakra you will become dis-ease free and have no fear of fire, being able to control this element". A balanced solar plexus chakra is shown when we are optimistic, self-confident, original, tolerant, flexible, adaptable and focused. The traditional sound for the solar plexus chakra is the *bija* mantra RAM in the Hindu tradition and a slightly altered and more powerful RANG in the Tantric Buddhist tradition of Nepal and Tibet.

The symbol for this chakra is the 10-petal lotus flower. The petals are yellow, representing wisdom, and the centre contains a deep red downward-pointing triangle surrounded by three *'svastikas'*, symbolic of fire. The three represent the combined energy of the three lower or physical realm chakras, because as we move into the higher chakras we shall move into the element of spirit. The creature associated with the solar plexus is the wild ram, which is an independent beast, not liking to be dominated or restrained, but it does have a remarkable sense of balance and poise and it is very powerful, much more so than in relation to its size.

Heart Chakra

Before we move into the heart chakra, we need to just recap on the three lower chakras. They relate very much to matter and the physical world of day-to-day survival, procreation, of energy manipulation and personal mastery over the physical realm. We are now moving into the presence of a magical quality we call love. There is no doubt that humans are preoccupied with this energy centre – there must have been thousands of songs written containing the word love – yet if you analyse all of them, very often you will find it is not the principle of true love they contain, but conditional love – which is the reason why so many of these love songs have reference to broken hearts and unfulfilled longings within their lyrics. Can a heart be broken? It can certainly feel like it, if you have attachments in your personal loving energy. Remember, human love never stands on its own, free of attachments – it is empowered by the energetic interplay of the first three chakras. Within the seven-fold chakra system it is only when we have fully merged the energy from the top three chakras through the heart and combined it with the energy of the lower three chakras that we can actually love unconditionally. If you can't love yourself and others unconditionally, how can you hope to create a pure home for God to dwell in?

When there is an ample balanced flow of energy from above and from below, the heart chakra is radiant with compassion or, as I like to express it, radiating compassion. The Sanskrit name for the heart chakra is *anahata*, which translates as unbeaten or unstruck. The sacred meaning of this word is 'a sound that is made without any two things striking'. We need to explore this a little further: in the intuitive understanding of Yogic tradition there exists at the very centre of each chakra a nucleus called the seed or *bija*. From this seed emanates a vibration: this is both a sound and an essential energy resonance pattern which governs that particular chakra. This seed sound governs the overall development of the particular energy centre. So when we meditate on the fourth chakra we must hold this concept uppermost in our minds. By sounding the mantra, we can develop our heart chakra in accord with our Divine cosmic blueprint. The sound, as the name *anahata* implies, is its creation come forth by no known means; it originates from the void and manifests in the heart chakra. Sound vibration is considered to be the originating power of manifestation in the universe. Whenever you choose to chant the *bija* mantra for each of the chakras, you are tuning your entire physical, emotional, mental and spiritual being to the exact sound of the chakra – and aligning yourself with the mysterious centre of your chakritic universe.

The heart chakra is located in the cardiac area, in the region of the physical and spiritual heart. It is associated with the element of air – or, as many people prefer to call it, prana. In ancient times the spiritual masters knew from direct inner revelation that each breath, and the air taken in with each breath, was magical, determining the quality of life and vitality in each individual. It was therefore decided that the air must hold a mystical, life-giving substance, which they termed prana. Prana has been described as the subtle all-pervading, Divine energy of eternal life – invisible but vital. A hundred years or so ago, the scientists discovered a substance called oxygen, which they explained does fuel our every movement on this planet – so is oxygen prana? In one way, yes, but in another, no. No-one fully understands what oxygen is. The scientists know some of its properties, but the deeper they look into its sub-atomic activities, the less they really understand the reality of the air we breathe. The mystery becomes bigger as the scientific knowledge grows more massive. The only real way to understand this mysterious substance called prana is through direct contact with it during meditation.

In Chinese philosophy underlying all aspects of Chinese medicine is an outgrowth of viewpoints on our relationship to the universe around us. The Chinese see human beings as a microcosm within the universal macrocosm. The principle demonstrated by the inner workings of humans is reflected in the universal relationships of energetic flow. They call this energy *qi* or *chi*; they give its explanation as a unique substance that flows from the environment into the physical body. The

Chinese feel that qi is an energy of both nutritive and cellular-organisational characteristics which supersedes the energetic contributions of ingested food and air. Therefore this qi is a type of subtle energy which permeates our environment. Since the heart chakra is closely tied to the expression of love and compassion, it is naturally considered to be an important centre of nurturing. Most of the organs associated with the heart chakra nurture and promote life and vitality throughout the rest of the body. The lungs take in air, oxygen or prana from the atmosphere. The heart pumps the blood to the lungs, where oxygen, prana or qi are taken in and distributed to the rest of the body's organs. In the digestive system, more nutrients are added to the bloodstream, where the circulation can distribute them to the rest of the physical body. The breasts are also located at the level of the heart chakra; they are dedicated in females to the nurture of another being. Therefore the ability to nurture oneself, as well as other people, is linked to the development of the love nature of the heart centre.

As the heart chakra becomes more open and free-flowing with cosmic pranic energy, the capability to unconditionally love oneself and others is substantially increased, along with a greater flow of life force or qi to all the organs it supplies. At a psychological level, the heart chakra deals with the emotions that bind individuals in various loving relationships. The act of nurturing is fed by the different emotional feelings generated by the heart chakra. Feelings of unconditional love, compassion and empathy are a direct outpouring of spiritual growth, therefore the heart chakra is important in developing higher levels of consciousness. When these elements are lacking in the personality, it indicates a severe dysfunction or energy block within the heart chakra. Interestingly, one of the most important links between the heart chakra and a physical organ is seen in the relationship between the heart chakra and the thymus gland. For years the medical profession thought it was 'normal' for the thymus gland to display atrophy in size and function as an individual grew older. This view is being revised, as physicians begin to delve into the energetic relationship between the heart chakra and the thymus gland. It is possible that the age-related involution of the thymus gland is not a universal phenomenon; in those who do have thymic-atrophy in later years it will be shown that there is a direct relationship between loneliness, depression, blockages of the heart chakra and glandular function. Researchers in the field of psychoneuroimmunology are examining the subtle-energetic links between emotions and immunological function. It has already been established that physiological links between human emotions and illness do exist – so it will not be long before full understanding of emotions and the thymus gland that plays an important role in the regulation of the immune system's response is finally accepted by the medical profession. Various researchers who have examined the link between emotions and illness have found a strong association between depression, grief and the overall suppression of immune functioning. But more importantly, dysfunction frequently arises from a lack of self-love. Persistent negative self-images and loss of self-worth do more physiological damage than is currently recognised.

The heart chakra is associated with compassion, empathy and love. It rules over our beliefs about love and relationships, one-ness, the physical heart, lungs, breasts, thymus, the immune system, lymph glands and the sensory channel of touch. Malfunctions include lung disease, asthma, heart disease; shallow breathing, high blood pressure, heart attack, tension and cancer; problems with arms, hands and fingers; fears about betrayal, co-dependence and melancholia. Negative heart chakra imbalances or states are demanding attention; being overly critical, possessive, moody, melodramatic, manic depressive; using money to control people, buying love or friendship; the martyr syndrome 'I have sacrificed myself for you', conditional love 'I will love you if', controlling love 'If you loved me you would'; or feeling sorry for yourself, the 'poor me' syndrome. Also indecisiveness, paranoia, fear of letting go, fear of getting hurt, feelings of abandonment, fear of rejection, feeling unworthy and feelings of shame and seeking constant reassurance and validation.

Your heart is the centre of your body – when your heart energy flows, your whole being follows. The heart centre allows you to transcend the limits of your ego and identify with other people, plants, animals, crystals, etc. – in fact all life. If you wish to 'heal' yourself and others, a requirement is an open balanced heart chakra. Very often I have found those who could feel 'nothing' from a crystal could feel 'nothing' from other people too. At some time in their development as a human being they had chosen to close off their heart chakra. Very often as therapists most of our work is to get people to allow their hearts to open and then heal.

The fourth chakra, the heart is experienced as feminine, loving, integrating, yin – and eventually the need to surrender the ego which allows the lower aspect of the soul, the *Nefesh*, to become fully entwined with the second aspect of the soul, the Ruah, which originates from the heart chakra. This will eventually bring you to the third aspect of the soul, the *Neshamah* – pure spirit.

The traditional sound for the heart chakra is the *bija* mantra YAM in the Hindu tradition and a slightly altered and more powerful YANG in the Tantric Buddhist tradition of Nepal and Tibet.

The traditional symbol is the 12-petal green lotus flower, the inner centre containing two intersecting triangles called *trikonas* in Sanskrit; they make up a perfect six-pointed star, demonstrating the balance between the downward-pointing spirit descending towards matter and the upward-pointing matter ascending towards spirit. Yet, if we care to look deeper, going into the heart further, we find that it is in the heart chakra that the triangle form is most strongly represented; by being made double it generates six smaller triangles aiming out in all directions, sending the *anahata bija* vibration out to all the other six chakras. The heart chakra represents *Bakti* Yoga – this closely resembles Christianity, in its devotional aspect. It is the Christian cross that helps us locate our heart chakra with ease: all you have to do is raise your arms out to each side and tune in to the midpoint in your chest where the horizontal meets the vertical – there is your heart.

The ultimate message of the kundalini goddess is that it is an act of surrender through enlightened willpower, not blind faith or subjugation, that brings the heart chakra into perfect alignment. Therefore, only by an of act of focused Herculean-will can we cause the full manifestation of the perfection of our being to be fully revealed in all dimensions and on all levels of our being.

The colour green is associated with the heart chakra, as well as the transmuting heart chakra ray of pink. Finally gold, which is the highest wisdom ray of the enlightened heart, will manifest in the heart chakra. The green ray is for soothing, healing, growth, balance, discrimination, ecstasy, unconditional love; merging the physical with the Divine; transmutation with love; the marriage of physical and spiritual. Meditation on the green ray of the heart chakra gives the sound of *anahata*, the 'primal sound' or *Sabdabrahman*. It also bestows pure qualities, cosmic love and various psychic powers. This central green heart chakra within the sevenfold system is the heart of our journey on the physical plane. It balances between the worlds of spirit and matter. Through this balance we relate compassionately and unconditionally with all life, with love. Remember, this 'love' is not dependant on others. It is not the tribal love of the root chakra or the sexual love of the sacral chakra, or the materialistic love of the solar plexus chakra, but is a state of being, enduring and constant. It also means self-love and self-acceptance.

The colour pink is for love and harmony in all our relationships; hope; being receptive, intimate; affection and kindness. It melts and dissolves resentment and any residual resistance we may have to healing. It will bring the activation of *Karuna* (compassion, pity, tenderness; it also implies devoted action to alleviate all suffering in ourselves and others). The gold is the Sun-gold ray of wisdom, knowledge and understanding – the end of the rainbow is the pot of gold that we all seek on our pathway to enlightenment. It aids the assimilation of knowledge, bringing spiritual vitality and spiritual abundance. It rids the body of parasites and parasitic energies on all levels.

Throat Chakra

The fifth or throat chakra is also known as the communication chakra. In Sanskrit the name is visuddha, which translates as pure; it also means purification. It is the first of the spiritual triad of higher centres and resonates most vibrantly with the blue ray. At the psychic level, this chakra is associated with clairaudience, or the ability to hear things at a subtle energetic level. It is located in the throat region, just above the base of the neck – directly situated over the thyroid gland. This is where our basic communication tool, the voice box or larynx, is situated also. This remarkable organ enables us to take the outflow of air through our windpipe and transform the torrent of air into a vibratory message for the outside world to respond to. The way people respond depends on the vocalisation you make. The human voice as a whole is very revealing; in fact it reflects the mental, emotional, spiritual and physical condition of a person.

Your voice, as you will come to recognise, is a direct expression of your soul. Understanding the voice is an excellent discipline of self-awareness and it is central to the art of active listening. The way you use your voice gives vital insight into your complete being; your vocalizations reveal how your energies, feelings, thoughts, emotions and intuition collaborate to produce your unique vocal style. This vocal style reacts to external influences as well as the feelings inside you. It evolves through time as your emotions and past experiences accumulate, develop and mature. Therefore the voice is diagnostic as well as therapeutic. By listening to the voices of others and by objectively tuning in to the nature of your own voice, you can find out many aspects of health and emotional well-being. Try listening to the individual words and their meanings in context, to the subtle layering of implications and associations behind the words and between the lines, to the pauses, gaps and silences; to the non-verbal utterances such as sighs and sobs, and to the voice itself – its pitch and tonal qualities, its rhythm and pace. In addition, look at the posture and the body language, as well as those more mysterious nuances of perception which we call intuition and instinct. Thus the nature of the voice reveals the nature of the soul; it can help us to identify and diagnose problems, which we can utilize to start the healing process.

A healthy voice reflects a healthy spirit. The signs of a healthy voice are sensitivity, compassion, warmth, joy, vitality, wisdom and purity of tone; it is clear, bright and open, with no hint of forcing or straining. Body language concerning the throat chakra is also interesting: if you observe someone who appears to have difficulty expressing themselves, see if their chin is held down towards the chest, obscuring the throat area. This shows that the person is very vulnerable or weak in the throat chakra. Such people frequently clear their throat, because esoterically they are being choked by the truths they have swallowed. Holding the head down towards the chest is also a sign of depression. If you raise your head and look upwards on a regular basis it will lift your energy. In fact this very movement of looking up will raise your energy. When we are sad or depressed we usually slump our shoulders and take very shallow breaths. If we sit up straight and breathe deeply it is much more difficult to stay sad or depressed. In this way, anything that makes us look physically upwards subtly makes us more open to feeling happy, optimistic and cheerful.

The throat chakra is concerned with all communication including the written word. We should remember that up until a few hundred years ago, with the invention of the printing press, the vast majority of human communication was through vocal exchange. The throat chakra also involves learning self-discipline or self-mastery over the incarnating ego's small-will. This controlled expression of the higher will is another important issue of the throat chakra. At a time when self-indulgence has become commonplace, the development of discipline in one's life is an important stepping stone towards any type of personal or spiritual transformation. Many people do not realise this communication is also with their guides, Angels, Masters and teachers, including their higher self. Long ago it was conjectured that there existed a fifth element beyond the four visible elements of earth, water, fire and air; the ancients called it the *akasha* in Sanskrit and 'ether' in the West. This fifth element was the realm where spirits were said to live. It was believed to be at a higher or faster vibration than the other elements, so it was only available to the adepts, those elite souls who could raise their vibratory rate sufficiently high or fast enough to encounter or view its elusive dimension.

The throat chakra also works with the sensory channel of sound. This is the most direct of the chakra correspondences and often the easiest for the Western mind to grasp. Talking about the Western mind – it shows how the throat chakra can become overactive to a detrimental degree. This is because the throat chakra is also intimately associated with the parts of the brain that generate complex thought-flows. My experience as a therapist and teacher has been that most people in our society fixate on the fifth chakra, living in a world of concepts, theories, ideas, dreams and fantasies.

When the communication chakra is inactive, we are mentally asleep, not thinking things through adequately in order to lead a productive, fulfilling life. These people tend to shut themselves off from society and normal human interaction. Conversely, when the throat chakra is overactive, it drains energy from all the other chakras and – worse – other people too! We have all encountered this negative draining effect of the person who does not know the meaning of the word moderation; silence can really be 'golden'. These souls who have hyperactive throat chakras can also be caught up in the energy of thinking-thinking-thinking, without tuning in to their heart enough (the affective domain) or the solar plexus chakra (the psychomotor domain) to give the necessary power to these ideas. Great thinker – ineffective doer. They can be manipulative too, always seeking the help of others to carry out their grandiose unrealistic plans.

The throat chakra can really become unbalanced through a severe lack of soul connection. The energy of the two higher chakras is needed to truly manifest your Divine path with heart. This will stop the abuse of the solar plexus power chakra and the throat chakra's cognitive abuse of the planet and its inhabitants. I do not mean in any way to demean the throat chakra's technological advances though; without the latest technology I would not be able to sit here at my computer and write this book. When technology is at its finest, it is used for the good of all that lives.

So to recap and explore further, the throat chakra is associated with communication, self-expression, sound, voice, speech, writing, typing, singing, chanting and active listening. It also relates to dreaming, imagination and out-of-body experiences and the astral realm. I have had so many clients over the years who were totally fixated with the astral dimension of the throat chakra. This is because not only does the throat chakra give out communication to others, it is where we receive communication from others. This includes the realm of 'spirit'. These non-physical realms contact us via our throat chakras; if our two higher chakras are unbalanced or non-functioning, we can spend our whole lives 'hypnotised' by low level entities. These lower level 'spirits', as anyone who has read a Carlos Castaneda book will know, can be fascinating but sometimes frightening. So it is very important when working with any chakra healing or vibrational therapy system to give equal attention to all the energy centres, so that they balance and complement each other. I should state, however, that visions are an integral part of the throat chakra; they relate very much to our own personal fantasies and unconscious activities, very much the way dreams do. If the visions come to you, it is perfectly fine; everyone has this capacity, just as everyone has the capacity to dream. The secret is not to fixate on them or become overly attached to them. The world of maya – illusion, of holding on to images and visions instead of moving beyond them – is a fifth chakra function. Always be ready to let go of your visions in order to move upwards into sixth chakra, non-conceptual, non-duality consciousness. Be open to immense fifth chakra visions that play out your conceptual imagery of spiritual awakening, but be ready to leave them far behind as you move onwards and upwards into the higher chakras.

Physically the throat chakra rules over the thyroid gland, parathyroid, lungs, vocal cords, jaw and breath. Malfunctions include stiff necks, colds, sore throats, thyroid and hearing problems, tinnitus, asthma. It also includes stiff-necked attitudes, dogma, religious dogma, the illusory masks of the self, perfectionism and the inability to express emotions in a constructive non-destructive manner; blocked creativity is also a result of an ineffective throat chakra.

The fifth chakra, the throat, is masculine, manifesting, logical and yang. Its symbol is the 16-petal blue lotus flower. As we progress through the chakras we find the colours becoming cooler and cooler and the vibrations of the colours faster and shorter. The warm earth frequencies (red) are the longest and slowest, as we would expect, and as we move heavenwards the cool blues begin to manifest. Contained within the lotus flower is a downward-pointing triangle representing spirit, within which is a circle representing the full silvery-blue moon. The moon represents the astral energy of the Akashic records. The moon's silver reflection is only an illusion of light. It contains no light of substance of its own. It is when we move into the third eye and crown chakras that the illusion vanishes, as duality and separation end. The sixteen petals of the lotus flower are very significant in this chakra; each petal represents a vowel of the ancient Sanskrit alphabet. This allows us to relate to the *Sabdabrahman* or original sound and it is through the throat chakra that we disperse the energy of all the other chakra mantras throughout our body and aura. Through the use of these primal *bija* sounds, the throat chakra has a vast potential to carry us towards enlightenment. The traditional sound for the throat chakra is the *bija* mantra HAM in the Hindu tradition and a slightly altered and more powerful HANG in the Tantric Buddhist tradition of Nepal and Tibet.

Anahata sounds or the melody are the mystical sounds heard by the meditator at the start of their cycle of meditation. They are called the voice of your inner God. This subject is termed *Nada-Anusandhana* or an enquiry into the mystic sounds. This is a sign of purification of the nadis, due to pranayama. These sounds are heard through the right ear, with or without closing the ears. The sounds are very distinct when heard through closed ears. The ears can be closed by introducing the two thumbs into the ears through the process of *yoni mudra*. Occasionally, you can hear the sounds through the left ear also. Practise to hear the sounds only through the right ear. The reason you should only hear distinctly with the right ear is to make sure your nadis are balanced. The solar (yang) pingala is on the right side of the nose. The *anahata* sound is also known as *Omkara Dhvani*. The sounds you hear are due to the vibration of *prana* in the heart.

There are 10 kinds of sounds. The first is *chini* (like the sound of the word chini) which resembles the sweet sound of a nightingale; the second is *chini-chini*; the third is the sound of a bell; the fourth is that of a conch – as the melodious song of an ocean-sprite imprisoned in its shell; the fifth is that of *tantri* (lute); the sixth is *tala* (cymbals); the seventh is that of a bamboo flute; the eight is that of *bheri* (drum); the ninth is that of *mridanga* (double drum) and the tenth is thunder.

The colour blue associated with the throat chakra gives communication with Divine guidance and right use of will. When this chakra is fully activated with the blue ray of wisdom you have a beautiful voice and your speech is clear and fluent. Your intellect increases, as does your understanding of the Divine scriptures. You have complete knowledge of the past, present and future. You have wisdom, patience, truth, mental attainment, good communication, contentment, artistic inspiration, deep meditation, spiritual and philosophical contemplation, personal integrity and loyalty.

Third Eye Chakra

The third eye chakra in Sanskrit is known as *ajna*, which means to command or to know. It is also known as the brow chakra. It is located right between and just above the physical eyes; it corresponds to the space between the eyebrows, the *trikuta*. All the chakras, except for the crown and root chakras, can be approached from the back as well as the front. Therefore the sixth chakra is also located in its rear aspect at the base of the skull, at the medulla oblongata. In the 'New Age' movement this position at the back of the head is sometimes called the 'causal' chakra. It is also known as the mouth of God; very often when you are going into deep meditation you may feel a strong pressure at this point, or even a pushing sensation on the roof of your mouth. These sensations are normal, although some people who have a fear-based mentality are afraid they are being 'taken over' – they are, by their Higher Selves – the 'ego-self' does not give in very easily and it can make you fearful; it really does not want to surrender anything, especially its hypnotic control of your senses. This is what the third eye is all about – the surrendering of your dualistic concepts and feelings of separation from your source of Divine wisdom, inspiration and bliss.

It is very difficult to talk about the third eye chakra, because we are using fifth chakra concepts throughout this book, or any book for that matter. In reality, the third eye, our sixth chakra, is beyond the fifth chakra's conceptual realm. Many people stay stuck in the fifth chakra their whole lives, thinking grandiose thoughts about the sixth chakra. Making the move upwards proves immensely difficult for many people. Ultimately the sixth chakra is beyond concepts. So, having said that, I shall give you just a few key points which you can reflect upon. The first primal chakritic concept that has existed for several thousand years is the Hindu and Buddhist understanding of the intricate workings of the kundalini system. There are two major conduits through which kundalini energy rises up the spine. These are the female *ida* and the male *pingala*, the yin and yang. Energy enters through the left side, ida, and exits through the right side, pingala. These female and male opposites intertwine intimately like lovers as they twist their way up through the first five chakras. Then something wondrous occurs: they merge in the sixth chakra. Sanskrit tradition says they integrate in the pineal gland or, as perhaps some modern neurologists hypothesise, in the pituitary. Here they generate the third eye, which lies within the brain, just behind the centre of the brow. It is here that the earthly duality ends, yin and yang unify to become whole. This marriage of opposites causes the manifest and un-manifest to merge.

As a human being finally lets go of concepts, of dualities, of opposites – which is to say when the ida and pingala merge – a great downpouring or flood of light comes into the body, caused by the awakening of the *bija* energy of the sixth chakra centre. The original concepts of duality, of darkness and light, come from our polar relationship with the Earth and Sun. In a very real sense it is this energetic relationship between these two force-fields that makes life on earth possible. By going into both the darkness of the centre of the earth and the unlimited brightness of the sun, we are guided into the unity of the third eye chakra.

So before the third eye opens you see through the two eyes; you experience a duality between your normal self *(Nefesh)* and your spirit *(Ruah)*. I don't believe you should force yourself to shed your ego-self. I believe with regular meditation practice on *all* your chakra centres you will eventually merge with your soul *(Neshamah)* and become one with the Divine through the activation of the crown chakra and the transcendental chakras above your head.

The Yogis say that the pineal gland is the seat of memory, so, as the three parts of the soul merge, your being is flooded with light and you have total access to all your past lives. You can let go of the multi-level veil of illusion, *avidya*, because you are no longer afraid, judgemental or full of guilt. You are flooded with compassion, love, wisdom and understanding for yourself and others. You view your past lives for what they are and you see yourself in everyone and everything. You no longer have any karmic debts; the merging has burned away all the debris of past lives by showing you they were the illusion of the ego or *maya*. The *Panchadasi*, an ancient Indian text, asserts: "Man's present miseries and sufferings, his pains and limited pleasures, births and deaths, are all due to his erroneous identification with the five sheaths and three bodies". The physical, astral and causal body make up the three bodies, while the five sheaths represent the first five levels of the aura and the first five master chakras along the spine; they are, in sequential order, the food sheath, emotional/vitality sheath, the mental sheath, the intellectual sheath and the bliss sheath. Even identifying with the bliss sheath means you have attachments – by wishing to become enlightened. It is only when you move beyond attachments into the sixth chakra that you can be free of maya; in other words, you are still trapped in *avidya*.

The sixth chakra, the third eye, is feminine, intuitive, mysterious and yin. It forms the final chakra in the triad of feminine yin chakras, the other two being the heart and sacral. They are each surrounded by masculine yang energy centres. As the energy flows upwards and, as you have discovered, downwards, it moves between the alternating male-female chakras. The feminine chakras are the driving force for the male chakras, with the ultimate balance of the whole being centred in the loving power of the heart chakra.

The third eye chakra is associated with intuition, the pituitary gland, left eye and base of the skull. In the sixth chakra the mind is looking directly at itself. The combined interaction of the pineal with the pituitary gland activates this chakra. The element is *avyakta*, the primordial cloud of undifferentiated energy and matter or light. Malfunctions include headaches, nightmares, eye problems, poor vision, neurological disturbances, glaucoma; also learning difficulties and hallucinations.

Its symbol is the pure white lotus flower which has two large pure white petals. The words on the petals are *ksham* and *ham*. They are on each side of a pure white circle, within which is a downward-pointing white triangle containing the *bija* seed letter *Om*. The white triangle represents the light of the soul in its downward path. When activated by the *Om*, it causes duality to vanish as the soul *(Neshamah)* illuminates the body.

The basic image also includes the vision of the ida and pingala energy upflows merging in the centre of white light. This mandala can also be seen to represent the two sides of the human brain, the opposing forces of cognitive and intuitive. Very often, as you feel the ida and pingala activating fully before merging (usually in deep meditation or when you sound the Om), you will be aware of soothing sensations in your temporal lobes. These sensations of the bliss that will be yours can be often felt and even recorded by instruments that measure brainwave patterns. The temporal lobes are your personal 'temples' where you are 'hard wired' before birth into the spiritual exploration of the energy we understand to be God. Your temples, when activated, give off a brilliant light which is often visible to those who are clairvoyant. With meditation practice comes the understanding and control of the brainwave patterns. Theta brainwaves are produced when you are in deep meditation. They are typically of even greater amplitude and slower frequency. This frequency range is normally between eight and five cycles a second. (For more information on brainwaves – see the section on Breathing and Brainwaves, page 129.)

The traditional sound for the third eye chakra is the *bija* mantra OM in the Hindu tradition and in the Tantric Buddhist tradition of Nepal and Tibet. You should devote a great deal of time to this mantra: it is the pathway to the great white light of brilliance. The associated creature of this chakra is the white owl – its natural mantra asks, who are you? This is similar to the Zen Buddhist *koan*, as a question that leads directly to spiritual realisation.

The colour ray associated with this chakra is indigo (a mix of dark blue and dark violet) which represents devotion to the truth – intuition and perception – the ability to look to the future. Indigo transmutes and purifies; it is the transformer. Indigo is the colour of the priest or priestess. When you meditate on the third eye chakra and it becomes fully activated, you can successfully destroy the karma of all past lives and become a liberated soul. Intuitional knowledge is obtained through this chakra; it is the seat of primordial power and soul. It is here that yogis consciously place their prana at the time of death. This is where the un-manifested and manifested meet. This is where yin and yang merge. This is where we move beyond dualism.

Crown Chakra

Infinite bliss or the crown chakra, as it is called, is so far beyond the mundane physical level and concepts that it defies an explanation. Any words used are merely a shadow play, a tiny reflection of the enormity of the encounter; it genuinely defies description. It should truly be encountered without preconceptions of any kind that will interfere with your direct personal experience. I can give the location and attributes though; these will help you to the direct encounter with your own personal experience of unlimited bliss, enlightenment, Christ consciousness, or samadhi as it is sometimes called. I think you should also be aware that just one momentary brief glimpse will enthral you, so you go further into samadhi, because there are levels of samadhi.

In *Nirvikalpa* samadhi the lower mind is withdrawn from the external objective world. The individual mind becomes one with the cosmic mind or *Hiranyagarbha* or the Oversoul, the Soul of the Universe, the 'One-Common-Thread Soul'. The functions of the intellect, the objective mind and the senses are suspended. The experience of enlightenment places the experiencer on a new plane of existence. All body consciousness falls away. Reading books and abstract reasoning will not give you samadhi. You need to practise meditation daily; this gives you direct personal experience, which is the source for higher intuitional knowledge or Divine wisdom. This experience is superconscious or transcendental.

The person who experiences Cosmic Consciousness acquires many *siddhis* or powers; these are described in the ancient *Raja Yoga Sutras* of *Patanjali Maharishi*. Though many people may originally seek enlightenment to gain these powers, if enlightenment happens these powers are then viewed as worthless, because at that point you have no desire for them. Cosmic Consciousness is the perfect awareness of the oneness of all life. The differentiating mind that splits everything up has gone, vanished. All barriers, all sense of duality, differences, separateness have disappeared. There is no time or space: you realize they are merely an illusion of the mundane mind. There is only eternity and supreme joy and bliss. This state is beyond description. You will have to realise this for yourself. The bliss state is not something we can force into existence in our minds. It comes only after we have prepared ourselves through meditation, prayer and purification. Even then, it comes when we are truly ready, in its own perfect moment.

As you move upwards through the chakras you will be aware that, as you align all your chakras to their highest potential, so you become aware of all the chakras at once. This can happen almost simultaneously after you become practised in mental expansion. The final expansion stage relies on resonance, the vibrating in harmony of all your chakras, which is a beautiful experience in itself – your personal symphony.

The Sanskrit name for the crown chakra is *sahasrara*, which means a thousand; it can also mean 'to multiply by a thousandfold'. The crown chakra through which you will experience samadhi is located at the crown of the head, known as the anterior fontanelle in a newborn child. It is called *Brahmarandhra*, the "hole of Brahma". At the time of death the advanced meditator separates him/herself from the physical body, it bursts open and the *prana* escapes through it. Please remember, although the crown chakra is situated at the top of the head, its swirling vortex of energy reaches far above the head. The crown chakra is associated with enlightenment, cosmic consciousness, the element of thought, right eye, cerebral cortex, pineal gland, upper skull and the skin. The malfunctions of the crown chakra are confusion, lack of clarity, depression, obsessional thinking, sensitivity to pollutants, chronic exhaustion, epilepsy and Alzheimer's. The seventh chakra, the crown, is masculine, pure bright light and yang. The crown chakra's sensory channel is experience – beyond self.

The seventh chakra's symbol is the thousand-petal lotus flower on which are repeated the fifty letters of the *Sanskrit* alphabet. It is represented as open in full bloom, which means you are fully open to the light of the soul. In the Sanskrit tradition it is the abode of *Shiva*. This is the seat of true wisdom, through deep meditation. When this chakra is fully activated you are filled with joy and develop a beautiful spiritual aura; your mystical light body has anchored onto the physical body, your DNA spiral of life has downloaded your personal keys to ascension and you have transformed into a rainbow warrior of light. In Buddhism the lotus is a token or symbol for that which transcends the mundane. It is the alchemy energy whereby we transmute our lower nature into our higher nature; thus we turn 'lead into gold'. It is also a symbol of spiritual receptivity. To understand the 'perfection' of wisdom we have to be prepared to stand under it and learn from it. In doing so we may even have to accept that we do not know anything about anything, spiritual or mundane. We need to discipline and develop our rational faculty, not try and dispense with it once we have fully trained our perfect intellect, then we can turn it to the perfect wisdom and let it discover for itself its inadequacy in apprehending reality. The rational mind has to be developed to a point where it can see through itself – and thus acknowledge its own limitations. The lotus is also known as the wisdom goddess, *Prajnaparamita* in Sanskrit, *Sherappkyi Pharoltuchinma* in Tibetan Buddhism.

The crown chakra colours are traditionally violet, gold and white. The violet ray represents those who search for the spiritual truth in all life. It is the ray of spirituality and spiritual service. It contains a balance of blue and red. It is the highest and fastest vibration in the rainbow. The body parts it rules are the pineal gland, top of the head, the crown, brain and scalp. It brings spiritual dedication and aids psychic abilities. It allows for full soul development and the clearing of karmic debris. It also allows psychic protection. The white ray of peace contains all other colours. It can also be the clear ray of brilliance, bringing enlightenment, cosmic awareness, blissful reunion with our source – allowing the 'Holy Spirit' to flow downward into our lives for the ultimate healing and inspirational power of the universe. We transcend our individual minds and enter into perfect conscious harmony with the infinite wholeness of the universe. Infinite love, infinite bliss. Enlightenment is to be filled with light, to comprehend the light, to function in the light, to radiate the light and merge with the light. When *Kundalini Shakti* is united with *Shiva* at the *sahasrara*, the *yogi/yogini* experiences extreme bliss. He/she attains the superconscious state and the highest knowledge. The clear ray of brilliance can be used anywhere on the body and aura. The sun-gold ray is of knowledge and Divine understanding – "at the end of the rainbow is the pot of gold". Its uses are that it aids assimilation of knowledge, brings vitality and spiritual abundance. It rids the body of parasites and parasitic energies on all levels (karmic debris and negative thought patterns, your own and those of others). It also brings the attunement to the Sun and Solar Lords of Light.

The traditional sound for the crown chakra is the *Bija* mantra of silence or silent OM. As you gently move from the sixth-chakra chanting of the OM to the seventh chakra, simply allow the Om chant to fall silent. This vibratory sound energy will continue throughout your chakra system. It becomes a silent but all-pervasive mantra; it is the sound of the universe singing your soul back home. It wakes up the bliss sensation in every cell of your body; just when you feel yourself entering this blissful state, stay aware of your breathing, so that it does not contract at the awesomeness of the experience; be aware, but do not control it; you will find that you become entrained in harmony with the universe. This is the bliss breath. Allow the universe to 'breathe' you. You will find this a joyful feeling of perfect abandonment. All your thoughts stop, there is only the Soul of the Universe.

In actuality no unified world tradition regarding the nature and overall functioning of the seven master chakras exists. The Hindu and Buddhist traditions of India, for instance, differ significantly from the Tantric and Taoist traditions found in Tibet, China and adjoining Buddhist regions. Significantly there are many diverse traditions regarding the human energy centres – descriptions of which can be found in every deep spiritual tradition of all tribes and civilizations throughout the world.

Chakra Correspondences

1. Root Chakra

Sanskrit name *muladhara* (*mula* = root, source; *adhara* = support, vital part). Also known as the base or earth chakra. Located in the perineum, the base of the spine, between anus and genitals. Associated with red, physical energy, physical health and fitness, gravity, self-preservation, survival, being grounded, adrenal glands, spinal column, all the solid elements of the body. Energy location: feet, ankles, legs, knees, thighs and large intestine. Energetic gateway between us and the earth, also energies of childhood and the past. When this chakra is developed, we are more grounded, solid and powerful at physical levels of survival. Knowledge of the past, present and future are bestowed when this chakra is fully activated.

Malfunction: osteoarthritis, obesity, haemorrhoids, constipation and problems associated with the feet, legs, bones and teeth. Mental lethargy, 'spaciness', being incapable of inner stillness.

The first chakra (Earth) is masculine; solid; earthly; yang.

Intake: protein.

Symbol: 4-petal crimson-red lotus flower, around a yellow square containing a downward-pointing triangle containing the *Bija* mantra Lam. Here also is the *Brahma granthi*, or knot of *Brahma*, which must be forced open through rigorous *sadhana* and intense purification for the *kundalini* to rise. It is also the location of the resting *Kundalini Goddess*: she is said to lie coiled three-and-a-half times around this chakra. The three coils represent the three stages of *avastha* (mind), namely *jagrt* (awake), *svapna* (dreaming) and *susuptiin* (deep sleep). There is a fourth level, *turiya*, combining and transcending the others, which represents the last half-coil. It is attained in *samadhi* (enlightenment).

Names of petals: vam, sam, sham, sam.

Sensory channel: smell.

Sound: *Bija* mantra – Lam (female) or Lang (male).

Musical note C.

Associated creature: elephant.

Gemstones: Ruby, Garnet, Zircon, Ruby Aura Quartz, Hematite.

2. Sacral Chakra

Sanskrit name *svadhisthana* (*sva* = vital force, soul; *adhisthana* = seat or abode). Also known as the water chakra. Located in the sexual organs and upwards towards the navel. Associated with vitality, attraction, magnetism, desire, emotion, creativity, sexuality, water. Bodily parts: all fluid functions of the body, ovaries, testes, womb. There is great cleansing potential in this chakra associated with personality disorders related to the emotions: unbalanced sex drive, emotional instability, feelings of isolation. Also relates to social awareness and partnerships. The colour orange is for creativity, wisdom and benevolence.

Malfunction: frigidity, impotence; bladder, kidney and uterine disorders; prostate problems, lower back pain, fertility. Also fear, shock and guilt.

The second chakra (Sex) is feminine; liquid; flowing; yin.

Intake: fluids.

Symbol: 6-petal orange-red lotus flower, containing a second lotus flower and an upward-pointing crescent moon. Within the moon lies the 'makara', a fish-tailed alligator with a coiled tail. When this chakra is balanced you will 'flow'. Use this chakra as a primal spiritual centre. When this chakra is activated fully you become healthy and full of vitality. Meditation on the crescent moon gives control over the water element and confers psychic powers, intuitional knowledge and knowledge of astral entities. Many impure qualities are annihilated.

Names of petals: bam, bham, mam, yam, ram, lam.

Sensory channel: taste.

Sound: *Bija* mantra – Vam or Vang.

Musical note D.

Associated creature: water dragon or a fish-tailed alligator with a coiled tail *(makara)* or crocodile.

Gemstones: Carnelian, Red Jasper, Orange Sunstone, Aragonite, Hessonite, Amber, Tangerine Quartz.

3.   Solar Plexus Chakra

Sanskrit name *manipuraka* (*manipura* = navel) situated in the navel; *manas* (mind) and *surya* (the sun). Also known as the power chakra or lustrous gem. Located between the navel and the solar plexus centre. Associated with fire, personal power, ambition, intellectual activity, combustion, anger, joy, laughter; astral force, mental power, pancreas and adrenals. Also central nervous system.

Malfunction: stomach ulcers and other digestive disorders, also diabetes, low vitality, chronic fatigue and allergies. Over-sensitivity to criticism, need to be in control, low self-esteem, addictive personality, aggression.

The third chakra (Power or *agni*) is masculine; wilful; yang.

Intake: starch, complex carbohydrates.

Symbol: 10-petal lotus flower. The petals are yellow; the centre contains a deep red downward-pointing triangle surrounded by three *'svastikas'*, symbolic of fire. The colour yellow is for meditative analytical thought, intellectual activity, abundance, manifestation of your dreams. If you meditate on this chakra you will become dis-ease free and have no fear of fire, being able to control this element.

There is another important chakra (manas) which lies between the manipuraka and anahata chakras. It is the seat of the emotions, igniting imagination and creativity. When the manas and anahata

114

chakras are activated together they strengthen the heart and help you develop devotion to your spiritual path or goal.

Names of petals: dam, dham, nam, tam, tham, dam, dham, nam, pam, pham.

Sensory channel: sight.

Sound: *Bija* mantra – Ram or Rang.

Musical note E.

Associated creature: ram.

Gemstones: Yellow Sapphire, Citrine, Golden Sunstone, Sunshine Aura Quartz, Amber, Amblygonite, Tiger Eye, Yellow Jasper.

4.   Heart Chakra

Sanskrit name *anahata* (= unbeaten or unstruck. A sound that is made without any two things striking). Located in the cardiac area, in the region of the physical and spiritual heart. Associated with compassion, love, beliefs about love and relationships, one-ness, heart, thymus and the immune system.

Malfunction: lung disease, asthma, heart disease; shallow breathing, high blood pressure, cancer. Problems with arms, hands and fingers. Fears about betrayal; co-dependency, melancholia.

The fourth chakra (Heart) is feminine; loving; integrating; yin.

Intake: vegetables.

Symbol: 12-petal emerald green lotus flower. The inner centre contains a green circle; two intersecting triangles make up a perfect six-pointed star, demonstrating the balance between the downward-pointing spirit descending towards matter and the upward-pointing matter ascending towards spirit. Meditation on the heart chakra gives the primal sound of *anahata* sound, the primal sound of *Sabdabrahman*. It also bestows pure qualities, cosmic love and various psychic powers.

Names of petals: kam, kham, gam, gham, nam, cam, cham, jam, jham, nam, tam, tham.

Sensory channel: touch.

Sound: *Bija* mantra – Yam or Yang.

Musical note F.

Associated creature: black antelope.

Gemstones: (Green) Emerald, Green Jade, Green Tourmaline, Green Aventurine, Moldavite, Peridot, Malachite, Chrysoprase.

(Pink) Rose Quartz, Morganite, Pink Tourmaline, Watermelon Tourmaline, Rhodochrosite, Kunzite, Smithsonite.

5.   Throat Chakra

Sanskrit name *visuddha* (= pure), which means purification. It is also known as the 'communication' chakra. Located in the throat region at the base of the neck. Associated with communication, self-expression, sound, voice, speech, writing; active listening, thyroid gland, parathyroid, lungs, vocal cords, jaw, breath. Dreaming, imagination and out-of-body experiences. The power of choice, harmony with others.

Malfunction: stiff necks, colds, sore throats, thyroid and hearing problems, tinnitus, asthma. Masks of the self. Perfectionism, inability to express emotions, blocked creativity.

The fifth chakra (Throat) is masculine; manifesting; logical; yang.

Intake: fruit.

Symbol: 16-petal blue lotus flower. Contained within the flower is a downward-pointing triangle, within which is a circle representing the full silvery-blue Moon. The colour blue gives communication with Divine guidance. When this chakra is fully activated you have a beautiful voice, your speech is clear and fluent. Your intellect increases, as does your understanding of the Divine scriptures. You have complete knowledge of the past, present and future.

Names of petals: am, am, im, im, um, um, rm, rm, im, im, em, aim, om, aum, am, ahm.

Sensory channel: sound.

Sound: *Bija* mantra – Ham or Hang.

Musical note G.

Associated creatures: white lion; Airavata, the many-tusked elephant.

Gemstones: Lapis Lazuli, Blue Sapphire, Chrysocolla, Blue Calcite, Azurite, Blue Lace Agate, Larimar, Aquamarine, Turquoise, Aqua Aura Quartz.

6a. Third Eye Chakra

Sanskrit name *ajna* (= command), which means to know. Also known as the brow chakra or intuitive chakra. Located right between and just above the physical eyes, it corresponds to the space between the eyebrows, the *Trikuta*. Associated with intuition, pituitary gland, left eye, the base of the skull. The mind is looking directly at itself. The combined interaction of the pineal with the pituitary gland activates this chakra. The element is *Avyakta*, the primordial cloud of undifferentiated energy and matter.

Malfunction: headaches, nightmares, eye problems, poor vision, neurological disturbances, glaucoma. Learning difficulties, hallucinations.

The sixth chakra (Brow) is feminine; intuitive; mysterious; yin.

Intake: air.

Symbol: 2 large pure white lotus petals on each side of a pure white circle, within which is a downward-pointing triangle containing the bija seed letter Om. The colour indigo (dark blue and dark violet) represents devotion to the truth – idealism, obedience, intuition and perception – and the ability to look to the future. Indigo transmutes and purifies, it is the transformer. Indigo is the colour of the priest or priestess. When you meditate on the third eye chakra and it becomes fully activated you can successfully destroy the karma of all past lives and become a liberated soul. Intuitional knowledge is obtained through this chakra; it is the seat of primordial power and soul. It is here that yogis consciously place their prana at the time of death. The colour violet represents those who search for the spiritual truth in all life.

Names of petals: ksham, ham.

Sensory channel: light, sixth sense.

Sound: *Bija* mantra – Om

Musical note A.

Associated creature: white owl.

Gemstones: Iolite, Amethyst, Tanzanite, Sugilite, Charoite, Lepidolite, Fluorite.

6b.   Fourth Eye Chakra

Sanskrit name *soma* (= water).

Located just above the third eye chakra in the centre of the brain.

This chakra controls the body temperature and balances the power chakra in the solar plexus, bringing the male/female balance to the whole body system. The balance is maintained via the breath. Erratic breathing causes imbalances in the body and upsets this polarity.

Sensory channel: light.

Sound: *Bija* mantra – Om

Musical note A.

Associated creature: eagle.

Gemstones: Amethyst, Tanzanite, Charoite, Lepidolite.

6c.   Fifth Eye Chakra

Sanskrit name *lalata* (= forehead).

Located at the top of the forehead. Its full activation brings man to be master of his own destiny.

Sensory channel: light.

Sound: *Bija* mantra – Om

Musical note A.

Associated creature: white dove.

Gemstones: Tanzanite, Diamond, Clear Quartz, Danburite, Phenacite, Azeztulite, Petalite, Clear Calcite, Selenite, Herkimer Diamond.

7.   Crown Chakra

Sanskrit name *sahasrara* (= thousand), which means 'to multiply by a thousandfold'. Located at the crown of the head, known as the anterior fontanelle in a newborn child; is called Brahmarandhra, the "hole of Brahma". At the time of death the advanced meditator separates him/herself from the physical body, it bursts open and the prana escapes through it. Associated with enlightenment, cosmic consciousness, right eye, cerebral cortex, pineal gland, upper skull, skin.

Malfunction: confusion, lack of clarity, depression, obsessional thinking, sensitivity to pollutants, chronic exhaustion, epilepsy, Alzheimer's.

The seventh chakra (Crown) is masculine; pure bright light; yang – violet, gold, white.

Intake: fasting (Prana).

Symbol: The thousand-petal white lotus flower, on which are repeated the fifty letters of the *Sanskrit* alphabet. It is the abode of *Shiva*. Brilliance, bringing enlightenment, cosmic awareness, blissful reunion with source. Allowing the 'Holy Spirit' to flow downwards into our lives for the ultimate healing and inspirational power of the universe.

Enlightenment is to be filled with light, to comprehend the light, to function in the light, to radiate the light and merge with the light. When *Kundalini Shakti* is united with *Shiva* at the sahasrara, the *yogi/yogini* experiences extreme bliss. He/she attains the superconscious state and the highest knowledge. This is the seat of true wisdom, through deep meditation. When this chakra is fully activated you are filled with joy and develop a spiritual aura. This is where the un-manifested and manifested meet. This is where yin and yang merge. This is where we move beyond dualism.

Sensory channel: experience – beyond self.

Sound: *Bija* mantra – of silence or silent OM.

Musical note B.

Gemstones: Diamond, Clear Quartz, Danburite, Phenacite, Azeztulite, Petalite, Clear Calcite, Selenite, Herkimer Diamond.

The Aura

The peoples of ancient cultures knew and understood that beyond its physical material form the human body is a pulsing, moving, dynamic field of energy. They developed a deep understanding of these basic fundamental energies, called Universal Life Force, prana or chi. This pool of energy is drawn into, surrounds and permeates the human body and surrounding energy field known as the *aura*. (*Aura* is a Greek word meaning breeze). The aura consists of seven levels, subtle bodies or *kosas* (body sheaths). The seven levels correlate to the seven master chakras. The aura begins with the seen (physical body) and progresses to subtle and more refined vibrations as we go further away from the physical. Awareness of the levels of the aura is gained through meditation. Often, as we open spiritually, we begin to perceive a glow around the physical body. This is the first level and the most easy to view.

The seven levels are as follows: each has a particular function, energy, awareness and realisation, which is reflected in the consciousness and is observable in all individuals. In Yoga it is known as the sevenfold knowledge and is to be integrated between the seen *(prakrti)* and the seer *(purusa)*. They are: integration of the body *(sarira samyama)*, the senses *(indriya samyama)*, energy *(prana samyama)*, mind *(mano samyama)*, intellect *(buddhi samyama)*, consciousness *(citta samyama)* and soul *(atma samyama)*. The Yoga Sutras of Patanjali (written 2,500 years ago) were the earliest – and are still the most profound and enlightening – study of the human psyche. In 11.27 he wrote *"tasya saptadha prantabhumih prajna"*. This roughly translates as "its sevenfold province holds supreme knowledge of consciousness". He was referring to the seven sheaths or levels of the aura.

The aura of an unevolved person will be very different to the aura of someone who is self-realised. All the stages in between these two vast polarities give myriad kinds and types of aura. When we progress spiritually we begin to find vast differences in the colour, quality, texture, resonance and vibration of each person on the planet. We do not have at the moment any totally accurate devices for measuring the aura. I am sure this will happen soon, but in the meantime we have our own awareness, which is automatic. I am sure we all know when we like someone or when someone is angry or sad: this we sense by direct contact of our aura with theirs.

All auras are different and change constantly as our thoughts, moods, environment and state of health change. The aura may become damaged by ill-health, negative thought patterns, environmental pollutants, stress or poor breathing techniques. This can be 'viewed' and the damage may be repaired with the correct use of Archangel essences and placement of gemstones. Sometimes we find debris in the aura when someone repeatedly holds a negative thought pattern or addiction for a long time. Some of these thought patterns and addictions take on a life of their own and act as a possession, negative entity thought form or negative entity thought form shape; in time these not only can influence the person they are attached to but can control other people's behaviour too. Colours and shapes are clearly visible within the aura, the colours reflecting which chakras are the most active or under-active, also where the person needs to pay special attention to restore pure colour or vibrancy. Any imbalances will cause trouble in the overall vitality of the energy field. If a person regularly has spiritual thoughts, the aura can be a very clear yellow or even gold, while a thought charged with anger and hatred is dark red.

The shapes and patterns in the aura represent energies which will block the spiritual, mental, emotional and physical health of a person. These can be removed with vibrational healing techniques. Karmic burdens and karmic pre-dispositions or miasms (crystallized patterns of karma) are also viewed within the aura. This debris is a past life carry-over and will cause problems, misery and mental or emotional instability. Very often we find damage in the aura caused by attachments, cords or ties. These are usually from outside causes, where one individual has damaged another. This can be very nasty to deal with, as it causes energy leakage or vampirism. These cords and energy drains need to be very carefully removed and the spaces where they have been need to be filled with healing energy which is positive, vital and loving.

The Seven Kosas

(Body Sheaths or Aura) and Corresponding States of Consciousness:

Sheath One

Element of earth

Sheath – physical body *(annamaya kosa)*

Related chakra – Root

State of consciousness – emerging consciousness *(vyutthana citta)*

Knowledge of body – integration of body *(sarira samyama)*

Appearance – Pale blue or light grey with tiny sparks of light moving very fast

State – Fixed

Close to the physical body

Level – One – Etheric (lower aspect)

Sheath Two

Element of water

Sheath – physiological body *(pranamaya kosa)*

Related chakra – Sacral

State of consciousness – restraining consciousness *(nirodha citta)*

Knowledge of energy – vitality, integration of senses *(indriya samyama)*

Appearance – Vibrant colours (when healthy and emotionally balanced)

State – Moving

2.5 – 7.5 cm around the physical body

Level – Two – Emotional/vitality body (lower base emotions aspect)

Sheath Three

Element of fire

Sheath – psychological body *(manomaya kosa)*

Related chakra – Solar Plexus

State of consciousness – individualized consciousness *(nirmana citta)*

Knowledge of energy – integration of energy *(prana samyama)*

Appearance – Yellow to gold depending on spiritual development

State – Fixed

7.5 – 20 cm around the physical body.

Level – Three – Mental body

Sheath Four

Element of air

Sheath – intellectual body *(vijnanamaya kosa)*

Related chakra – Heart

State of consciousness – tranquil consciousness *(prasanta citta)*

Knowledge of energy – integration of mind *(mano samyama)*

Appearance – Pastel colours; when fully developed, a pastel rainbow infused with rose pink

State – Moving

15 – 30 cm around the physical body

Level – Four – Astral

Sheath Five

Element of ether

Sheath – the body of joy *(anandamaya kosa)*

Related chakra – Throat

State of consciousness – attentive consciousness *(ekagrata citta)*

Knowledge of energy – integration of intellect *(buddhi samyama)*

Appearance – Vivid bright blue

State – Fixed

30 – 60 cm around the physical body

Level – Five – Etheric blueprint

Sheath Six

Element of spirit

Sheath – the body of consciousness *(cittamaya kosa)*

Related chakra – Third eye (brow)

State of consciousness – fissured or rent consciousness *(chidra citta)*

Knowledge of energy – integration of consciousness *(citta samyama)*

Appearance – Bright gold light flowing down from the higher self, when fully developed

State – Moving

60 – 75 cm around the physical body

Level – Six – Celestial

Sheath Seven

Element of thought

Sheath – the body of the self *(atmamaya kosa)*

Related chakra – Crown

State of consciousness – pure consciousness *(paripakva citta or divya citta)*

Knowledge of energy – integration of soul *(atma samyama)*

Appearance – Silvery-blue to shimmering gold (the original blueprint)

State – Fixed

75 – 112 cm around the physical body (until self-realisation)

Level – Seven – Luminous egg

The Meridians

The ancient Chinese meridian theory, based on acupuncture channels through which qi flows, was discovered many years ago. It arose from thousands of years of medical practice in China. The word meridian, as used in Chinese medicine, came into the English language through a French translation of the Chinese term jing-luo. Jing means 'to go through', or 'a thread in a fabric'; luo means 'something that connects or attaches' or 'a net'. In traditional Eastern medical systems – notably the Chinese healing system and the Indian Ayurvedic system – it has long been accepted that health is based on the continuous harmonious flow of energies. These systems believe that an intricate realm of subtle energy flows permeates the universe and that the physical, material world is but a gross manifestation of these energies. In Chinese and Ayurvedic medicine, health is seen as the fluent and harmonious movement of energies at subtle levels. In the East, energies have various names. The Indian yogis call it prana; to the Tibetan lamas it is lung-gom. It is known as sakia-tundra or ki to the Japanese Shinto and the Chinese call it qi or chi. In the West it is loosely translated as 'life force'. This energy is considered as having clearly distinct and established pathways, definite direction of flow and characteristic behaviour as well defined as any other circulation, such as blood and the vascular system. Oriental medicine seeks the underlying cause of the disease by concentrating on the quality and flow of qi. The qi flows through the channels in the body, feeding each cell, which helps to maintain balance (homeostasis). The channels also connect the chakras and aura. This ancient system of vibrational medicine provides protection to the physical bodies' inner mechanisms.

There are twelve pairs of major channels in the body, plus two extra channels which run up the torso and head on the front and back. All channels flow near the surface of the skin. These twelve regular meridians correspond to each of the five yin and six yang organs. Together these constitute the body's energy system, which works to maintain the health of the whole organism. There are also many finer smaller net-like meridians called luo meridians. These meridians are pathways through which the energy of the universe circulates throughout the body organs and keeps the body and the universe in harmony. Traditional Oriental medicine does not treat the symptom of a disease; it looks for the underlying cause of it. This is always expressed as a disruption of the flow of qi. Illness or pain occurs when the channels become blocked, overactive or underactive, thereby disrupting the energy flow and breaking the body's harmony.

Although it is one integrated system, each channel has a starting point and an end point, which indicate direction of flow and function. Each meridian is named after an organ or function, such as lung, spleen or liver, but these 'names' can be very misleading, as the physical organ is only one tiny aspect of the type of energy over which a meridian has influence. The functions ascribed to physical organs by the Chinese rarely have any recognisable correlations to Western medicine and it is difficult not to get completely confused by trying to tie in the two very distinct systems. Meridians are not straight lines; their pathways have curves; they curl and sometimes zig-zag across the body. The Chinese, in acupuncture, developed the use of needles to unblock these pathways. In shiatsu, the Japanese use direct thumb and finger pressure on acupuncture meridian points to achieve similar results. Reflexologists also work on acupuncture and acupressure points, but only those found in the feet. Through increased awareness of meridians one can practise vibrational therapy more effectively, as meridians provide profound insight into the disease pathway and are therefore a most useful diagnostic tool. Vibrational therapy encourages positive changes throughout the body by stimulating the body's own healing potential, which is believed to be the result of stimulating and revitalizing this energy flow. Once you have identified which meridian(s) are dysfunctional, it is easy to bring them back into balance. However, always remember to think of the meridian system in its entirety and how each one works in harmony with the others to bring a complete sense of well-being. Each meridian operates at a unique, optimum frequency, which determines its vibrancy and flow. However, this frequency can be detrimentally affected through receiving too much or too little from the Universal Life Force.

Yin and Yang

The Chinese use the concept of yin and yang to express the idea of balance within the bodies' energy flow. Good health depends on the smooth flow of qi along the channels; this in turn requires the body, mind, and spirit to be in harmony.

Yin is negative, passive, female, interior, soft, downward, cold and dark.

Yang is positive, active, male, exterior, hard, upward, hot and light.

They are a pair of complementary qualities, constantly interacting and changing, and neither can exist in isolation from the other. Their affinity to each other has a direct effect on health, harmony and well-being. The meridians connect the interior of the body with the exterior.

Cause of Disease

Positive thoughts, feelings and emotions strengthen the meridians, whilst negative thoughts and emotions weaken the meridians. According to Oriental medicine, disease is brought about by three different means. These three categories are internal (emotions), external (the weather) and various causes such as bacteria, viruses, drugs, poisons, pollutants and diet.

Emotions

Disease caused by emotional disturbances are usually the hardest to treat.

Fear: Diminishes the energy of the kidneys and brings a lack of self-confidence.

Anger: Affects the liver; prolonged anger can then affect the spleen.

Joy: Normally is strengthening, but too much excitement overstimulates the heart.

Grief: Impairs the energy of the lungs.

Sadness: Affects the heart.

Worry: Depletes the spleen, which interferes with digestion.

Shock: Depletes the heart and interferes with the harmony of the mind.

Weather

This normally only affects people when their resistance is low.

Wind: Normally affects the head, causing colds, coughing or runny nose.

Damp: Weakens the spleen's function.

Cold: Obstructs the function of the blood.

Dryness: Causes disruption in body fluids.

Other Causes

The symptoms caused by bacteria, viruses, drugs, poisons, pollutants and diet are usually the easiest to treat. If ignored they can produce far-reaching problems.

Central Meridian (Conceptual Vessel)

Begins at the perineum and flows up the front centre of the body and ends just below the lower lip on the outside of the body, but actually ends at the tip of the tongue. This is a yin vessel which has a governing effect on all the other yin meridians. It has a major effect on conception. The yin meridians and organ functions – heart, pericardium, spleen, lungs, kidneys and liver – are related to storing vital essence. They are associated with generation, regulation, transformation and storage of energy, blood, fluids and spirit (shen). The specific connecting point for all yin meridians is the base of the sternum, where according to the Nei Ching all the energies are collected. This area of the solar plexus is very important for the overall well-being of the body.

Governing Meridian

The yang channel (the Governing vessel) begins at the perineum and flows up the back centre of the body, over the top of the head and back down to the roof of the mouth. On the outside of the body it ends at the centre of the upper lip. This is the main yang meridian and as such has a governing effect on all the other yang meridians and organs – small intestine, bladder, triple burner, stomach, large intestine and gall-bladder. The yang organ functions are primarily active and relate to breaking down food and fluids and the absorption of nutrients from them, the circulation of the derived 'nourishing energies' around the body and the secretion of unused materials. Located right at the crown of the head, known as the anterior fontanelle in a newborn child, is a unique connecting point for all yang meridians. The name of the point is 'Baihui' which means 'meeting point for 100 points'. This point governs all other points and all meridians in the body; according to Chinese philosophy it is a point of contact of the heavenly yang.

Qi Circuit

The tongue connects these two important currents when touched to the highest point in the roof of the mouth. An easy way to open and connect this energy channel is to sit in a relaxed posture. Allow your energy to complete the loop by letting your mind flow along with it. Start in the mouth and mentally circulate your attention with the energy. Eventually the current will begin to feel warm in some places as it loops around. Relax, try to bring your mind directly into the part of the loop being focused on. Experience the actual feeling of the flow of qi in that part of your body. Once the circuit is going smoothly, inhale as you go up the spine and over to the third eye and exhale as you go down from the third eye to the perineum.

Gall-bladder Meridian

Begins at the outer edge of the eye and finishes at the outer end of the fourth toe. It has a descending pathway (yang). As it circulates around the ear, it therefore directly relates to the ear.

The gall-bladder meridian penetrates the lungs, liver, gall-bladder, spleen, large intestine and hip area. Meridian disorders include problems with the lungs, liver, gall-bladder, spleen, large intestine and hip area. Stores and empties the bile from the liver.

Liver Meridian

Starts at the outside of the big toe and ends just above the bottom of the ribcage, either side of the sternum. It has an ascending pathway (yin) and an internal branch which runs through the throat and affects the thyroid. Meridian disorders include eye pain, obstructions in the throat, chest tightness, lung conditions and tightness in the solar plexus area. Regulates emotional harmony.

Bladder Meridian

Begins at the inner canthus of the eye and ends on the outer edge of the little toe. It has a descending pathway (yang). It is the longest meridian line in the body. Meridian disorders are eye weakness, for example, red, itchy, weak or squint eyes; headaches in the crown of the head or in the forehead crossing over the head, and headaches caused by neck tension; forehead sinus; hair loss; pain and stiffness along the spine; haemorrhoids; bladder and kidney problems. Transforms and excretes body fluids.

Kidney Meridian

Begins at the ball of the foot and ends where the collarbone and breastbone meet. The kidney meridian also penetrates the uterus/prostate in the body and, according to Chinese medicine, the kidneys store the jing, a vital essence involved in reproduction. It has an ascending pathway (yin). Meridian disorders include uterus/prostate disorders, bladder weakness, digestive problems in the small intestine or colon, solar plexus and diaphragm problems, breast problems, lumps in the breast on the inner side, asthma; lung conditions and kidney pain. Also determines will-power.

Large Intestine Meridian

Begins on the face by the outer edge of the nostril and ends on the inner edge of the index finger. It has an ascending pathway (yin). Problems associated with this meridian are herpes, cold sores, colic, toxins, constipation and diarrhoea.

Lung Meridian

Begins just below the coracoid process on the shoulder and ends on the inner end of the thumb.

It has an ascending pathway (yin). The lungs regulate respiration and are therefore responsible for the qi of the entire body. Combines qi from air with qi from food; it then spreads this throughout the body via the channels and blood vessels. Also distributes defensive qi against pathogens. Imbalance in this meridian will result in all kinds of chest and skin problems; also asthma.

Stomach Meridian

Begins below the eye at the inner edge of the orbit and finishes at the outer end of the second toe.

It has a descending pathway (yang). It affects the sinuses, throat, lungs, diaphragm, spleen, liver, gall-bladder, stomach, pancreas, duodenum, adrenal glands, kidneys, large intestine, small intestine and pelvic region; also the appetite and digestion. If the stomach is out of balance, whatever is taken in, be it physical or psychic food, will not be utilized correctly; energy depletion, lethargy, weakness and debilitation are the results.

Spleen Meridian

Begins at the inner edge of the big toe and ends at the side of the chest just below nipple level. It has an ascending pathway (yin) and affects the spleen and pancreas. It is the crucial link in the process by which food is transformed into qi and blood. Emotional problems are also related to this meridian, for example depression, PMT, irritability and concentration problems. Correct functioning aids concentration and memory.

Small Intestine Meridian

Begins at the outer end of the little fingertip and ends at the start of the upper edge of the ear in a small hollow of the cheek. It has a descending pathway (yang). Meridian disorders are any heart condition, abdominal distension, headaches, poor circulation in the legs, indigestion, constipation, feeling cold and weakness in the legs.

Triple Heater Meridian

Begins at the outside end of the ring finger (third) and ends at the outer edge of the eyebrow. It has a descending pathway (yang). Distributes and regulates warmth. Meridian disorders include ear problems, loss of hearing and earache; spontaneous perspiration for no reason; mental confusion; weakness and lack of energy.

Heart Meridian

Begins at the forward edge of the armpit and ends on the inner edge of the little finger. It has a descending pathway (yang). The heart and small intestine meridians are coupled. The heart meridian gets its qi from the spleen meridian and in turn passes it to the small intestine meridian. If the heart meridian is strong and healthy, the emotions will be balanced. Circulates blood, houses the mind, influences long-term memory and clear thinking. Imbalances in this meridian will affect the skin and cause weak wrists, angina and palpitations.

Heart Protector

Begins at the outer edge of the nipple and finishes at the inside of the middle finger. It has an ascending pathway (yin). Meridian disorders include hot flushes and rapid heartbeat, heart pain and endocrine-related problems.

Three Techniques

Tonifying, dispersing and calming all restore the body's equilibrium.

Tonifying: To strengthen weak qi.

Dispersing   For blocked or stagnant qi.

Calming   For overactive qi.

Transcendental Chakras – Soul Star

The transcendental or transpersonal chakras, also known as the eighth to fourteenth master chakras, are situated above your head in your etheric body. The first of these is the eighth 'master' chakra which is sometimes called the 'soul star'. It is located about 15 to 17 cm above the top of your head. You have another six transcendental master chakras or energy centres also above your head. The soul star chakra is the one that gives you access to all the others. When the soul star chakra is aligned and activated by your higher self, a remarkable light energy will flow down into you. This flow downwards into your body fills each chakra with the sensation of bliss. Meditators experience it as bliss, even though the words bliss, ecstasy, exhilaration, elation, are wholly inadequate.

Light Body

The key to experiencing the crown chakra and the fourth dimension and beyond of the non-physical chakras above your head and leaving your physical body – this is sometimes called astral travel or astral journey – so you materialise there by drawing the necessary materials either from *Asmita (Ahamkara)* or the universal storehouse (ocean of elements), is a thorough understanding and knowledge of your master chakra system which is embedded into your physical body. As you access your soul star chakra, your 'light body' will also be activated. Many people also visualise the eighth to fourteenth master chakras above their head as a tube of light.

Star Gateway

The ninth master chakra is sometimes called the 'Star Gateway' and by the time you are fully aware of this energy centre you will have access to the celestial realms and be Angelically guided on a daily basis, having balanced and aligned all your chakras on the physical body and be beyond the limited concepts of the third dimension. This will also give you access to the fifth dimension and all the higher dimensions of light.

I am often asked about the eighth to fourteenth transcendental chakras and how to access them, but it is outside the scope and limitations of this book. However, I can say that once your soul star chakra is activated by your higher self you will have instant access to the higher dimensions and worlds of light. Perhaps when you view your transcendental chakras you will perceive them as others have before you – that it is a structure which does have a central column of energy centres, but these are very much like only looking at the middle pillar on the kabalistic Tree of Life and forgetting about the rest of the Tree of Life structure, which is not a tube but a multi-dimensional sacred geometry structure consisting of harmonics and ratios. This structure can also be viewed as a vehicle which gives access to higher and even more refined energy centres.

Part Five

Breathing, Meditation and Relaxation

Breathing, Meditation and Relaxation

One of the keys to successful meditation and relaxation is your breathing; because breathing is such a fundamental function for our survival we always take its power for granted. We constantly overlook this primary tool with which we can increase our own perfect health, vitality and overall sense of well-being. The process of breathing is governed by your automatic nervous system. This means you do not have to think about breathing, you will do it anyway. In fact the physical function of breathing is far more than just breathing in and out. The in-breath carries the life-force, which is also known as qi, chi or prana. When you are stressed, tense, angry or fearful, your breath is short, fast and shallow. When you are peaceful and relaxed your breath is long, slow, deeper and charged with pranic life-force. The chest expands when we breathe deeply and fully: this assists the release of inner tensions and toxins as we exhale. You can also augment the release process by using the focused power of your mind through your intent, by focusing your intent on releasing not just toxins, anxiety and stress, but stagnant life force as well, which may be the underlying cause of disease.

So, by becoming aware of the connection between your breath, your nervous system, your brain and your intent, you have a tool with which to enhance all areas of your life. This will help you maintain optimum health, vitality, relaxation, balance, harmony and spiritual growth. Conscious breathing changes your breathing patterns permanently. By deeply breathing into the abdomen you can change your state of mind from being stressed out and fraught to having a sense of peacefulness and well-being. By becoming more mindful of your breathing and conscious relaxation you can take control of all aspects of your life. In most meditation practices the breath is also used to aid your focus of attention. Your focused awareness naturally follows what you are paying attention to. You furthermore associate what you are doing with your breathing, so that your breathing reinforces what you are doing. Therefore you associate the two fundamental steps of breathing, inhaling and exhaling, with your focus. This activates your focused intent and energy always follows your intent.

Meditation Space

A dedicated room you keep solely for meditation, relaxation and breathing exercises is best, as it soon acquires an ambience of peace and tranquillity. This room should be comfortably warm but well aired, especially if you use candles or incense which burn up oxygen. Keep it clean and simple: this will heighten your concentration by cutting out distractions. Have a regular time, place and practice; the most effective times are dawn and dusk. A simple altar can be a useful focus – see page 22.

Posture

Try to sit cross-legged, or in the half lotus or full lotus posture; these classic forms make a triangular path for the energy field and stop it dissipating in all directions. For long meditations choose to sit in a comfortable steady posture with the spine and neck held erect but not tense. This means that the base of the spine needs to be higher than the knees, thus tilting the pelvis forward to a position where the spine naturally remains upright when relaxed. The easiest way of doing this is to put a small, firm cushion beneath the base of the spine. The psychic current must be able to flow unimpeded from the base of the spine to the top of the head. When sitting, face north or east to take advantage of favourable magnetic vibrations. You can also lie on your back, on the floor sometimes, and it will give you a different meditation experience – usually sensory ventures into other states are heightened when lying down in a sleep posture. These trance-like dream meditations can be very intense. If you choose to lie down, use an exercise mat for comfort. Keep your arms and legs straight but relaxed. If sitting on a chair, choose a straight-backed chair to give you support and stop your diaphragm cramping. Your feet should be flat on the floor, your hands resting palms up on your knees. Do not let your heal loll forward as this will restrict your breathing.

Simple Meditation to De-stress

Before you begin the 'Temple Meditations' in each chapter, perform the following exercise if you often feel stressed due to incorrect breathing patterns. This exercise is quick. It is done seated, so it can be performed anywhere and at any time, at work, at home etc. Use it often to restore vitality, reduce stress, aid relaxation, prepare for meditation and focus your intent.

1.   Sit in a chair with your back straight but not rigid, using the chair back for support if necessary. Your feet must be flat on the floor.

2.   Relax your shoulders by stretching them up and down several times; this releases tension and stagnant qi.

3.   Close your eyes and begin releasing tension in the neck by rolling the head slowly from side to side.

4.   Open your eyes and shake out your hands vigorously for a minute to cleanse your emotions and stimulate the flow of qi to your hands.

5.   Place the palms of your hands on either side of your abdomen.

6.   First it is vitally important to exhale completely through your nose by releasing all the air from your lungs as you would normally and then exhale completely by forcing the remaining air out of your lungs.

7.   Then let your inhaling be the natural result of your exhaling, as you fill your lungs completely with air by inhaling very slowly through your nose, drawing your breath first through your abdomen to fill and expand it and then up through your middle and finally expanding your chest by raising your breastbone. When exhaling, contract your abdomen first and then your middle and chest by lowering your breastbone. Repeat seven times.

This is a potent exercise and should be done in moderation at first. Performed regularly over time it can enhance your vitality and help to reduce your stress levels. We will call this exercise of 'conscious breathing' a 'meditation intention breath'.

Here are some more breathing exercises to help you develop your meditation practice.

Alternate Nostril Breathing

To maintain balance and harmony in the heart chakra and help you de-stress yourself you should practise alternate nostril breathing on a daily basis. It is an ancient discipline as taught by the great Yoga teacher Patanjali. It is just as fresh and potent a vehicle for spiritual development today as it was when he taught it several thousand years ago. This technique brings the integration of the lower three chakras with the heart chakra, which will energise the physical body.

1. Sit comfortably with your spine straight and just focus on your normal breathing pattern for several breaths – just watch your breath coming and going.

2. Now, raise your right hand to your nose, palm towards your mouth. Place your thumb beside your right nostril and your forefinger beside your left nostril, so that you can close off one air passage or the other, with slight gentle pressure.

3. Now move your focused attention to your three lower chakras: you are going to energise them with a downflow of loving heart energy from above. Simply close the right nostril with your thumb, while you exhale through the left nostril.

4. At the bottom of your exhale, simply be empty for a moment, send your focus of attention as far down to the root chakra as possible…then release the thumb from the right nostril and press with your forefinger on the left nostril, so that you inhale through the right nostril.

5. At the top of this inhale, keep your fingers the same as on the inhale, and exhale through the same right nostril until you are empty of air…hold on empty…

6. Now reverse the process…by releasing your forefinger from your left nostril and pressing your thumb on the right nostril…inhale through the left nostril…hold at the top a moment, keep your fingers the same, then exhale through the same left nostril.

7. Continue in this pattern, where you inhale and exhale on one side only, then switch nostrils.

8. Inhale fully, do not switch nostrils…exhale fully from the same nostril…

    Now switch nostrils…inhale…exhale

    Now switch nostrils…inhale…exhale

    Now switch nostrils…inhale…exhale

9. Continue in this pattern for 12 to 20 rounds.

Practise this exercise until you can do it automatically and you are clear about the process.

Simple Candle Meditation

Establishing good meditation practice is vital, especially when you are just beginning to train yourself in the habit of sitting quietly and focusing your mind. This simple basic candle meditation is not very demanding, but it will aid your powers of concentration if you practise it daily for five minutes.

Sit in your chosen posture, preferably cross-legged on the floor.

Allow your breathing to be natural.

Focus on a lighted candle flame, then gently soften your gaze, so that you are actually looking beyond the flame.

When you feel you have the candle flame as a picture in your mind's eye, allow your eyes to close.

At first the afterglow may fade, but with practice you will be able to retain the image for several minutes.

When you can retain the image, allow yourself to become one with the flame so that there is no separation between you and the flame.

Enjoy the feelings of expansion and space; when you are ready, open your eyes and bring yourself back to normal everyday waking reality.

Sacred Presence

This primary whole-body meditation is a process of consciousness expansion. It will help you to experience yourself as a whole unified entity. We can employ our awareness of our breathing experience, heartbeat and balance to lead us into whole-body awareness. Whole body consciousness prepares us for the fundamental act of focusing our power of undivided attention on our master chakras, our energy centres along our spinal column.

1.   Begin with the awareness of the physical sensation of the air rushing in and out of your nostrils with every new breath; feel the pranic life energy filling your lungs.

2.   Expand your awareness to include the movement of your chest and stomach as you breathe.

3.   Expand your awareness to include your heartbeat and allow your attention to come alive in the present moment.

4.   Experience your muscular sense of balance in the present moment; feel the energy of Mother Earth's gravity, her Divine force field.

5.   Expand your awareness to include your whole body at once; effortlessly experience yourself in the present moment.

6.   Now, while maintaining awareness of your whole-body presence, expand your awareness to focus on each of the master chakras in turn, allowing seven breaths for each chakra.

7.   Now let go of individual chakra-focusing and be aware of all the chakras together as one energy system. Feel your entire energy system at once, including your aura. Open yourself to experience whatever energy is flowing around you…allow yourself to make contact with the actual energy of yourself, your personal 'sacred presence'.

8.   As you experience your sacred presence, begin to breathe in 'cosmic pranic life force'. Feel your body supercharged by this energy. It will increase your spiritual growth and 'light-body activation'.

9.   When you have finished, ground, centre and focus yourself.

Universal Consciousness Expansion and Contraction Exercise

Place the palms of your hands on either side of your abdomen. Take a 'meditation intention breath' and as you exhale imagine that your consciousness is flowing outwards, expanding into the vastness of the universe. Really feel it extending outwards from the centre of your being in all directions. Allow yourself to become vaster and vaster, reaching out in all directions; keep reaching out further with each exhalation. Allow yourself to merge into the universal consciousness. As you inhale deeply, feel your consciousness converging into your solar plexus. Envisage it as the central point from which the whole universe manifests itself. Practise this expansion and contraction for as long as you wish. Bring yourself back to everyday normal awareness and normal consciousness by changing the focus of the direction of the breath, directing your consciousness back into your physical body as you exhale.

Ascending into Cosmic Consciousness and Descending into Matter Exercise

Place the palms of your hands in the *Namaste* mudra (prayer position at the heart chakra). Do a complete 'meditation intention breath'. Then close your eyes and focus them upwards towards your third eye. At the same time, press your tongue up against the roof of your mouth, just behind your teeth. As you inhale, allow your consciousness to rise upwards; see yourself as a being of light rising upwards. Allow yourself to be drawn from your body higher and higher through all the spheres and planes of existence. With each inhalation allow yourself to rise ever higher and higher. As you exhale, imagine that you are bringing pure celestial energy down into your physical body, being conscious of descending, of incarnating. Be aware that the celestial energy centre is your heart chakra; this is where it combines with the earth energy of your inhalation and becomes pure light which radiates in all directions. Practise this ascending – descending meditation for as long as you wish. Bring yourself back to everyday normal awareness and normal consciousness by changing the focus of the direction of the breath, directing your consciousness back into your physical body. This process activates your 'Light Body'.

Aura Awareness and Chakra Presence

Place the palms of your hands in the *Namaste* mudra (prayer position at the heart chakra). Do a complete 'meditation intention breath'. When you exhale, be conscious of your aura. When you inhale, be conscious of your personal chakra system.

Elemental Purification

A.   Take three 'meditation intention breaths', inhaling through the nose and exhaling through the nose. This corresponds with the fixed crystalline element of Earth. As you inhale, consciously focus upon the sensation of energy flowing up from the earth into your root chakra and then on upwards through each chakra. Then, as you exhale, open up to receive a spontaneous flow of celestial light energy from above. Feel it flowing downwards through each chakra until all your chakra centres are lit up and you feel grounded, vital and alive, with a strong sense of well-being.

B.   Take three 'meditation intention breaths', inhaling through the nose and exhaling through the mouth. This corresponds with the fluid, flowing, cleansing element of Water. As you exhale, imagine water flowing down through your chakras, cleansing and purifying them. As you inhale, imagine pure water flowing up through your chakras like a natural spring flowing out of the top of your head. This cleanses your emotional body.

C.   Take three 'meditation intention breaths', inhaling swiftly through the mouth and out through the nose. This corresponds with the transformational element of Fire. As you inhale, concentrate on your solar plexus chakra and feel it becoming very hot, as if the air is blowing on your personal internal fire. As you exhale, imagine that the fire from your solar plexus is radiating light, as your consciousness is transferred to your aura. This energises the solar plexus and burns off any negative mental attitudes which may have lodged in your auric shell.

D.   Take three meditation intention breaths, inhaling through the mouth and exhaling through the mouth. This corresponds with the uplifting element of Air. Focus on your heart chakra...as you exhale, feel as though you are being dispersed into the universe; as you inhale, realize that you are the product of the convergence of the universe upon a point. This reconnects you to the Universal web of life.

Angelic Guidance Meditation

The following meditation will put you in touch with the celestial realm and help you find your Angelic guide. You may wish to light a white, pink or purple candle. You must purify your energy space. Soothing Angelic music is also useful, if it does not distract you too much. Flowers are very acceptable as energy offerings to the Angels. They also like bells. You could hold a crystal, such as rose quartz, seraphinite, danburite, angelite or selenite. Purifying your physical body by taking a shower or bath and putting on clean clothes can also make you feel more receptive and in tune; after all, you are going to invite an Angel or Angels into your life. Angels will be very happy to work with you and very often you will feel emotions of excitement and happiness even before you begin the meditation. All the people I know who truly work with Angels are very joyful, happy souls who have a light in their eyes, a smile on their lips, a glow in their aura, joy in their heart and unconditional love for all.

1. Sit in a comfortable steady posture, with the spine and neck held erect but not tense. This helps steady the mind and aids concentration. If you cannot sit cross-legged, sit on a straight-backed chair with your feet flat on the floor, your knees level with your hips and your spine upright. You can also lie on your back. I would suggest you try both, which will lead to balance in your Angel meditation practice. Many people prefer to sit upright to begin the day in meditation and to lie down to finish the day with a more dream-like meditation.

2. Place your hands on your thighs, palms upward, and join your thumbs to your index fingers. Now pull the shoulders back ever so slightly and the chin in a little, so that there is a small pull on the back of the neck; this will ease the blood flow to the brain. Close your eyes and, with the mouth ever so slightly open, rest the tip of the tongue on the roof of the mouth just behind the teeth. This placement of the tongue is vital because it naturally maintains the flow of energy to the head whilst keeping the jaw relaxed. There are two major energy channels (acupuncture meridians): the Yin channel (the conception vessel) begins at the perineum and flows up the front centre of the body, ending at the tip of the tongue; the Yang channel (the governing vessel) begins at the perineum and flows up the back centre of the body, over the top of the head and back down to the roof of the mouth. The tongue connects these two important currents when touched to the highest point in the roof of the mouth.

    An easy way to open this energy channel is to sit in a relaxed posture. Allow your energy to complete the loop by letting your mind flow along with it. Start in the mouth and mentally circulate your attention with the energy. Eventually the current will begin to feel warm in some places as it loops around. Relax, try to bring your mind directly into the part of the loop being focused on. Experience the actual feeling of the flow of chi in that part of your body.

3. Once the circuit is going smoothly, inhale as you go up the spine and over to the third eye, and exhale as you go down from the third eye to the perineum. Complete seven of these circuits (seven is a mystical number and it will serve to clear your chakras).

4. Bring the energy up your spine as you inhale and send it up to heaven. With it send gratitude for all the good things in your life.

5. Imagine an overcast day. See the clouds part, as a ray of cosmic white/gold light comes through and settles directly on your head. Absorb that brilliant Celestial Light into your being through the top of your head. This is your link with the Divine Source...your connection with everything that ever was, is, or will be.

6.   Allow this Celestial Light to pour in through your body; feel it nurturing every cell, every fibre of your being…with pure consciousness. Bring in the blessings that are meant for you. Feel this good energy coursing through your body…as you receive your Divine Blessings, sit with the energy. Bask in it. Allow it to bathe your body internally and externally.

7.   Now focus on your third eye or crown chakra and feel your Divine connection. Stay with this energy for several minutes.

8.   Allow this consciousness that transcends normal thought and the ordinary senses to begin to take you…beyond space and time…into a state of deeper awareness. This is your link with an unlimited realm of Angelic understanding and knowing…you are becoming enlightened…the process of unlocking your enlightenment code has started.

9.   It is now time to make contact with your Angelic guidance…from the deepest centre of your beautiful heart chakra send out your longing for an Angel (or Angels) to be your guide to help you in your spiritual development…really feel your longing going out into the Angelic realms of love, light, joy, healing and Divine understanding…ask for an Angel (or Angels) who will be your very own special guide and companion.

10.   Feel your Angel(s) drawing closer…feel the change in your energy signature as your Angelic guide draws close…

11.   You may wish to ask for guidance…or even your Angel's name…be still and wait for an answer…if necessary, tell your conscious mind to step aside. Breathe deeply.

12.   When you receive an answer, give thanks. Always give thanks. Focus on your gratitude towards the Angel(s) that has answered your call and answered your question(s) instead of getting caught up in thinking about how wonderful you are because you can do such a thing.

13.   Now it is time to come back to everyday waking reality, but before you do…make an appointment to meet your Angel(s) again…

14.   Allow yourself plenty of time to come back to everyday reality…centre and earth yourself.

15.   Keep a written record of the experience.

16.   Keep your appointment to meet your Angel(s). The more you practise this meditation, the stronger your links into the heavenly Angelic realm become.

Basic Relaxation, Breathing and Visualisation Techniques for Clients

Client Relaxation – It is very important that you, as a therapist, can relax your client because this relieves their stress, anxiety and tension, which allows their life force to flow freely. As your client's body relaxes, the heart, brain and lungs are slowed down, calming the emotions, which begins the healing process. One of the best ways of relaxing your client is by using guided imagery, which is helpful to teach them to relax. Many people do not know how to relax. They are very tense, so it is up to you to be as calm and relaxed as possible. This will help them relax also. When you use relaxation techniques you are working with the unconscious mind. This contains all the wisdom, memories and intelligence. It is the source of creativity. It regulates body maintenance and autonomic processes like breathing, blood circulation and tissue regeneration. The conscious mind cannot heal a cut or accelerate your heartbeat to the correct rate; the unconscious mind does. It is the seat of your emotions and directs nearly all your behaviour. Everything that has ever happened, you and everything that you have ever imagined, is stored as a multi-sensory recording in your unconscious mind. You can use relaxation techniques to go into the unconscious mind and reveal details of incidents that happened many years before, all of which are filed away somewhere.

You may use relaxation techniques to help your client relax in between therapy sessions. The following exercises could also be used for self-healing.

Full Body Relaxation – A good way to help your client release tension is by teaching them to relax each part of their body, starting at the feet and working up to the top of the head: Your client will be lying flat on the floor, bed or therapy couch, with their eyes closed. Their legs should be apart and arms slightly away from the body. Their head should be supported and if necessary a pillow placed beneath their knees.

1.   Begin by guiding them to breathe deeply and slowly, inhaling to the count of three. Hold for the count of three. Exhale to the count of three. Hold on the out-breath for the count of three. Ask them to do this balancing breath three times.

2.   Now begin to guide your client into consciously relaxing every part of their body. Get them to use the out-breath as a release of tension. You can also ask them to use the mental command 'relax' as they breathe out. Begin at the feet and move slowly up the body until you reach the top of the head.

3.   Ask your client to imagine that their body is now becoming heavier and heavier. This may take several minutes.

4.   Then ask them to allow themselves to become lighter and lighter, until they feel they are gently floating on a beautiful white cloud that is soft, warm and so very comfortable.

5.   Allow your client to stay on this beautiful white cloud for as long as they need to as you begin the therapy process.

Visualisation

Visualisation is basically a process whereby we internalise our view of the world and by using specific techniques alter our outer world; this includes our health and overall experience of life. Nearly all visualisations begin with getting us to view something with our mind's eye. Many people get worried that they cannot visualise. Don't worry, everyone can visualise; just think of a time when you were happy. Picture the scene, whether it was a party, holiday, wedding or whatever comes to mind. A mental picture will come into your mind and that is visualisation; you may even be able to remember sounds, smells, feelings and emotions.

Colour Visualisation

This simple technique can be used for yourself or with a client. It can be used for healing, pain relief, relaxation, balance or as a 'tonic'. Begin with the relaxation technique, whereby you relax each part of the body, starting at the feet and working up to the top of the head. It is important to take the in-breath through the nostrils. Exhale through the nose – unless the pain or condition is acute, in which case the out-breath should be through the mouth. This is applicable for shock or pain of any kind, physical, mental or emotional. You may use the colour breath to fill the whole body or just part of the body. This applies to pain or any area of the body that particularly needs healing.

If you wanted to, you could just breathe the colour or colours you are intuitively drawn to. There are endless variations and combinations. You could try breathing mixed colours such as pink or turquoise. You could even use the colour breath, for instance, in a stressful situation, when blue would be very calming or turquoise would help with protection and communication.

1. Make yourself comfortable in a chair or lie flat on the floor or therapy couch.

2. Allow your eyes to close.

3. Begin breathing deeply, consciously relaxing every part of your body. Begin at the feet and move slowly up the body until you reach the top of your head.

4. Imagine each part becoming heavier and heavier. This may take several minutes.

5. Then allow yourself to become lighter and lighter, until you feel you are completely relaxed.

6. Remain in this relaxed state and visualise the air around you filled with the colour violet.

7. Breathe in for the count of three, visualising yourself inhaling the colour violet as you do. Visualise this strongly. Actually see yourself pulling the colour in through your nose, out of the air, and watch it going away into your body.

8. Hold your colour breath for the count of three.

9. Exhale for the count of three.

10. Repeat 7, 8 and 9 twice more. This will complete the first three-breath colour cycle.

11. Now visualise the air around you filled with the indigo colour. Breathe in for the count of three, visualising yourself inhaling the colour indigo as you do. Visualise this strongly. Actually see yourself pulling the colour in through your nose, out of the air, and watch it going away into your body.

12. Hold your colour breath for the count of three.

13. Exhale for the count of three.

14. Repeat 11, 12 and 13 twice more. This will complete the second three-breath colour cycle.

15. Continue with this process of three-breath cycles, going through all the remaining colours of the rainbow in reverse order:

   Blue
   Green
   Yellow
   Orange
   Red

16. When you have finished the process, you can either concentrate on breathing in clear white light, or just relax and allow your body to come back very slowly.

Be aware of any areas that would not absorb some colours, or any areas that absorbed lots of colour; these are parts of the body that may need more attention in the healing process.

I gave you the colours in an order that would be a grounding experience, from the fastest colour vibration of violet to the slowest of red. You could also try the reverse – starting with red and moving through to violet. Going from the slowest to the fastest colour vibration would be much more suitable before meditation practice.

Sound

Today the modern therapist or meditator has unlimited access to a plethora of amazing musical experiences. These range from ancient chants and mantras to drumming or the sounds of nature. There is even music composed specifically to activate healing, relaxation or spiritual growth, so it is vital to suggest to your client that they purchase a suitable music CD. You will probably be quite familiar with the full range of music on offer and be able to guide them in their choice.

Instruct your client to lie down and relax for thirty minutes once a day or fifteen minutes twice a day whilst listening to the music. You could also give them an Angelic essence to use in their aura just before the relaxation session which would support the healing process, such as Archangel Raphael's Dream or Angel of Light. Also the relaxation/healing experience can be greatly enhanced by giving your client two clear quartz single-terminated crystals to hold in their hands. The crystal in the left hand should point inwards, while the crystal in the right hand should point away from the body. Each crystal must be cleansed under running water before the session and then programmed by misting it with the Angelic essence.

Breathing and Brain Waves

There are four categories of brainwaves, Alpha, Beta, Delta and Theta, ranging from the most activity to the least activity. Each brainwave is associated with different activities of the mind. An electroencephalograph measures brainwaves and biofeedback machines monitor the state of mind and mental activity.

Beta brainwaves are produced when the brain is aroused and actively engaged in mental activities. These beta waves are of relatively low amplitude and are the fastest of the four different brainwaves. The frequency of beta waves ranges from 40 to 15 cycles a second.

Alpha brainwaves are produced when you are relaxed, under hypnosis or light meditation or reflection. Alpha brainwaves are slower and are higher in amplitude. Their frequency ranges from 14 to 9 cycles per second.

Theta brainwaves are produced when you are day-dreaming or in deep meditation. They are typically of even greater amplitude and slower frequency. This frequency range is normally between 8 and 5 cycles a second.

Delta brainwaves are produced when you are asleep. Here the brainwaves are of the greatest amplitude and slowest frequency. They typically centre around a range of 4 to 1.5 cycles per second. Deep dreamless sleep would take you down to the lowest frequency, typically 2 to 3 cycles a second. When we go to bed and turn off the lights and close our eyes, our brainwaves will descend from beta to alpha to theta and finally, when we fall asleep, to delta. For meditation practice we aim at the theta range of 8 to 5 cycles per second.

Part Six

Therapy Section

Using the Angelic Essences – Preparing for an Angel Therapy Session

The way you prepare yourself and your client before an Angelic therapy session will have an enormous effect on not only the quality of the experience, but also the final outcome. It will also minimise any healing crisis. So to help you get the most from your therapy sessions here is a very comprehensive list of advice.

You must be relaxed and confident before starting a therapy session: if you are tense, your client will feel it and become tense also. You must allow yourself time to attune to the Archangel essence you will be using for the session, as well as allowing yourself plenty of time to attune to your client's energy field to gain energetic rapport. If at any time you feel threatened or drained by something attached to your client, such as lower vibrational entities, immediately spray your crown chakra and the back of your heart chakra and back with Archangel Michael's Empowerment aura essence.

You should wear loose white cotton clothes which are comfortable and allow freedom of movement for both giving and receiving a treatment. Synthetic fabrics interfere with the energy flow of the meridian channels, as well as potentially holding negativity within the chakra system. Dark or drab coloured clothing will interfere with the therapy session by lowering both your energy field and that of your client. If you or your client have chosen to wear pastel-coloured clothing, make sure it is compatible with the Archangelic energies you have chosen to work with: this will maximise the overall effectiveness of the therapy session. Black clothing is not recommended for giving or receiving a therapy session as it creates a holding energy.

Unless otherwise specified, use white bedding until you gain more experience with the Angelic webs. When you gain confidence, explore the use of different coloured cloths to lie on or place over the client. For some Angelic webs certain colours have been suggested.

Please make sure you have a clean, safe space to work in. Cleanse it energetically with the 'Angel of Light' essence mist – see the section **Purification – Creating A Sacred Space**. It is very important that all crystals are cleansed before and after use if you are using the 'process' method. This will guarantee that any residual disharmonies are removed from the energy field of the stones.

Asking your client to drink plenty of fresh pure water, just before and especially just after each therapy session, will ease the removal of energy blocks and toxicity. These are always released with the integration of new energy patterns and information (as you return the body back to the original blueprint of perfection and resonance). You must also drink plenty of fresh water to help your energy field before and after giving a therapy session.

Heavy meals should be avoided immediately after a vibrational therapy session as blood is diverted to the gut to help with the digestion process. The blood plays a very important role in the healing process, so this diversion will disrupt the body's ability to heal by releasing toxins.

Wash your hands in cool flowing water before and after each client. This will remove any residual energies.

Ask your client to remove contact lenses, glasses, all jewellery, belts, coins from their pockets and any metal objects like keys etc. Also ask them not to wear to the therapy session clothes which have metal buttons or hooks, as metal gives a false energetic field. Be sure to clear all jewellery before wearing it again after the therapy session.

Normally your client lies on a massage table or therapy couch. They should be made comfortable with a pillow supporting the head and, if your client has back discomfort, a pillow needs to be placed behind the knees to support the legs. Your therapy couch needs to be wide enough and long enough to accommodate your client so that their arms can relax easily at their sides and their feet are on the couch. You must stress to your client not to cross their arms or legs during the therapy process as this will block the energetic flow. Your client can be covered with a white blanket if at any time during the session they feel cold.

Unless specified otherwise, all Angelic webs should be laid out so that the head is aligned with magnetic north. This places the individual's bioelectromagnetic field in harmony with the flow of the earth's energy field, which will augment any therapy session.

Please note, warn anyone who has had any 'new device' fitted into their body since birth that they may have problems with it (discomfort). This is due to the original blueprint being reinstated back into the body. Do not worry though, the energy will equal out and healing will still occur (new device = fillings in teeth, caps on teeth, hip replacements etc).

Your client may need less medication than before. They should inform their GP that they are receiving therapy and that they may need to make the necessary adjustments in managing their medication.

Always allow yourself and your client plenty of time and space. Never rush a therapy session. Allow your client several minutes of quiet time before beginning the session. This will allow the possibility of a clearer experience and the increased ability to notice any changes more easily.

You must be able to relax your client prior to the commencement of a therapy session. It would be wise to practise 'delivering' the basic breathing and relaxation meditation – see the section **Breathing, Meditation and Relaxation – Basic Relaxation, Breathing and Visualisation Techniques for Clients.**

Your experience will probably differ for each session. Angel essences always work in the same way, but your client will always have a different experience. This is due to the different issues, thoughts, feelings, miasms, emotions etc. within each person's energy field.

Always allow your client plenty of time to come round to everyday activities slowly. Ideally they should have three times the length of time they have been receiving Angel therapy before they need to do anything focused. This will allow their body to integrate the energies it has experienced into its normal everyday functioning. Tell them to allow any feelings of agitation, anxiety, fidgeting, anger, resentment, annoyance, heat, stress, cold, fear or restlessness to dispel before they resume normal activity. The same would apply if you used Angel therapy for self-healing: give yourself plenty of time. For self-healing make sure you will not be disturbed during the session or during the rest period afterwards: take the phone off the hook etc.

As you gain in confidence and competence with the Angelic essences you can easily incorporate them into every other therapy and treatment regime you use on your clients or yourself.

Also, for self-healing sessions, if at any time you feel discomfort whilst in a Angel web, quietly get up and find somewhere to rest and relax until the sensations disappear. Re-enter the Angel web when you are ready, or terminate the session.

For general grounding, earthing and centering at the end of a Angel therapy session, use Angel of the Animals aura essence on your legs and feet.

Establishing rapport and trust by communicating with your client plays an integral part in any therapy session. During the consultation at the start of the session try to ask open-ended questions – use words such as 'how' or 'what'. At some point ask the key question 'Do you wish to be healed?' This may seem obvious, but sometimes a person does not really want to let go of a problem and find a resolution. Healing is a very personal process and each person must deal with core issues at their own pace, so be sure you receive an affirmative response. If you receive a negative, fearful or non-committal response in any form, whether verbal, physical or psychic, it is not wise to continue with the Angelic therapy session. It would be better to discuss with your client their hesitation. Please do this in a non-judgemental, non-threatening way. Also, it is wise to have completed a counselling course before giving 'advice'. If you have completed a counselling course, you would know not to give advice: all we can do is to facilitate the client in finding a deeper understanding of the cause of their dis-ease.

After receiving a positive affirmation from your client, it is now time to merge with the Archangel's energies – link yourself totally with this energy and ask for the highest possible good of all. Ask for help and guidance in all your Angel therapy work. Allow yourself to be completely surrounded by this Angelic energy and allow yourself to be totally protected and guided. Please remember that the most important energies to work with are love and compassion. If your heart is not open and loving, you are not coming from the right energy. Do not allow your mind to wander to other things while you are treating your client. Stay focused.

If there is no reaction to Angel therapy after several sessions, the body could be unreceptive due to external factors such as heavy medication or psychological attitude, blocking the therapeutic process. As long as reactions are positive, there is value in continuing the treatment. (This applies to all therapy procedures, not only Angel therapy).

You must take responsibility for your actions and the well-being of your client. Remember, when they are in the Angelic web or Angel energy field, you are responsible for maintaining the purity and integrity of the energy field.

You must develop methods for monitoring/checking quality and depth of the Angel therapy session, such as monitoring electrical skin responses (biofeedback), visual observations of physiological change, verbal check with client, touch, pre-arranged distress signal. The client's safety must be monitored at all times.

Self-awareness is essential: the kinds of physical, mental and emotional health issues for the practitioner which can affect therapy, such as coughs, flu, stress, unresolved emotional issues, fatigue or any medical condition which is unresolved.

Finally, but most important: you must be able to differentiate between your own internal world and that of your clients.

Manifestation of the Archangel Essences

Each Angelic essence contains the energetic signature of the Archangel or Angel that the essence is dedicated to and guided or over-shadowed by. To capture and bind in stable form the subtle vibrations of the Archangels to a material substance requires thorough preparation. Each Archangel was previously attuned to over a prolonged period of time – usually many years as in the case of Archangels Michael, Gabriel, Metatron, Sandalphon, Raphael, Seraphiel and Uriel, who actually approached me over 30 years ago during the meditation practice which always followed my daily yoga sessions. Each Angelic contact brought about an expanded state of consciousness which allowed my mind to detach from my body, allowing me to experience timelessness in pure serenity.

The other Archangels have also frequently contacted me during meditation, invocation, dreams, visions or prayer.

Preparation

Each Archangel then supplies all the preparation details that will capture their perfected signature. The alchemical process used to bring about the metamorphosis includes the most auspicious day, time, length of time in full unclouded morning sunshine (sun potentizing), gemstones, purified water, essential oils, colour filters, invocations, visualisations and harmonic sound frequencies. The gemstones chosen by the Angels are always the finest quality available on the earth plane; sometimes they are etherically potentized or etherically restructured. Pure quartz singing bowls tuned to the crown chakra B or soul star chakra C# are used. Glass containers are inferior and not recommended for producing Angelic essences. All gemstones used are physically and metaphysically cleansed, dedicated and, if quartz, programmed. High quality purified water, alcohol and essential oils are used in the aura sprays. The production space and all equipment used in the process is physically and metaphysically cleansed, purified, energised and dedicated. The bottles and atomiser caps are also suitably cleansed, purified, energised and dedicated. After filling, the bottles are sealed and potentized once more, before the specifically designed labels are added. The entire process is completed by hand in a silent, calm, meditative state of mind.

Why Did the Angels Choose Gemstones?

Gemstones have been specifically chosen by the Archangels to 'capture' and bind their Angelic energy signatures because they have a unique molecular arrangement of geometric symmetry which is perfectly balanced due to the three-dimensional pattern of atoms known as the crystal lattice. Gemstones have a stabilizing energetic influence on cellular systems within the physical body. Their harmonic range resonates with certain key points within the human anatomy. This energetic influence affects all levels of the subtle anatomy as the body, chakras, aura and meridians are totally interconnected. Angelic essences can also bring about transformational spiritual growth and understanding of Divine universal laws which relate to soul initiations.

Why Use the Archangel and Angel Essences?

When we are experiencing joy, love, peace and health, our vibratory pattern will be high and in balance; illness, dis-ease and negative emotional states of mind are lower or a disrupted unbalanced frequency. This is where the Angelic essences can come to the rescue and act as a catalyst for change. In order to therapeutically alter our physical and subtle bodies, we must administer energy that vibrates at a higher stable frequency. Holistic healing with Angelic essences allows the vibration of the Angel to interact with our own energy field. Through their balanced superior higher vibration we quickly find the imbalance will be alleviated at a core level. This, in turn, stimulates the body's own capacity to heal itself by bringing it back into alignment with the higher self, which is a pathway to inner peace and an expansion of consciousness.

How Do the Archangel, Angel or Ascended Master Essences Work?

Angelic essences can be categorised as highly refined stable vibrational medicine. They always have an effect and they work in a myriad different ways and on all levels, from the gross physical body through to the highest spiritual level. This is because we store negative thought patterns, dis-ease, frozen emotional miasms etc, in different areas of not just the physical body but all the subtle bodies as well. Each person is unique, so are their dis-eases; therefore the Angelic essences, because they are vibrational medicine, will work on everyone in a unique way to transform dis-ease. During the process of transforming through releasing dis-ease you may become acutely aware of the patterns the dis-ease has caused in your energy field; this is often in the form of remembering the initial experience or emotion. You may even find your behaviour becomes a little erratic as the dis-ease patterns and associated toxins are released. Once they are released, though, you will find an energy renewal as your body, mind and spirit then have immediate direct access to the energy that has been stored in the miasm, emotion, etc, as well as the energy your body has invested in the storage of the miasm, emotion, etc. As you release more and more dis-ease, your vibrational rate will rise; this, too, brings more energy of a highly refined soul quality, which means you just attract even more of the same high vibrational energy through the process of entrainment. At this point you will find yourself on an upward spiral of joy and renewal, rather than the downward slippery slope into negativity and dis-ease which you may have been on. The simple truth is that the more negativity you feel compelled to hold onto, the more will be attracted; just like a cancer it grows and swamps you on all levels until you feel totally choked to death by it. Likewise, light attracts light, so it is always your free choice – you choose moment by moment what vibratory pattern you choose to hold onto.

The Effects of the Angelic Essences

The Angelic essences are transformational catalysts which provide a new system of healing as part of the human evolution on planet Earth. We, as holistic vibrational therapists, find our role is to transform energy that is causing a disruption in our client's energy field. The Archangel essences are specially prepared and Angelically guided remedies. Each Archangel essence carries an Angelic vibratory signature. These Angelic signatures or themes will address a different feeling, emotion, thought pattern or physical symptom.

Promoting Spiritual Growth

The Angels also specifically designed the essences to promote spiritual development through soul initiations or karmic lessons. We, as souls (individualised aspects of God that are pure spirit), have chosen the experience of dwelling in a human body as part of our soul's development. The experience of being 'human' is to assimilate our spiritual nature into physical form, thereby becoming the embodiment of God on earth. It is an amazing undertaking, especially when each of us goes through the process before birth of amnesia – that is the act of forgetting our true nature. We are given the amnesia so that we can, for the first part of our lives, integrate into the earth plane and bond with our families. Unfortunately most of us forget our true nature for too long and ignore the whisperings of our soul. We become earthbound and locked into the material pleasures and addictions of the earth plane. It is not until our overall dis-ease becomes critical that we finally 'wake up' to our true nature and soul's purpose. So in fact dis-ease can be seen in a very positive light and used as a catalyst for change.

Transformation

Our journey through life can sometimes feel painful to us as our soul searches for its authenticity and maturity. Some of the comments I hear over and over again from the people who attend the Angel seminars are the feelings they experience of coming home, of feeling themselves, of being connected, of remembering who they truly are. Frequently during the Angel seminars tears of release flow; these tears are always a positive experience. Although the Angel essences are definitely not a quick fix, some people experience immediate and permanent change. Through attuning to the Angels you will find your true purpose in life and your pathway home. I usually suggest 'Archangel Uriel's Initiation', which brings Angelic peace and wisdom as it illuminates your path through life; it is wonderful for those who feel lost, abandoned, rejected or alone.

Path of Growth

As part of the transformation process you have to integrate yourself once more into your surroundings and current lifestyle. This includes the people around you on whose lives you impact. The people closest to you – your partner, children, family, friends, work colleagues – are not always comfortable with the 'new' you; it often means that they will have to change too and they may not be ready for this change. Just think back to a time in your life when change was forced upon you; perhaps this change was due to bereavement, divorce or job loss. I am sure you remember how uncomfortable the process was. So it is important to be self-reliant and single- minded through your transformation, for others may even perceive you as selfish. It is important that you seek out those who will support you and encourage your spiritual growth and health renewal. You will derive a great deal of support from the Angelic realms, but you must ask for the help, as the Angels can never interfere with your free will.

Dosage

How often and for how long you use an Angelic essence will depend on how quickly your body integrates the essence's vibration. This will also depend on the circumstances surrounding the emotions/feelings/dis-ease, etc. you are administering it to. If your dis-ease is merely transitory or you are in a small crisis situation, such as a job interview or driving test, you may require only one dose/application, but if you have been feeling the same dis-ease for a longer period, there is no set time limit for how long you can use your chosen essence or essences. If you are using the Angelic essence for treating a long-standing or chronic condition, I have found it is best to review the essence and its actions at least once a fortnight. This is the time when you will decide whether to change the essence for yourself or your client or to continue for another two weeks.

If you are in a crisis situation it is perfectly safe to use the essences every hour until you begin to experience relief. Angel of Light is especially recommended in acute or crisis situations. It is our most popular essence and the one most people use first.

Spiritual Development

If you are taking an Angelic essence for spiritual development, you may need to review it more often, as they can be integrated very quickly by those who are energy aware (we are talking about minutes and seconds, rather than days). Also, if you are taking the essence in a group situation, especially for group meditation or spiritual attunement or alignment, the integration period is very fast, almost instantaneous. This is due to the amplification of the overall group energetic dynamics. If you are taking the Angelic essence in an Earth 'power' area, such as Stonehenge, Glastonbury, Sedona or the Pyramids in Egypt, the essence will be amplified and the integration period substantially reduced.

Pathways

Each Angelic essence will work in its own unique way, but generally they clear miasms outwards and through the aura, although some discharge downwards into the earth. Others work through the water element and will discharge the miasm when you are taking a shower or bath. It is fascinating to watch the process. If you cannot see the energy movement yet, you will still be able to feel or 'know' what is happening.

Safety

Angel aura essences are beneficial to all living things. They can be used by anyone of any age; they are safe and effective for pets; even flowers, trees and plants have been known to benefit. As they work in harmony with your body and they are self-adjusting and 100% natural, they can be used with any conventional or complementary medicines and treatments. For different methods of using an Angelic essence, see the section – **Application: Using the Angelic Essences on Yourself.**

Mixtures

Each Angelic essence is complete in itself and will work very well in clearing patterns of dis-ease. So by using the Angelic theme (signature) and during the process of attunement to a particular Archangel you will readily get used to the signature; this engenders confidence in the Angelic realm.

But I have also found that by combining two or three essences (which can be misted into the aura at the same time) chakra integration occurs much more quickly. Very often I have found severe dysfunction in one chakra is so great that it needs to be realigned with the chakras above and below before total alignment will occur.

Likewise, if you are working spiritually with the Tree of Life model and experiencing each sephirah in turn, you may wish at some point to work with a triad such as the first one:

Kether or Crown – Archangel Metatron (Divine)
Chokmah or Wisdom – Archangel Raziel (Ratziel) (Cosmic Father)
Binah or Understanding – Archangel Tzaphkiel (Zaphkiel) (Cosmic Mother)

By choosing to work with the first triad, which starts with *Kether* (Crown) and begins the activity, it has all the power and potential of creation. It then forms *Chokmah* (Wisdom) and *Binah* (Understanding). These first three spheres are the Divine trinity and traditionally relate to the realm of the intellect. These first three spheres also form pillars, which act as support for the next seven spheres to bring the energy of the Divine down to *Malkuth* or Kingdom.

This combination of essences would give you the trinity of wisdom, understanding and knowledge of the ascension process. Also it would stabilise and support the downflow of light energy via the three pillars, which would, in turn, support the whole structure of your own personal tree of life and give you an intellectual understanding of the descent of energy into matter .

So in the end analysis it is up to your intuition to guide you in using individual Angelic essences or a mixture.

Causes of Dis-ease

Harmony and health can be viewed as the continuous harmonious flow of vital energy between the body, mind, spirit, soul, subtle bodies and the universe. When we become dis-eased, we block the flow of vital energy on all levels of our being. We are all in a constant state of change and personal growth; remaining in harmony with our soul is a constant balancing act. Every day we are bombarded by our own and others' negative thought patterns, media manipulation, environmental pollutants, emotional stress, modern living conditions, addictions, bacteria, viruses, poor diet and inadequate breathing techniques, lack of exercise; even the weather can adversely affect us. All these factors have an effect on us and a good vibrational therapist will be able to compile an energetic profile of the whole being which takes into account all the damage which has accumulated over the years. Many people go along life's path with little regard for their health because all seems well, but the damage is there and it accumulates until the whole system breaks down and really severe health problems are diagnosed. Very often when someone develops severe health problems they choose to look at the larger picture and this brings them to unprecedented spiritual growth and personal development, as well as seeking ways to become responsible for their own health and emotional well-being.

Positive emotions strengthen your energy field, bringing health, balance and vitality, whilst negative emotions or stress bring sickness, instability, mood swings and low energy. This is called the body-mind connection. From the moment of conception onwards (as you developed in your mother's womb you would be subject to her thoughts, emotions, feelings, diet and environment), your life experiences accumulate and combine with all the other factors, like the layers of an onion, to develop the individual you are today.

Any form of healing or therapy allows qi (energy) to be redirected by the healer, which clears the patterns of dis-ease which have blocked the harmonious flow in relationship to the universe. Researchers in the field of psychoneuroimmunology are examining the subtle energetic links between emotions and immunological function. It has already been established that physiological links between human emotions and illness do exist. Various researchers who have examined the link between emotions and illness have found a strong association between depression, grief and the overall suppression of immune functioning.

Reactions and Growth

Holistic healing resolves many different issues which have caused blockages in the overall energy flow of the physical and subtle bodies. So by working holistically we bring harmony back to the body, mind, spirit and soul; this is something everybody aspires to. Emotional problems caused by becoming detached from our inner guidance often lodge in a frozen or crystallised pattern, which is often referred to as a miasm.

Healing Crisis

Healing crisis or contra-actions or symptom substitution or emotional disturbance or self-sabotage etc. – these reactions are all part of the process of holistic healing. We will explore the different sensations experienced during and/or after complementary therapy sessions. You may also experience other sensations not listed. Everyone is unique. Whatever the reactions, they are a necessary part of the healing process and will pass.

Negative Sensations

Aching head – Drink plenty of water. Direct your awareness towards your feet. Use Angel of the Animals aura essence for grounding. Check your diet for allergies and vitamin deficiencies. Check your environment for strong perfumes etc.

Bloated stomach – Too much energy in the solar plexus. Check your diet and vitamin deficiencies.

Feeling 'spacey' – Not grounded enough. Drink plenty of water. Check your diet for allergies. Check your environment for strong perfumes etc.

Detached from reality – Not grounded enough. Drink plenty of water. Check your diet for allergies and vitamin deficiencies. Check your environment for strong perfumes etc.

Self-sabotage – Does the client really want 'healing'? Suggest seeing a good holistic counsellor.

Positive Sensations

Sweating – Normal. A sign that the body is cleansing itself of toxins. Drink plenty of water.

Numbness – Normal. A sign that Qi is flowing.

Increased urination – A good sign. The kidneys are stimulated to produce more urine, which may be darker and stronger smelling, due to the toxin content. Drink plenty of water.

Symptom substitution – Normal. A sign that natural healing is taking place. But be aware of the deep process your client is undergoing. (In standard allopathic medical treatment, symptom substitution is very common. This is due to the nature of allopathic treatment, which only treats the symptom, not the cause of the disease).

Aggravated skin conditions – Good sign, particularly in conditions which have been suppressed; increased perspiration and pimples. Drink plenty of water.

Improved skin tone – Good sign, due to improved circulation.

Increased secretions – Good sign. Increased secretions of the mucus membrane in the nose, mouth and bronchial area. Drink plenty of water.

Disrupted sleep patterns – Good sign. This means the body is re-balancing itself and old energy patterns are breaking down.

Aggression or feelings of irritation or agitation – Normal, this means that Qi is flowing and the body is releasing toxins. Anger is a good way to release stored emotions, so healing can begin. Find a safe, positive way to release the anger, though.

Temporary outbreak of a disease which has been suppressed – A sign that Qi is flowing. Drink plenty of water.

Tiredness – A sign that Qi is flowing, toxins are being released and the body needs rest. Drink plenty of water.

Depression – Overwhelming desire to weep. A good sign, this means that Qi is flowing. Weeping is a good way to release stored emotions, so healing can begin. Drink plenty of water.

Tingling – Normal. A sign that Qi is flowing. Drink plenty of water.

Body heat – Normal. A sign that Qi is flowing. When energy flows it heats the body. Drink plenty of water.

Trembling – Normal. A sign that Qi is flowing and negative patterns of dis-ease are being released. Drink plenty of water.

Shivering – Normal. A good sign that the body is releasing blocked energy.

Feeling asymmetrical – Normal. A sign that the body is trying to rebalance itself.

Yawning – A sign that you are able to relax but perhaps you are too tired.

Flatulence and Burping- A good sign. The body is discharging toxins. Drink plenty of water and check your diet for allergies and candida overgrowth.

Diminished or no sensation – This may happen after a while. This is a sign that the meridian pathways have opened up and qi is flowing smoothly.

Aching old injuries – A good sign. It means you are healing on a deeper level.

Principles of Good Practice

As a therapist you have certain legal and moral obligations to your clients. Health care is delivered through direct interaction between individuals. Those who come into contact with practitioners in the complementary health care sector expect that these practitioners will undertake their duty; this includes being caring and honest, avoiding harm, showing integrity and not exploiting or abusing their power. Complementary medicine practitioners should show respect for the human condition and its complexity, acknowledging each person's essential humanity. We should welcome our individuality and diversity as the wealth of human experience and hence the need to take the holistic view. This holistic view should include that each human being has a right to expect an environment that is conducive to health and social well-being and that of future generations.

Performance Criteria

1. The practitioner monitors her/his own physical, mental and emotional health and any conditions which may impede effective therapy.

2. The practitioner's personal presentation aims to promote client confidence and ease.

3. All necessary equipment is available and in good order ready for use.

4. Heat, light, and ventilation are set and maintained at a level to optimise client and practitioner comfort during therapy.

5. The work area is arranged and prepared in a suitable way to enhance the client's confidence in vibrational therapy and to take into account the client's requirements.

6. Work areas comply with relevant current legal and organisational health and safety requirements. Such as Health and Safety at work Act 1974. Health and Safety (First Aid) Regulations 1981. Local Government Act 1982. The Fire Precautions Act 1971. The Consumer Protection Act 1987.

7. Furniture and equipment are arranged in such a way as to facilitate effective therapy.

8. Foreseeable interruptions to the therapy session are eliminated.

9. The client is offered the opportunity to use the toilet before the start of the therapy.

10. The client is encouraged and enabled to optimise her/his comfort, without adversely affecting the practitioner's ability to monitor and work with her/him during therapy.

11. Any factors which may cause discomfort or danger to the client during the therapy session are identified and the appropriate action is taken to minimise the risk they pose.

12. Where the practitioner is unable to see the client at the agreed time, the client is given clear information on the likely extent of the delay and any necessary alternative arrangements are agreed.

13.   Confidential materials are stored securely when not in use.

14.   Clinical records are kept accurately. Bearing in mind that, by law, these notes may be accessed by the client on request. Therefore post session notes should be brief and to the point. Subjective opinions and descriptions should not be included.

15.   Ensure continuing self-support by joining a therapist support group in your area.

16.   Develop ways of enabling understanding of the therapeutic process with clients, their companions, partners, relatives, friends etc. by interaction, e.g. face to face, by telephone, in writing (e.g. letter, information sheets, diagrams).

Practice Management

Your practice management will also include legal and ethical issues such as client confidentiality. You will also have to be aware of the ways in which holistic treatment differs from conventional treatment. You must also be aware that it is illegal for non-medically qualified personnel to treat sexually transmitted diseases (except Aids) and you cannot claim to be able to cure a disease (e.g. cancer, Brights disease, etc). Also under current UK law, healers are not allowed to attend the mother until ten days after the birth of her baby.

Selection of the Appropriate Angelic Essence

From the sixteen Angelic essences available as energy sprays I have found overall that the selection of the appropriate Angelic essence is very much a matter of personal choice or practitioner preference.

I also truly believe, because the essences are Angelically guided and each essence has an effect, that there can be no wrong choices – just different pathways to inner peace to explore. However, sometimes certain essences may well prove a stronger catalyst than others to initiate the healing process. It all depends on the client's (and sometimes the therapist's) core energetic blocks and therefore which pathways are more 'open' to us for accessing these obstructions in the overall energy flow. Many people also use the Angelic essences for spiritual or soul development and so choose an essence which has the theme they are addressing at that time.

Before we explore the different techniques used in the selecting and prescribing of the appropriate Angelic essence I would like to examine the simple six groupings I have been guided by the Archangels to use on our updated internet site. The website is designed for Angel therapy practitioners and their clients to use during the consultation process, but it can be used by anyone who needs immediate help in choosing an appropriate essence which will help with their current life situation.

We have, over the last three years, provided a free service which enabled us to study in depth the types of problem areas which concern people the most through the key questions they ask us personally. We have literally been asked thousands and thousands of questions, mainly on the following six themes: Relationships, Well-being, Spiritual growth, Protection, Guidance and Cosmic connection. As each Archangel also has a unique signature which has an underpinning theme – such as Healing, Wisdom, Love, Protection, Peace, Freedom, etc. – this has been included in the overall formula.

Relationships

Archangel Chamuel's Embrace – Angelic Love (God's Love)
Archangel Jophiel's Illumination – Angelic Wisdom
Archangel Raphael's Dream – Angelic Healing
Archangel Gabriel's Call – Angelic Guidance

Well-being

Archangel Raphael's Dream – Angelic Healing
Angel of Light (Seraphim) – Healing and Angelic Protection
Archangel Uriel's Initiation – Angelic Peace
Angel of the Animals – Animal Healing (Grounding, supportive and nurturing for all that lives)
Archangel Sandalphon – Guardian of the Earth

Spiritual Growth

Archangel Shamael – The Angel of Sacred Sound
Angel of Ascension – Cosmic Consciousness and Light Body Activation
Archangel Tzaphkiel's Contemplation – Cosmic Contemplation
Archangel Raziel's Secret – Secret Mysteries

Protection

Archangel Michael's Empowerment – Angelic Protection
Angel of Light (Seraphim) – Healing and Angelic Protection
Archangel Zadkiel's Joy – Angelic Violet Flame of Freedom
Archangel Haniel's Glory – Angelic Communication.

Guidance

Archangel Gabriel's Call – Angelic Guidance
Guardian Angel – Attune to Your Guardian Angel
Archangel Haniel's Glory – Angelic Communication.
Angel of Ascension – Cosmic Consciousness and Light Body Activation

Cosmic Connection

All the Archangel essences – Cosmic choice

Prescribing Angelic Essences

The consultation process is an excellent way of choosing an Angelic essence for your client, especially if you are familiar with the full range: you can then prescribe from them. Therefore, if you, as a therapist, have experienced very positive results consistently with a particular essence – such as Archangel Raphael's Dream for initiating the healing process – then you may well use it as a 'first time' essence with all your clients.

Conducting an Angelic Essence Consultation

You must be relaxed and confident before starting a therapy session; if you are tense, your client will feel it and become tense also. So prior to the meeting allow yourself some quiet time to calm, focus and centre yourself – this should include cleansing the therapy room and your own aura. You must also place protection around yourself – through visualisation, wearing a protective crystal, Reiki or Archangel Michael's Empowerment essence. Establishing rapport and trust by communicating with your client plays an integral part in any therapy session.

Through the simple act of listening attentively to your client during the consultation process, it is possible to select an Angelic essence that they will find beneficial. During the consultation try to ask open-ended questions – use words such as 'how' or 'what'. Notice your client's tone of voice throughout the consultation and be aware of their body language. Listen for key words and pay special attention if the client mentions them more than once. A consultation form which includes your client's medical history and lifestyle must be completed at the beginning of the first session. This must include a client declaration section. You must ensure that the client reads and signs this section. Reassure your client that confidential clinical records are kept accurately and stored securely.

The consultation process should take about twenty minutes. During this time explore, agree and in further session review with your client the goals they wish to achieve through Angelic therapy. You will need to examine with your client factors relating to their physical health, emotional well-being and current lifestyle that will support Angelic therapy treatments. Try to find out how the client reacts to their life experience in different situations. You will also want to explore with your client current contributing factors which are affecting their current state of health and emotional well-being – perhaps through observation or guided discussion. You may wish to suggest to your client ways to de-stress or take up an exercise regime, or recommend yoga, t'ai chi, relaxation exercises, visualisation or simple breathing techniques.

You will need to explain very simply the process of Angel therapy, including the physical, mental, emotional and spiritual process of holistic healing. This will help to reassure a nervous client. A treatment plan containing the client's expectations of the treatment and your objectives is recommended to ensure your client is satisfied with the therapy process. It will also enable your client and their family and friends to understand the nature, scope and limitations of Angelic therapy. Information sheets can be given to your clients which contain all relevant information about the therapy, plus contact details, phone number, e.mail, etc.

Once the consultation is complete you can now move on to investigate with your client their presenting symptoms through external scanning. This examination is of the subtle bodies. Aura scanning, etc. and other intuitive information gained during the therapy session is an energetic profile. It is not a medical diagnosis and should never be taken as one. Unless you are a medical doctor it is illegal to diagnose an illness. The consultation, plus the subtle body scanning, will help you to select an Archangel essence or essences which you will use to treat your client during the therapy session. You can verify the suitability of an Archangel essence with your client – very often your client will say that they have felt particularly drawn to that Archangel recently or they will relate to the Archangel energy signature theme. Verifying your choice with your client will make them feel more involved in their treatment and responsible for their own healing journey. Then all that will be left for you to do is facilitate your client's own use of the Archangel essences for maintenance between visits.

Selecting Essences for Others

The other methods of selecting an Angelic essence are intuition, scanning, kinesiology and dowsing. Some therapists use a mixture of methods to prescribe the correct essence. Each method has its own virtue and each method develops spiritual growth, as we shall find as we explore each technique.

Intuitive Diagnosis

Your intuitional development is directly linked to the conscious evolution of your soul. An intuitive diagnosis is therefore obtained by tuning into the three aspects of your soul. So we can say – intuitive diagnosis is obtained by tapping into your inner knowing, inner feelings or instinct.

Inner knowing – Third eye chakra – *Neshamah*

Inner feelings – Heart chakra – *Ruah*

Instinct – Root chakra – *Nefesh*

You will, in your life, have hopefully developed your inner knowing, your inner feelings or your instinct. Most people are very strong in one of these areas; as you read the descriptions below, try to think of times in your life when you have experienced your intuition working.

Instinct – This is a survival skill that dwells in the root chakra. You will have developed a strong gut reaction to people and situations. This intuitive ability is very often motivated by ego's need to feel good and be wanted and most of all to be admired.

Inner feelings – This is the "it just felt good syndrome". We have all experienced this: it has a 'feel good' factor to it – which makes our heart lift and take wings.

Inner knowing – Perhaps the most elusive of all, as it is never logical, but Divinely inspired. It is in those moments in your life when you say something will happen that is totally illogical and everyone either thinks you have gone completely mad, or challenges you straight out with "that will never happen in a million years", yet what you expressed not only does come true, but usually in the most unexpected way.

You probably have experienced all three, but are stronger in just one area. To fully develop the highest level of Divine intuition you need to balance and merge both sides of your brain; this can be done by altering your brainwave patterns and activating your 'temples'. Your temples are on each side of your forehead – they are also known as the 'temporal lobes' of the brain. Current scientific investigation using electromagnetic waves is finding that the temporal lobes are your personal pre-programme to activate your 'God' awareness. You can think of them as being your brain's area of operation that is 'hard-wired to God'. When your temporal lobes are both stimulated and resonating in balance, your crown chakra is fully open. All advanced meditators have been found to have the ability to alter their brainwave patterns to fall in to the frequency of theta brainwaves, which are produced when you are day-dreaming or in deep meditation. This frequency range is normally between 8 and 5 cycles a second.

Left and Right Brain

Your brain has two sides, left and right. The left side deals with logic and reason and is male orientated. The right deals with creativity and intuition and has female orientation. The two sides, just like yin and yang, polarise each other with male and female attributes. We live in a very male-orientated left brain society which needs desperately for the female side to become more dynamic and active. When you meditate, you use your feminine side and quieten your dominant male side. This brings what is commonly called an altered state of consciousness. Also, by developing your female intuitive side, you will find that you can balance both sides of your brain to the same resonance, which is a prerequisite for fully opening the crown chakra.

Intuitive Selection

We will look at two simple techniques that will enable you to select an Angelic essence using your intuition. These methods can be used for yourself or your client. Having a clear question in your mind is vital to the outcome. For example, this could be "Which Archangel should I invite into my life to help with my current situation?" If you are choosing an essence for your client, it is crucial you focus your intent upon the client and do not allow your mind to drift. Also, you must always work from the pure intent of the outcome being for the highest good of your client.

Technique 1:

For this technique you will need the full selection of Angelic essences positioned comfortably at arm's length in front of you. This technique relies on your 'higher self' to guide you – it overrides your logical mind by tapping into your subconscious mind.

1. Sit in a comfortable steady posture, with the spine and neck held erect but not tense. This helps steady the mind and aids concentration.

2. Ask your 'higher self' to send down a sphere of pale blue light surrounded by pale golden light. Visualise or feel it positioned directly above your crown chakra.

3. Take several very deep slow breaths – with each out-breath release all negative thoughts and emotions. With each in-breath, breathe in the light. Continue releasing negativity and breathing in the light of your soul until you feel full of light and have a strong connection to your higher self.

4. Allow your body to relax and your mind to drift into a dreamy meditative state.

5. Focus completely on the Angel essences – look at them one by one. Which essence is your eye drawn to? Keep focusing on your question. One of the essences should seem to draw your attention and resonate with you. Of course you may need a mixture of essences, so it is perfectly all right if more that one 'jumps' out at you.

Or

6. Hold each Angel essence in your left hand and feel the energy resonance; if it intuitively feels 'right' to you it will be. Once again you may need more than one Angel essence, so allow your intuition to guide you.

7. When you have finished, ground, centre and focus yourself.

Technique 2:

Intuitive selection can also be obtained merely by reading a description of the Angelic essences. You just 'know' which is the 'right' one (or two if you need a mixture of essences).

Or

You can also 'feel' which is the right Angelic essence just by looking at a photograph of the Archangel essence bottles.

Your higher self may also guide you to the correct essence by sending you a dream about a particular Archangel. I have even been told of people who have been magically guided to enter 'New Age' stores and found what drew them inside was the Angelic energies of the Archangel essences.

Scanning

Another method of selecting an essence is to use the attunement process of scanning. By passing your hand slowly over all the Archangel essence bottles you will soon detect which essence strongly resonates with you. Having your question very clearly in your mind is vital to the outcome. For example, this could be "Which Archangel should I invite into my life to help with my spiritual development?" If you are choosing an essence for your client, it is crucial you focus your intent upon the client and do not allow your mind to drift.

It may be impossible in one session to scan all sixteen essences, so it would be a good idea to read through the theme of each essence before you begin scanning and make a short list of just four.

The most appropriate four for spiritual growth might be:

Archangel Shamael – The Angel of Sacred Sound
Angel of Ascension – Cosmic Consciousness and Light Body Activation
Archangel Tzaphkiel's Contemplation – Cosmic Contemplation
Archangel Raziel's Secret – Secret Mysteries

So to help you develop your intuitive scanning ability:

1.   Raise the sensitivity in your hands by washing them in warm water, then dry them thoroughly.

2.   Begin to sensitise your hands by shaking them; this releases blocked energy.

3   Briskly rub your hands together; this begins to concentrate the qi into your hands and sensitises them.

4.   Hold your hands with your palms facing each other, about nine inches apart. Feel the energy radiating and vibrating between your hands; play with this energy.

5.   Begin to form this energy into a sphere and visualise it yellow in colour. When it feels right, place this yellow ball into the solar plexus area. This energises your mental body, allowing you to perceive the energy of the essences more easily.

6.   Now take a very deep breath and release all negative thoughts and emotions, still your mind and focus completely on the essences.

7.   Pass your left hand slowly over each Angelic essence and begin to feel their energy signature. Gradually work along each essence, observing the energy in any way you can, via heat, cold, tingling, vibration, pulse or reactions within your physical body or subtle bodies etc. If you are left-handed, work with your right hand.

8.   When you have finished, ground, centre and focus yourself. Then write down the experience for future reference.

Kinesiology

The technique of kinesiology, or muscle testing, is one very effective means of selecting an Archangel essence. This very simplified version really is extremely useful for developing your intuition. You also need to find a partner to work with. One of you will be the test person and the other the tester.

Technique 1:

1. The test person must take a sip of water before being tested.

2. The test person lifts their right arm to shoulder height to make a right angle to the body (either in front or to the side).

3. The tester then will establish the test person's normal muscle strength by resting two fingers on the test person's extended arm and pressing down gently but firmly while the test person resists.

4. Once normal muscle resistance has been established, the test person will be passed each Angelic essence in turn. It is normally held in the left hand. Also, holding the essence to the witness area, which is at the thymus (the area where your physical and etheric bodies meet) greatly enhances the results.

5. The tester then asks a question, such as "Is this the best Angelic essence to support (name of test person's) spiritual growth?" or "Is this the right Angelic essence for (test person) to use for self-healing?

6. The test person's arm will remain strong when the correct essence is chosen. If the arm becomes weak, try again with another essence. Continue the process of evaluating all the essences until the tester establishes the test person's strongest response. If more than four essences are being evaluated at any one session, a rest period should be allowed, as the test person's arm can tire.

Technique 2:

An even simpler kinesiology technique which also has the advantage of being self-administered is to make a circle by joining the tips of the forefinger and thumb of the left hand. Insert the first two fingers of the right hand into the circle. Focus your mind on an Angelic essence or have it near you and ask your question, such as "Is this the best Angelic essence to support me in my spiritual growth?" Try to break the circle of your left thumb and forefinger by pushing them apart as you separate your right forefinger and middle finger. Normally for a strong "yes" answer the circle of your thumb and forefinger remains strong. A negative "no" answer will weaken your energy and the circle will break.

Dowsing

Dowsing or divination by the use of a 'pendulum' is a useful technique to master, as it really connects you with your higher self. It is also, in my opinion, the best way of confirming your 'consultation' choice of Angelic essence for your client by tuning into their higher self.

Pendulums

There are dozens of different types, styles, weights and sizes of pendulums readily available today. They can be fashioned from wood, glass, base metal, silver, gold or a myriad different varieties of crystal. It can be very confusing for those who are new to dowsing to choose a pendulum that is right for them and will prove easy to attune to.

A simple clear quartz crystal pendulum 5 to 7 cm long, symmetrically cut and balanced, which is suspended on a silver chain, is the best and only choice in my opinion, because it can be suitably cleansed, dedicated and programmed for choosing Angelic essences.

Also, because it is quartz, you will find one that has the natural affinity of entrainment with your energy field and by holding it near your solar plexus you will feel the resonance very strongly. Your pranic energy flows into the clear quartz pendulum and into its energy field; this energises it. This combined field of the quartz pendulum and your energy then interacts with your higher self, causing the clear quartz pendulum to move.

How it Works

As a beginner you will need to establish that the pendulum of your choice is resonating with your energy field or you may find it impossible to establish your 'yes' and 'no' answers, which can be very frustrating! This dialogue with your pendulum will be unique to you. Some people find their pendulum swings clockwise for 'yes' and anti-clockwise for 'no'. But your pendulum movement may be different; as long as you know what is your 'yes' and what is your 'no', that is all that really counts. You must also check at the beginning of each dowsing session that your 'yes' and 'no' pendulum movements have not changed.

Attuning to Your Pendulum

There are many schools of thought on dowsing using a pendulum and each experienced dowser has their own methods of getting a beginner to dowse. I have been teaching dowsing as part of the courses I run since 1986 and it can be very traumatic for a student if their pendulum decides it does not want to 'talk' or if the student has tried dowsing before and had no success at all – this can quickly shatter your confidence! The most common faults in non-communication between the student, pendulum and higher self are that the student has the wrong type of pendulum, which is why once we change them over to the clear quartz crystal pendulum style I described above and find the right size and resonance for their energy field by a process of attunement, all is well. The next most common problem is the non-higher-self-connection. This can easily be remedied by taking the student on a guided meditation to align with the higher self. The next most common problem is that the student's chakras are out of balance, which can be quickly remedied by tapping the witness point (thymus) seven times; this will temporarily align the seven master chakras. One more problem that causes havoc is that sometimes students slump forwards (especially when using dowsing charts). A straight spine with head held erect works wonders for your energy flow and confidence.

Technique: Resonance

Hold your pendulum's chain (about 13 cm from the top of the crystal) between the thumb and forefinger of your right hand. Hold your left hand directly underneath your pendulum. Make sure that your pendulum is perfectly still; if you have the correct pendulum for you it should start to 'tremble'. This is a direct sign that it is in entrainment with your energy field by going into resonance. If it does not immediately go into resonance, try holding it just in front of your solar plexus chakra. If that does not work, move it upwards towards your heart chakra.

Still your pendulum and ask mentally or aloud for your pendulum to show you your 'yes' movement. Take a few moments for this movement to become firmly established.

Still your pendulum and then ask it to show you your 'no' movement. This will be different to your 'yes' signal.

Once you and your pendulum are working in harmony and you have a strong clear 'yes' and 'no' you must test your link to your higher self by asking a succession of 'yes' and 'no' questions, to which you already know the correct answer.

Once you have gained confidence in your pendulum's answers, ask the question "Am I tuned in to my higher self?" If you get a negative answer, ask to be "tuned in to your higher self". Keep asking and making sure your energy is flowing and your posture has not suddenly become contorted by slumping forwards, thereby blocking your energy flow.

The next question you need a 'yes' answer for is asking if you are "clean and ready for divination practice". You must obtain a 'yes' answer before continuing with the dowsing session. You can ask your higher self to send cleansing energies to assist you.

The next question you must ask is "Is my pendulum clean?" Once again you must obtain a 'yes' answer. If not, ask your higher self to send down cleansing energies for your pendulum.

If you are using a chart to dowse over (like the one at the back of this book), make sure your chart is clean and you obtain a positive 'yes' answer.

You must keep checking throughout your dowsing session that you are receiving reliable answers. You can do this by frequently asking your pendulum "Is my dowsing accurate?"

Now you are ready to begin dowsing:

When you are dowsing the Angel essences for your client you can dowse directly over the bottles by holding your pendulum over each bottle in turn and asking a question such as "Is this the correct essence for (name of client) at this time?" If your client is not present, you can still obtain reliable answers by linking into their higher self or using a 'witness' – this can be a photograph of them, a piece of their hair, a small blood sample or even their name on a piece of paper. All you have to do is check with your pendulum that you are tuned into them and then proceed as normal. The 'witness' sample works very well for your pets and animal clients. For more details on animal healing, see the section **Angel of the Animals – Animal Healing.**

If you do not have the full range of Angelic essences to dowse over, you could use the Angelic pendulum chart at the back of this book. Please remember, dowsing is very effective, so much so that it is easy to become complacent instead of actually experiencing by learning about the essences or taking a full client consultation.

A few more really important points:

1.   Never be tempted to wear your pendulum round your neck. It is a precision healing tool and needs to be kept sacred.

2.   Try not to be tempted to dowse in unsuitable places where the energy may not be sacred.

3.   Keep your pendulum stored safely in a suitable drawstring pouch.

4. Do not let others touch your pendulum, because if you have the 'right' pendulum for you there is every chance it will not 'perform' for someone else.

5. Also, suitably close, seal, protect and ground your energy field after each dowsing session.

Purification – Creating a Sacred Space

Angelic Space Clearing

The **Angel of Light** aura essence spray has been successfully used by thousands of people to create a harmonious, sacred, safe, Angelic healing environment. This powerful essence dynamically clears and releases spaces with built-up negative emotional, psychic and mental energies. It has been used for initiating the body's own healing process, Angelic attunement, meditation practice and clearing karmic debris or miasms. The essence has also been successfully used for clearing crystals of stagnant energy and clearing homes of geopathic stress and lower astral entities.

Daily use is recommended for sensitive individuals; morning and evening are best. Or if you are the type of person who is easily drained by the constant and unnatural demands of modern environments such as computers, electrical equipment, mobile phones etc, or the stressful emotions of others, pollution, crowds and noise, it can prove of enormous benefit. Therapists or those who care for others should use it between clients, as it will cleanse and protect their aura.

To cleanse a space thoroughly, begin by opening the windows: this allows any negative energy an exit route and it will air the room. Then go back to the entrance door and walk slowly clockwise around the room, spraying the essence into any areas where you feel it is required. Pay special attention to the corners. Once you have completed a full circuit of the room you will notice an immediate change in the quality and integrity of the energy.

Violet Flame of Angelic Transformation and Joy

Zadkiel is the Archangel of Divine joy. Zadkiel's name means the 'Righteousness of God'. He is the Angelic guardian of the violet flame of transmutation, transformation, joy and freedom. This high frequency spiritual energy known as the 'violet flame' instantly transforms lower energies into positive life-affirming energy. This miracle flame was brought down for us by Saint Germain, who is an Ascended Master. Zadkiel is the Archangel of mercy, who teaches us to trust in God's benevolence. He brings comfort in our hour of need and helps us understand the underlying karmic lessons we need to acknowledge, accept, control, release and transmute with the violet flame of freedom.

Archangel Zadkiel's violet flame of cosmic freedom can be invoked and used in numerous ways. This God flame has the highest vibrational frequency which, when summoned, brings soul freedom and joy by releasing you from your own limiting behaviour, concepts and karmic miasms, including past life memories which may have been carried over to this lifetime. Use it often to cleanse all areas of your mind, body and aura. It instantly purifies all the chakra centres, giving relief from addictions and addictive traits within the personality. It works as an amplifier of healing and spiritual energies. When consciously directed by Archangel Zadkiel it will break down and transform blocked or stuck energies, such as those which have been caused by anger, hatred, resentment, bitterness, jealousy, intolerance, blame, fear and guilt. It also helps protect from over-indulgences which have lodged in the emotional body, it calms the mind and touches the Divine spark within you, thereby aiding spiritual and personal growth, giving understanding into the cause of the indulgence. Using the Archangel Zadkiel essence before meditation practice instantly purifies your body and aura, which will enhance the meditation experience, helping to calm the mind and bring the necessary stillness which is most desirable for enhanced spiritual growth. The essence can also be used for clearing planetary miasms and planetary or group karma.

Personal Energy Field

Begin by spraying the essence high above your head; this will filter down through your aura starting the transformation process. You can now visualise the violet flame in your auric shell, feel it burning away all that needs to be transmuted. Sense the freedom and joy that is now yours as you step forward into the future with a positive mental attitude.

Personal Space

Start at the entrance of the space and walk slowly clockwise round the room, spraying the essence into any areas where you feel it is required. You can visualise the violet flame of transformation burning very brightly transmuting all the negative energy, so that you are ready to step forward into the future with hope and joy. Pay special attention to the corners of the room. Once you have completed a full circuit of the room you will notice an immediate change in the room's atmosphere.

Angelic Attunement and Aura Cleansing

The following exercise is simple yet powerful, especially when performed for the first time – it is life-changing. You will be using the Angel of Light (Seraphim) aura essence. The Angels of Light bring forward a healing energy known as 'brilliance' – it is pure 'cosmic iridescent rainbow light' and contains all the colours and 'rays'. The Seraphim, whose essence is perfect love, direct the 'Divine' energy which emanates from the first creative source. Seraphim means 'the inflamer', from the Hebraic root word *saraph*, which means burning. They are the angels of 'Divine' fire. In the Bible they bring a glowing coal to cleanse Isaiah, by placing it on his lips. In that moment he is cleansed of all karma. It says in Revelation 4.8 that if we call on their power, our being is flooded with infinite love, light, joy and peace. In fact working with the Seraphim is like becoming pure iridescent cosmic light. Enoch, a Hebrew prophet, reported that Archangel Seraphiel is the most brilliant of all the Angelic beings.

The brilliance Angel of Light carries is an extremely high vibration of the supreme ray; it works to stimulate the third, fourth, fifth eye and crown chakras, plus the 8th to 14th chakras in the etheric body. Angel of Light can also initiate immediate activation of the 'heart' chakra and integrate it with these higher energies. Angel of Light will connect you to the highest communication currents of the Angelic domain. It will also help you develop lucid dreaming. In everyday use, Angel of Light essence will provide a joyful connection to the Angelic realms, giving access to serenity and inner wisdom in your daily encounters. It is useful to those who wish to consciously access inner guidance. In meditation, Angel of Light is powerful; it aids the attainment of higher states because of its natural resonance with the higher frequencies of the perfected human vibrational spectrum. We use Angel of Light when we want to bring about change, major or minor, in our lives. It allows us to wipe the slate clean, to start again. The energy will allow us to move on in a new direction. This can be on any level: physical outer changes, emotional changes or spiritual changes. It is good for those who are making the transition from life to death.

Because Angel of Light aura essence has the power to modify any condition some therapists see it as a 'cure all' – it is – it will bring 'healing' in the 'Angels' wake'. It is the same energy as *Johrei*, which is a Japanese word meaning the act of spiritual purification by focusing the Divine Light of God. Angel of Light has been frequently used to alleviate allergies and chronic conditions; it helps

159

with the removal of toxins from the body, which allows healing energy to flow to the liver, kidneys and gall-bladder.

Angel of Light aura essence has also been used to clear karmic burdens, negative karma patterns, crystallised planetary miasms and habitual memory patterns which have been caused by the ego-self. The ego-self is a construction of the un-enlightened mind which the individual believes to be real and have permanence. The ego-self gets you to focus all your life-force on negative emotions and actions. Remember, never feel discouraged about past events; do not allow yourself the indulgence of dwelling on negativity. Every event in your life has been a perfect learning opportunity. Be humble, check your motivations and intentions. Be prepared to move forward spiritually when you work with the Seraphim, as they direct the radiant light of God which has the power to clear the spiritual body of impurities and toxins.

The Angelic attunement aura cleansing ritual can be used any time you feel the need of it. You can also use it before giving a therapy session or before meditation practice. It works by first dispelling any darkness which shrouds a person's light. Consciously attuning to its energies you can instantly see the difference in the aura within seconds. It is fast and swift. If you perform the exercise correctly you will find it clears, calms and stills the mind and is a complete meditation in itself.

1.   Spray the Angel of Light aura essence on your left hand, then spread the essence over the palms of both hands. As you do so, establish contact with the Angels of Light. You are now ready to cleanse and smooth your aura. Most people are aware of the different aura layers; they are also acutely aware of any energy which is not smooth and light. If you find any stagnant, sticky, prickly or heavy energy, just allow the essence to transform it and allow it to be carried away by the Angels of Light. You need to use gently sweeping movements. If you find any cords, hooks or attachments within your aura, just ask Archangel Seraphiel or one of the other Seraphim to remove them and transmute them with unconditional love, before filling with positive beneficial energy the spaces where the cords etc. have been.

2.   Firstly you need to cup your hands over your nose and inhale deeply three times. This brings the Angelic energy instantly into your physical body, which will start the cleansing process. With each inhalation you could mentally say a positive affirmation such as "I invoke the mighty Angels of Light to assist me in releasing all negative karma as I now allow Angelic healing to manifest in my life".

3.   Now raise your hands above your head and begin to cleanse your aura, starting with the crown chakra; as you do so, ask that your crown chakra be blessed and filled with Angelic light.

4.   Move downwards to your third eye chakra and gently cleanse away all that has kept you from allowing your intuition to guide you, asking for an Angelic blessing to be placed over your third eye.

5.   Cleanse the whole of your head, your eyes, nose, mouth and ears, asking for a blessing to be placed over your eyes – so you can see the beauty of God all around you; your ears – so that you hear with clarity the whisperings of your soul; your mouth – so that you communicate with truth and integrity; your nose – so that all your senses are attuned to God.

6.   Now cleanse your throat chakra and shoulders. Include the back of your neck where the causal chakra is situated. As you cleanse your throat, ask for a blessing to be placed over your throat chakra so that it remains pure and can express what is truly in your heart. As you cleanse the causal chakra, also ask for it to be blessed, requesting understanding to flow through you.

7. Now cleanse your heart chakra, lungs and arms, asking for a blessing to be placed over your heart chakra that will allow you to interact with others with heartfelt compassion.

8. Now cleanse your solar plexus chakra and the waist area, including your internal organs. See your solar plexus chakra glowing as brightly as the sun. Ask for a blessing to be placed over your solar plexus, so that you can retain your own personal space with integrity and not intrude upon other people's power or they on yours.

9. Move down to the sacral chakra, the seat of your creativity, and gently cleanse this area, including the area at the back. Ask for a blessing to be placed over your sacral chakra, so all that you create is filled with the beauty of God.

10. Move down to your root chakra and cleanse it, including the area of your lower back. Ask for a blessing to be placed over your root chakra to give you balance, poise, grace and stability.

11. Continue downwards, cleansing both your legs and beneath your feet. Cleanse the area you are standing on. Touch the floor with the tips of your fingers and connect with the consciousness of the Great Mother. It is she you live upon, who nurtures your physical body and allows you this wonderful opportunity of life – this amazing gift that you can use for your spiritual growth and ultimately the spiritual growth and liberation of others, who you can influence by your living example.

12. Now stand up and raise your arms high above you. As you do so, I want you to visualise yourself with your feet standing firmly on the earth and your head in the highest heaven. Feel your body connecting heaven and earth. Now stretch your fingers upwards and, as you do so, feel the Angelic hands of the Seraphim come downwards – allow them to place their hands in yours. This is a special experience and you may wish to bask in the Angelic contact for a few moments. When you feel ready, ask for a blessing of healing to be placed on your hands; this will empower your Angelic therapy work. Feel you are now truly blessed, supported, nurtured and guided.

13. When you are ready, allow your Angelic wings to grow out of the space between your shoulder-blades. Feel them growing upwards and outwards. Sense how they feel, what they look like. Are they fluffy and covered in white feathers or are they gossamer, as light as air? Let your wings unfurl fully. However you sense them, allow your body to adjust to the experience of having wings. Very often you will feel a shift in your overall energy field as your vibrational rate is raised and you grow accustomed to the experience of having wings. See if you can move your wings. Ask for a blessing to be placed on your wings and allow them to help you 'fly' through life, raising you above the everyday worries and concerns of ordinary mind, which has in the past dulled your senses to the beauty of God all around you.

14. Now I want you to bring your arms down and place your hands on your heart centre. Your left hand is diagonally across your heart, with your right hand diagonally over the left. Your hands should cross and form the shape of a cross. At this point you can say a silent prayer to the Anima Mundi, the World Soul, the One-Thread-Soul of the Universe, of which your soul is a microcosm. You can ask for healing, spiritual growth or help for yourself or others. You can stay in this energy as long as you like. You can now sit or lie down and go fully into Angelic meditation or you can, when you are ready, go about your Angelic therapy work.

As an embellishment to the 'Angelic Attunement and Aura Cleansing' ritual you could have a special mat or cloth that you always stand on to do the exercise. It must be kept only for this ritual or Angelic meditation. I use a beautiful piece of violet and gold silk sari fabric. Over time mine has become imbued with very special energies which enhance my commitment as an aspiring angel.

Aura Cleansing

You can also use the Angel of Light essence to do a quick aura cleanse.

1.   Spray the Angel of Light aura essence on your left hand, then spread the essence over the palms of both hands. As you do so, establish contact with the Angels of Light. You will normally feel the energy of the Seraphim (Angels of Light) pouring in through your crown chakra and flooding out of your palm chakras. Allow yourself to be completely surrounded and supported by this energy. You are now ready to cleanse and smooth your aura. Most people are aware of the different auric layers; they are also acutely aware of any energy which is not smooth and light. If you find any stagnant, sticky, prickly or heavy energy, just allow the essence to transform it and allow it to be carried away by the Seraphim. You need to use gently sweeping movements. Allow the tips of your fingers to glide through the aura. If you meet any stagnant energy, use your fingertips to rake it away. If you find any cords, hooks or other attachments within your auric shell, just ask Archangel Seraphiel and the Seraphim to help you to remove them with the radiant luminosity of God.

2.   Cup your hands over your nose and inhale deeply three times. This brings the Angelic energy instantly into your physical body, which will start the cleansing process. You are now ready to cleanse and smooth your aura.

3.   Raise your hands above your head and begin to cleanse all the levels of the aura and chakras. Start with the crown chakra, then the third eye, throat, heart, solar, sacral and root chakras.

4.   Continue downwards, cleansing both your legs and beneath your feet. Cleanse the area you are standing on. Touch the floor with the tips of your fingers and connect with the earth.

5.   Place your hands at your heart centre in the Namaste Mudra – stay in this energy as long as you like.

You can also use the Angel of Light essence to cleanse your client's aura – before, during or at the conclusion of a therapy session.

Aura Cleansing – Your Client

Your client can be standing, seated on a stool or lying face up on a treatment couch or massage table. If your client is lying down you may like to treat the back directly, especially if they have problems in this area. Ask your client to gently turn over on the couch for the second half of the aura cleansing treatment. You will have already cleansed your own aura with Angel of Light before your client arrives for the therapy session.

1.   Spray the Angel of Light aura essence on your left hand, then spread the essence over the palms of both hands. As you do so, establish contact with the Angels of Light. You will normally feel the energy of the Seraphim (Angels of Light) pouring in through your crown chakra and flooding out of your palm chakras. Allow yourself to be completely surrounded and supported by this energy. You are now ready to cleanse and smooth your client's aura. Most people are aware of the different aura layers; they are also acutely aware of any energy which is not smooth and light. If you find any stagnant, sticky, prickly or heavy energy, just

allow the essence to transform it and allow it to be carried away by the Angels of Light. You need to use gently sweeping movements. Allow the tips of your fingers to glide through the aura. If you meet any stagnant energy, use your fingertips to rake it away. If you find any cords, hooks or other attachments within your client's aura, just ask the Seraphim to help you to remove them and transmute them with unconditional love, before filling with positive beneficial energy the spaces where the cords etc. have been . You may have to go through the aura layer by layer. This process can take an hour or more, especially if this is the first time your client has experienced Angelic aura cleansing. It can also be a long process if your client has been going through a lot of intense karmic lessons; therefore the cleansing process will become a complete treatment in itself for some of your clients.

2.   Firstly you need to cup your hands gently a few inches away from your client's nose and get them to inhale deeply three times. This brings the Angelic energy instantly into their physical body which will start their cleansing process. With each inhalation you could mentally say a positive affirmation for them such as "I invoke the mighty Angels of Light to assist me and my client in releasing all negative karma, as my client now allows Angelic healing to manifest in their life".

3.   Start about 50 centimetres above your client's crown chakra and move downwards through all the chakras in sequential order. When you get to the heart chakra, cleanse the arms and hands. Then return to the solar plexus chakra and continue downwards until you have cleansed all the chakras and the sides of your client's body.

4.   Continue downwards, cleansing the legs and feet. Cleanse at least 50 cm beneath the feet.

5.   You can now ask your client to gently turn over whilst you proceed to cleanse their back. Start at a distance of about 50 cm above their head and work downwards through the chakras in sequential order, layer by layer. You must also cleanse the arms, legs and the sides of the body.

6.   To finish the treatment on your client's back, stroke the aura to smooth it out. Start above the head and finish beneath the feet. You will need to walk around your client as you do this, to make sure you cover all the aura.

7.   You can now ask your client to turn over and smooth the front of the aura, starting above the head and working downwards to the feet. Be aware of any areas where you have removed stagnant energy, cords, hooks or other attachments. These areas need special attention. You must make sure your client has no holes, gaps or fissures in their aura. If you find auric gapping, be sure to fill the area with positive energy. Try to finish the auric cleansing session with long smooth strokes, working down through all the layers until you reach the physical body. Here you need to stroke down the legs to the feet. Position yourself at your client's feet and draw your client fully back into their body. Feel your client returning to normal waking consciousness.

8.   At the end of the session your client's aura should feel smooth and buoyant to the touch. Your client should have no excess energy in any of the chakras or different auric layers.

9.   Allow your client time to return to normal everyday waking reality. Offer a drink of water. Asking your client to drink plenty of fresh pure water, just before and especially just after each therapy session, will ease the removal of energy blocks and toxicity. These are always released with the integration of new energy patterns and information. You must also drink plenty of fresh water to help your energy field before and after giving a therapy session.

Subtle Body Attunement

This external examination is of the subtle bodies. Aura scanning etc. and other intuitive information gained during the session is an energetic profile. It is not a medical diagnosis and should never be taken as one. Unless you are a medical doctor, it is illegal to diagnose an illness.

Radiant health can be viewed as the continuous harmonious flow of vital energy between the body, mind, spirit and soul. While anatomically unrecognized by current Western medical science, the subtle energy systems are nevertheless metaphysically connected with all the different systems within the physical body. The subtle anatomy is composed of the chakras, aura and meridians. These subtle systems are invisible to most people, although this talent can be developed. Most therapists can, with practice, develop the ability to scan the subtle bodies with their palm chakras. As with all other systems, and even the gross physical system, a tiny change in one area will create a larger overall effect, so care must be taken to become proficient at understanding subtle energy.

Because all human beings are extremely different in their vibratory rate and harmonic frequency range, when you attune to (scan) a client you will experience a sensation that is wholly appropriate to them. As we evolve spiritually and our vibratory rate raises, we begin to find vast differences in the aura's colour, quality, texture and harmonic resonance. The aura is a pulsing, scintillating, moving, dynamic field of energy. This pool of energy is drawn into and surrounds and permeates the human body and surrounding energy field and is totally interconnected by the meridian system. The seven aura levels correlate and are penetrated by the seven master chakras also.

The aura begins with the slowest vibration, the seen (physical body), and progresses to subtle and more refined (faster) vibrations as we go further away from the physical. The seven levels are as follows: each has a particular function, energy, awareness and realisation, which is reflected in the consciousness and is observable in all individuals. In yoga it is known as the sevenfold knowledge and is to be integrated between the seen *(prakrti)* and the seer *(purusa)*.

They are: integration of the body *(sarira samyama)*, the senses *(indriya samyama)*, energy *(prana samyama)*, mind *(mano samyama)*, intellect *(buddhi samyama)*, consciousness *(citta samyama)* and soul *(atma samyama)*.

All auras change constantly as our thoughts, feelings, moods, environment and state of health change. The aura may become damaged by ill-health, which is caused by negative thought patterns, environmental pollutants, stress, poor dietary habits, alcohol, drugs or poor breathing techniques. Sometimes we find debris, stagnant energy, stickiness, prickly or spiky areas in the aura, when someone repeatedly holds a negative thought pattern or addiction for a long time. Some of these thought patterns and addictions frequently take on a life of their own and act as a possession, negative entity thought form or negative entity thought form shape; in time these can influence not only the person they are attached to but attempt to control other people's behaviour too. Colours and shapes are clearly visible within the aura, the colours reflecting which chakras are the most active or underactive, also where the person needs to pay special attention to restore pure colour or vibrancy.

Any imbalances will cause trouble in the overall vitality of the energy field. If a person regularly has spiritual thoughts, the aura can be a very clear pale-yellow or even gold, while a thought charged with anger and hatred is dirty dark red. The shapes and patterns in the aura represent energies which will block the spiritual, mental, emotional and physical health of a person. Cords and energy drains need to be very carefully removed and the spaces where they have been need to be filled with positive loving Angelic healing energy.

Client Care

Your client can be standing, seated on a stool or lying face up on a treatment couch or massage table. If your client is lying down you may like to scan the back directly, especially if they have problems in this area. Ask your client to gently turn over on the couch for the second half of the subtle body scanning. You will have already cleansed your own aura with Angel of Light before your client arrives for the therapy session.

Scanning

You will be scanning or sensing the energetic integrity and overall structure of all seven layers of the client's aura in turn with your palm chakras. You can use your left or right hand or both hands simultaneously. Whichever hand(s) you choose, remember to keep your palm chakras pointing towards your client. As you work through all the levels and find debris within your client's aura, it is helpful to use both hands together as a diagnostic tool; this will give you a clear definition of the shape and size of the problem. The debris normally will be through more than one level of the aura and if there are attachments involved (hooks, cords etc) you may find you need to trace them back to the connection.

Palm Centre Activation

To raise the receptiveness in your hands, wash them in cool water and dry them thoroughly. Begin to sensitise your hands by shaking them vigorously; this releases blocked emotional energy and opens your heart chakra. Then rub your palms together rapidly in a circular motion several times to build up the surface qi.

Mental Body Activation

This next exercise increases your perceptive power by energising your mental body, allowing you to experience the energy field of your client with ease. This is especially important when you are just learning the scanning technique. In time you will not need to energise your mental body and your palm chakras will develop an amazing energetic structure.

1. Raise the receptiveness in your hands, wash them in cool water and dry them thoroughly. Begin to sensitise your hands by shaking them vigorously. Then rub your palms together rapidly in a circular motion several times to build up the surface qi.

2. Hold your hands with your palms facing each other, about 22 cm apart. Feel the energy radiating and vibrating between your hands; play with this energy.

3. Begin to form this energy into a sphere and visualise it bright yellow in colour. When it feels strongly pulsing with life-force, place this sunshine-yellow sphere into the solar plexus area. This quickly energises your mental body.

You can augment the mental body activation by using Archangel Jophiel's Illumination – Angelic Wisdom essence on your hands as you energise them.

Quick Palm Centre Activation

Alternatively, you can open and close both hands simultaneously (make a loose fist). Do this quite rapidly until you feel the surface qi building up.

Personal Development – Aura Sensing

For those of you who are new to sensing energy fields and making an energetic diagnosis, here is a basic development exercise. The structure of the human aura is vast and at the higher soul levels we are all One. For this exercise we will only be working with the first seven levels. By using Archangel Raphael's Dream – Angelic Healing aura essence you will increase the effectiveness of your energetic diagnosis.

For this exercise you will need a partner to work with. Your partner should be standing with their feet at least thirty centimetres apart. Their knees should be relaxed and slightly bent, so that there is no tension in the legs; this will help their energy to flow more smoothly. Their breathing should be relaxed and normal. Their eyes can be open or closed; if the eyes are open, tell them not to watch what you are doing.

Stand at least two metres away from your partner and energise your palm chakras. Now turn to face your partner, hold your hands up in front of you with palms forwards and begin to walk very slowly in their direction. Try to place all your awareness into your palm chakras. You can imagine your palm chakras as another set of eyes you can see out of. Hold your focused intent on your partner and try to sense the 'edge' of their energy field. This is normally oval in shape, but can be distorted. As soon as you are aware of the field – most people feel a resistance, change in temperature or tingling – begin to move around your partner, defining the edge with your hands. Allow your hands to move upwards above the head and downwards to the ground, then go all around your partner still sensing their energy field. Make a mental note of how their energy felt and the overall shape.

Allow yourself to relax for a few moments, then try to feel the next auric layer. Keep going through all the auric levels, allowing yourself to relax for several moments between layers. At the end of the session you can make notes and, if appropriate, share with your partner what you perceived. Give your perceptions in a positive presentation. Also, was your partner aware of anything during the sensing exercise?

Personal Development – Sensing the Chakras

Chakras pick up cosmic vibrational energy and distribute it throughout the body and aura via the nadis (meridians). These amazing moderators of subtle energy are envisioned in classic lore as a 'lotus' flower. Each chakra's lotus has a different number of petals. The chakras must always be seen as a complete system. Each chakra is aware of all the other chakras through the etheric consciousness known as the aura. Each chakra 'anchors' a particular layer of the subtle body to the physical body.

For this chakra sensing exercise you will need a partner to work with. Your partner should lie face up on a therapy couch and be made comfortable with a pillow supporting the head. If your partner has back discomfort, a pillow needs to be placed behind the knees to support the legs. Your therapy couch must be wide and long enough to accommodate your partner so that their arms can relax easily at their sides and their feet are on the couch. You must stress to your partner not to cross their arms or legs during the chakra sensing process as this will block the energetic flow. Their legs should also be slightly apart. Your partner can be covered with a white blanket if at any time during the session they feel cold. Their breathing should be relaxed and normal. Their eyes can be open or closed; if the eyes are open, ask them not to watch what you are doing. By using Archangel Raphael's Dream – Angelic Healing aura essence you will increase the effectiveness of your chakra sensing exercise.

Take a deep breath and relax yourself. Release all negative thoughts and emotions, still your mind and focus completely on the energy field of your partner. Remain non-judgemental and positive throughout the whole subtle body examination. Allow yourself several minutes to gain energetic rapport with your partner: this attunement process is vital.

Start about 20 cm above the top of your partner's head in the crown chakra area. Raise your hands upwards, palms towards them; your hands should be about 50 cm apart. Slowly lower your hands towards the top of their head, at the same time bringing your hands together. Stop immediately you feel a resistance. With your hands, explore the crown chakra energy field. Do this very gently, as most people on the spiritual path have very sensitive crown chakras. Frequently the crown chakra is sensed at a distance of 15 cm, but it all depends on your sensitivity and your partner's spiritual development.

The soul star chakra is positioned about 25 cm above the crown chakra and you may have sensed this. Check you have the crown chakra and have not been sensing the soul star chakra. In fact you have seven transcendental chakras above your head; in time you will be able to sense these too. See the section – **Transcendental Chakras** (page 126).

Now move to the brow chakra and position your hands as high as you can above the brow area; your hands should be about 50 cm apart. Slowly bring your hands down and together until you feel a resistance. With your hands, explore the brow chakra energy field. Do this very gently, as most people on the spiritual path have a very sensitive third eye.

Raise your hands as high as you can and move to the throat area. Repeat the process. Continue sensing all the chakras in this manner until you feel you have located all the seven master chakras: crown, brow, throat, heart, solar, sacral and root.

The root chakra is the slowest energy and the easiest to sense. You may need to stand at your partner's feet. Position your hands just beneath and between your partner's feet. Very slowly move your hand towards your partner until you feel a resistance.

At the end of the session you can make notes and, if appropriate, share with your partner what you perceived. Give your intuitive perceptions in a positive presentation. Also, what did your partner feel during the exercise?

Personal Development – Advanced Sensing of the Chakras

For this chakra sensing exercise you will need a partner to work with. Your partner should be lying face up on a therapy couch etc.

Start about 20 cm above the top of your partner's head in the crown chakra area. Raise your hands upwards, palms towards them; your hands should be about 50 cm apart. Slowly lower your hands towards the top of their head, at the same time bringing your hands together. Stop immediately you feel a resistance. Do this very gently, as most people on the spiritual path have very sensitive crown chakras.

Now just use one hand to explore the crown chakra – choose the hand you feel is the most intuitive. Ask yourself the following questions about the chakra:

Is it spinning smoothly?
Does it feel out of balance?
Are one or more 'petals' damaged?
Is the energy strong or weak?
Does it anchor the relevant subtle body to the physical?

How far from the crown of the head does the energy of the chakra extend?
Does the chakra feel split into two or more segments?
Are there any cords, hooks or other 'alien' energies attached to this chakra?

Once you have gained an energetic profile, move on to the brow chakra and repeat the process.

Continue sensing all the chakras in this manner until you feel you have an energetic profile of all the seven master chakras: crown, brow, throat, heart, solar, sacral and root.

At the end of the advanced chakra sensing session you can make notes and, if appropriate, share with your partner what you perceived. Give your intuitive diagnosis in a positive presentation. Also, what did your partner feel during the exercise?

Complete Sensing of the Energy Field

By using either Archangel Raphael's Dream – Angelic Healing aura essence or Archangel Gabriel's Call – Angelic Guidance aura essence you will increase the effectiveness of the subtle body sensing exercise and energetic diagnosis.

1. Give your client reassurance on the procedure.

2. Relax your client using your chosen method.

3. Take a deep breath and relax yourself. Release all negative thoughts and emotions, still your mind and focus completely on the energy field of your client. Your intention will be known to your client even if this is only on a subtle level – so please remain non-judgemental and positive throughout the whole subtle body examination. Allow yourself several minutes to gain energetic rapport with your client. This attunement is a vital step, especially with a first-time client.

4. Begin by scanning your client's energy field approximately 2.5 cm above the physical body. Start at their feet and legs, move upwards over the sides of the body. Then scan the fingers, hands and arms, going finally over the body scanning the seven major chakras. Finish at the crown chakra. Remember the chakras are energetic gateways, opening communication not only between the different layers of a person's aura, but between other dimensions of light, love and inspiration.

5. Observe your client while you are getting an energetic diagnosis.

How did this first level feel?

Was it balanced?

This sheath *(annamaya kosa)* relates to the element of earth. It is pale blue or light grey in appearance, with tiny sparks of light moving very fast.(It can also be deep blue in very physical level-orientated individuals who are not in the least bit interested in spirituality). It is a fixed level which corresponds to the root chakra – the integration of the physical body *(sarira samyama)* and anchoring of the first level of the aura to the physical body. It is the lower aspect of the etheric. It is associated with the colour red, so it relates to the blood, skeletal system, physical health, survival, being grounded, adrenal glands, spinal column and all the solid elements of the body.

6. Move your hand to about 5cm above the physical body. Repeat the scanning process as before.

How did this second level feel?

Was it balanced?

This sheath relates to the element of water – the physiological body. It has a moving appearance full of vibrant colours (when healthy and emotionally balanced, otherwise it can be streaked with grey, black or muddy colours. I have also seen this level turn completely grey in appearance when someone is very ill or has just had a really bad shock). This level corresponds to the sacral chakra and is the anchor point of the second level of the aura to the physical body. It is also the start of the male/female balance through the integration of the root chakra with the sacral. It is associated with energy, vitality, integration of senses and lower base emotions. It rules all fluid functions of the body, kidneys, bladder, lymphatic system, reproductive system, breasts, tongue, fat deposits and skin. It links the physical and mental energies.

7.   Move your hand to about 15cm above the physical body. Repeat the scanning process as before.

How did this third level feel?

Was it balanced?

This sheath *(manomaya kosa)* relates to the element of fire. It is a fixed layer, yellow or gold in appearance. (I have seen this layer with massive holes within its structure as the mental processes break down; these holes allow lower astral entities to attach very easily to the physical body). This level corresponds to the solar plexus chakra. It deals with the integration of energy as the psychological or mental body and is the anchor point of the third level of the aura to the physical body. It is associated with the logical functioning of the mind. This means it also rules our intellectual prowess, thought processes, will-power and energy manipulation on all levels. It deals with the assimilation of energy from the pancreas and adrenals; also the central nervous system, stomach, liver, gall-bladder, spleen and eyesight.

8.   Move your hand to about 28 cm above the physical body. Repeat the scanning process as before.

How did this fourth level feel?

Was it balanced?

This sheath *(vijnanamaya kosa)* relates to the element of air. It is a moving layer of the intellectual body; in appearance it should be full of pastel colours and, when fully developed, a pastel rainbow infused with rose pink. (I have seen this layer filled with grey, red or black streaks when an individual has a blocked heart chakra). It corresponds to the heart chakra and is the anchor point of the fourth level of the aura to the physical body. It deals with the integration of the mind and the astral body. The word *astral* comes from the Latin for 'star', *astron*. When balanced it brings tranquil consciousness *(prasanta citta)* and compassion. It relates to the physical heart, lungs, breasts, thymus, the immune system, lymph glands and the sensory channel of touch.

9.   Move your hand to about 45 cm above the physical body. Repeat the scanning process as before.

How did this fifth level feel?

Was it balanced?

This sheath *(anandamaya kosa)* relates to the element of ether. It is a fixed layer that is vivid bright blue in appearance, corresponds to the throat chakra and is the anchor point of the fifth level of the aura to the physical body. It deals with the integration of the intellect – the body of joy. It is frequently called the etheric blueprint level. It governs the thyroid gland, parathyroid, lungs, vocal cords, jaw and breath.

10.   Move your hand to about 60 cm above the physical body. Repeat the scanning process as before.

How did this sixth level feel?

Was it balanced?

This sheath *(cittamaya kosa)* relates to the element of spirit, *Avyakta*, the primordial cloud of undifferentiated energy and matter. In appearance it is bright gold light which flows down from the higher self, when fully developed through meditation. It has movement, corresponds to the brow chakra and is the anchor point of the sixth level of the aura to the physical body. It is a celestial level which allows the integration of consciousness *(citta samyama)*. This level governs intuition, the pituitary gland, left eye and base of the skull.

11.   Move your hand to about 75 cm above the physical body. Repeat the scanning process as before.

How did this seventh level feel?

Was it balanced?

This sheath *(atmamaya kosa)* relates to the element of thought – pure consciousness *(paripakva citta* or *divya citta)*. It governs integration of the soul. It is a fixed level; in appearance it is silvery-blue to shimmering gold (the original blueprint). It relates to the crown chakra and is the anchor point of the seventh level of the aura to the physical body. It is the 'luminous egg' often seen around those of a highly developed spiritual nature such as Saints or Masters. It is associated with enlightenment, cosmic consciousness, the element of thought, right eye, cerebral cortex, pineal gland, upper skull and skin.

At the end of the subtle body scanning session you will have gained a full energetic profile and intuitive diagnosis which you may wish to make notes on. The subtle body scanning also prepares your client's energy field to receive healing. In time you will learn to use your clairvoyance and with practice you will be able to view the many auric levels. To be able to see the aura you have to train your vision, both inner and outer, and mentally state your intent as to which level of the aura you wish to view.

Also during the session you will have found yourself going through all the different auric levels to establish the full extent of the damage, debris, cords etc. You will need to confirm on what level the problem starts and how much the aura may be breached. It is not unusual to find holes, rips and tears in the aura. Very often you will find damaged chakras where they have split. Some of the chakras may be functioning at very low levels while others are overactive. Any imbalances will cause trouble in the overall vitality of the energy field. You must check each chakra is actually anchoring the relevant subtle body to the physical body. Cords, hooks, entities etc. or energy drains will need careful removal. The spaces where they have been need to be filled with positive loving Angelic healing energy. So this is the next step. For removing cords, hooks, thought-forms, entities etc. see the section – **Energy Sweep.** *The energy sweep is performed, if needed, during the scanning process, if attachments are found in the client's aura –* see page 186.

The client consultation, plus the subtle body scanning, will help you to select an Archangel essence(s) which you will use to treat your client during the session. You can verify the suitability of the Archangel essence with your client. Verifying your choice with your client will make them feel more involved in their treatment. For how to choose an Angelic essence see the section – **Selection of the Appropriate Angelic Essence** (page 149).

Intuitive Sensing of the Energy Field

Intuitive sensing of your client's energy field is something Reiki practitioners like to do before and after giving a full Reiki treatment to see what changes have taken place. You can use either hand or both hands and begin at the head or the feet. Allow yourself to be drawn to any area where you are guided. This simple yet powerful technique can also be used on yourself to gain a deeper understanding of your own energy field.

Angelic Essences – Using the Essences on Others

You can use the Angelic essences on your clients in many different ways. If you are a Reiki practitioner you can easily incorporate the Archangel essences into your practice by using them in your client's aura or on your hands during the Reiki energy transmission. The Angelic energy can be included in every type of treatment, both conventional and complementary. I know of the Angelic essences being used with hypnosis, shiatsu, acupuncture, reflexology, soul retrieval therapy, Reiki, past life therapy, sound therapy, crystal therapy, massage and colour healing. Remember, as you gain in confidence and competence with the Angelic essences, you can easily incorporate them into every other therapy and treatment regime you use on your clients or yourself.

Many people also use the Angelic essences to enhance their meditation practice, while others use them to gain artistic inspiration. I also know of several Reiki Masters who use them during the Reiki attunement process. However you feel drawn to use them, it is best if you do it in a conscious way by inviting the Archangels into your life to bring harmony, support and spiritual growth.

Vibrational Transmission

A simple way of using the essences on others is to transmit the vibration through your palm chakras. Your client can be standing, seated on a stool or lying face up on a treatment couch or massage table. You will have already cleansed your own aura before your client arrives for the therapy session. You can work in the aura, chakras, meridians or directly on the physical body. Allow your intuition to guide you.

Alignment

Align yourself with the source of healing energies you will be using by spraying the chosen Archangel essence on your left hand, then spread the essence over the palms of both hands. As you do so, establish contact with the Archangelic energy. You will normally feel the energy pouring in through your crown chakra and downwards to your heart chakra, before flowing down your arms into your hands and flooding out of your palm chakras. Allow yourself to be completely surrounded and supported by this energy. You are now ready to transmit the Angelic vibration towards your client.

Establishing Contact

Establish contact with your client for the energy transmission to commence by standing about 80 cm away from them. Hold your hands out in front of you, palm chakras towards them. Allow their aura to be completely flooded by the energy.

Auric Transmission

You may choose to go through the aura layer by layer. Spend some time observing how the energy is flowing around your client. Allow your hands to guide you. You may use sweeping movements in the aura or be guided to place specific symbols in the aura. Remember, this whole process is intuitive and can take an hour or more, especially if this is the first time your client has experienced Angelic energy transmission. Allow your intuition to guide you as you infuse the Archangel energy and celestial light into your client's auric shell and their aura has completed its process of absorption.

Chakra Transmission

When you are ready, you may feel intuitively guided to work through the chakra centres. You could start with your client's crown chakra and move downwards through all the chakras in sequential order. Or you may be guided to work on the chakras in any order or combination. The aim is to infuse each chakra with the Archangel energy and celestial light until the chakra feels it has completed its process of absorption.

Physical Transmission

To work on the physical body, allow yourself to be guided to either your client's head or feet.

Here is a sequential list of hand positions you may choose to use. They start at the crown of the head and work down the body; you can reverse them if you are guided to start at your client's feet. The hand positions also assume your client is lying down on a therapy couch. If your client is seated you will have to adapt the hand positions to suit the situation – or you may be intuitively guided to place your hands in any position required. The length of time you keep your hands in each position is entirely up to your intuition, but three to five minutes is a good guideline. Each hand position draws the Archangel energy and celestial light into the meridian system before anchoring it down into the skeletal system.

Hand Positions

Position yourself at your client's head. You can be seated for these first five hand positions.

a)   Place the palms of your hands gently on the crown of their head.

b)   Place your hands gently over the recipient's eyes.

c)   Place your hands underneath your client's head. Allow your hands to gently cradle the head.

d)   Place your hands with the heels of your palms on the side of the neck and your palms and your fingers lightly on the throat.

e)   Place your thumbs just below and aligned with the collarbones and your palms towards the breastbone.

Move to the side of your client for treating the heart, solar plexus and stomach areas.

f)   Place both hands over the rib-cage in a straight line across the base of the sternum.

g)   Place both hands in a straight line just above the waist.

h)   Place both hands just below the waist, level with the pelvic bones (hips).

Move to the legs.

i)   Move down the legs in as many stages as you feel is required – normally thighs, knees, shins and ankles. You can work on each leg separately or both at the same time by placing one hand on each leg.

Move to the feet and position yourself at the end of the therapy couch.

j)   Treat the tops of the feet.

k)   Place your hands on the soles of the feet.

l)   Move your hands off the feet and place your palms about 10 cm beneath the soles of the feet; now use your intuition to observe your client's male – female polarity balance. The right foot represents the male polarity and the left foot the female polarity. Hold your hands in this position until all energy movement ceases. This position strengthens the skeletal structure and draws your client fully back into the physical body, which signals the end of the treatment. The vibrational transmission is now complete and you have worked in the aura, chakras and meridian system.

m)   Remain positioned at your client's feet, place your hands back on the ankles and draw your client fully back into their body. Feel your client is returning to normal waking consciousness.

At the end of the session your client's aura should feel smooth and buoyant to the touch. Your client should have no excess energy in any of the meridians, chakras or different auric layers or the physical body.

Allow your client time to return to normal everyday waking reality. Offer them a drink of water. Asking your client to drink plenty of fresh pure water, just before and especially just after each Archangel vibrational transmission, will ease the removal of energetic blocks and emotional toxicity. These are always released with the integration of new energy patterns and information. You must also drink plenty of fresh water to help your energy field before and after giving a vibrational transmission. If you like, you can express your gratitude to the Archangel you have been working with.

Extra Hand Positions

If you have time you can include the shoulders, arms and hands in the treatment. Treat your client's left hand first because energy enters through the left side and leaves through the right side in healthy balanced individuals.

Left side: Position your right palm on the left shoulder and hold your client's left hand with your left hand (as though you were shaking hands with them).

Right side: Position your left palm on the right shoulder and hold your client's right hand with your right hand (as though you were shaking hands with them).

Spine: When your client is sitting up on the therapy couch at the end of the treatment it is good to place your hands at the top and base of the spine; this balances the energy along the spinal column.

You may use this technique as many times as your client requires it. Try using different Archangel essences for each session; this will help your client to harmoniously release their core energetic blocks on all levels. Try not to overdo this procedure though; remember to allow your client's subtle bodies time to integrate their new energetic flow and celestial light information before attempting another session. Please also recognise that everyone processes healing energy at their own pace. Some people choose to take the Archangel infusion and integrate it very quickly, others may take longer. We are all unique and each disease is unique, so allow the healing process to be natural to your client.

Also, there is a growing awareness in the power of group work. So you may decide to work with other therapists, all of you using the same Archangelic transmission technique – your shared vision and intention will create a truly wonderful experience for your clients.

Angelic Essence Vibrational Transmission with Crystals

Angelic Essence Vibrational Transmission with Crystals gives a complete chakra realignment, aura cleansing and meridian cleansing which facilitates wholeness, good health and emotional well-being. This specific system produces an energy vortex of healing over each chakra, which results in higher octaves or frequencies of energy and light becoming more pronounced within them. The aura is cleansed and breaches, holes and gapping etc. are filled. The aura is then sealed and protected. Please note: No healing crisis should result if the client drinks enough water before and after the session. (This applies to all the different healing techniques.)

Crystals, Angelic essences etc. required

Crystals: 4 clear quartz medium-size points are needed. They should be as clear and free from damage as possible and at least 9 cm long with perfect terminations.

Use 3 medium clear quartz points in a triangle configuration to form a crystal web of light (2 level with the ankles, 1 at the soul star chakra about 18 cm above the crown chakra).

Use 1 clear quartz point (known as the control or master crystal) held in your hand with the termination pointing towards the client.

You can replace the 3 quartz points with the Star of David (Merkaba) large meditation pieces – female side upwards.

You can replace the clear quartz point (control) with a faceted crystal wand or liquid light wand.

Archangel Michael's Empowerment – Angelic Protection aura essence.

Reiki (useful but not essential).

You can use Angel of Light – Archangel Seraphiel – Healing and Angelic protection essence to cleanse your crystals before, during and after the therapy session.

You can use Archangel Raphael's Dream – Angelic Healing or Angel of Light, Archangel Seraphiel – Healing and Angelic Protection essences for the therapy session.

You can also use during the session:

Archangel Chamuel's Embrace – Angelic Love
Archangel Haniel's Glory – Angelic Communication
Archangel Zadkiel's Joy – Violet Flame of Freedom
Archangel Uriel's Initiation – Angelic Peace.

You should use Angel of the Animals or Archangel Sandalphon aura essence to ground your client at the end of the session; alternatively use a smoky quartz point beneath each foot or a pair of Boji stones TM, one beneath each foot, to ground your client.

You can also incorporate an Archangel Web of Light – see the section **Process** – or give a Reiki session. The crystals for the Archangel Web of Light would be used/placed on the body once you have completed number 19.

A lit candle can be useful to dispose of the negative energy.

1. Raise the sensitivity in your hands. (Wash them in cool water, dry them thoroughly, then rub your hands together in a circular motion several times to build up the surface qi in your hands).

2. Align yourself with the source of healing energies you will be using, e.g. by spraying the Archangel aura essence of your choice on your left hand, then spreading the essence over the palms of both hands. As you do so, establish contact with your Archangels and feel them overshadowing and guiding you. You will normally feel the Archangelic energy transmission pouring in through your crown chakra, coming down to your heart chakra, flowing down your arms and flooding out of your palm chakras.

3. Make sure your own personal energy system is now flowing smoothly and you are completely surrounded and guided by the Archangels; you should feel grounded, centred and in perfect balance.

4. Ask your client to lie down, face upwards, on the therapy table. Make sure that they are comfortable.

5. Relax your client and give reassurance on the procedure and arrange a distress signal.

6. Allow a few moments to gain energetic rapport with your client before you begin scanning.

7. Begin by scanning your client's energy field using your left hand or right hand (or both), starting with level one approximately 2.5 cm above the physical body. Start at their feet and legs, then the hands and arms, going finally over the body scanning the seven major chakras. Finish at the crown chakra.

8. Keep scanning all the layers of the aura, including the chakra centres, until you are satisfied that you have a good knowledge of your client's energy field. Always move your hand in the same forwards direction when scanning; never go backwards and forwards over an area when you are doing the initial scan (if you do go backwards and forwards you will begin the process of chelation and this will start to release the 'negative energy'. This should only be done when you are doing an energy sweep). If you need to re-check an area, lift your hand upwards and then go back to the original point of auric entry for that level.

9. If you find problem areas within the aura you can also begin scanning at a distance of several metres. This may seem a long way from the client's physical body but it is a vital step. You must identify the edge of problem areas. Work your way downwards through the various sheaths of the aura, moving down through the emotional sheath to the sheath which is closest to the body, i.e. the physical.

10. Your subtle body scanning is searching for: energy blocks, stagnant or stuck energy, weak energy, gaps, holes, breaks, tears, heat, cold, body armouring, auric gapping and, most important of all, 'metal'- especially spikes, knives, needles, spears or in fact anything sharp. (These will feel as if they are protruding from your client and will frequently hurt your hand as you scan over them). Some clients have 'vortexes' of negative energy attached to them. Check that each chakra is spinning correctly and none of the petals are damaged or that the chakra is not split or deformed and that the chakra is actually anchoring the relevant auric layer. Some of the chakras may be functioning at very low levels, while others are overactive. Any imbalances will cause trouble in the overall vitality of the energy field.

11. See **'Energy Sweep'** for complete directions on aura cleansing. Once you have finished the aura sweep (if it is appropriate), you can proceed to number 12.

Please note: if at any time during the therapy session you uncover very sharp objects or entities you must do a complete 'Energy Sweep'.

12. The client consultation, plus the subtle body scanning, will help you to select an Archangel essence or essences which you will now use to treat your client during the crystal transmission. You can verify the suitability of an Archangel essence with your client – very often your client will say that they have felt particularly drawn to that Archangel recently or they will relate to the Archangel energy signature and overall theme. By verifying your choice with your client it will make them feel more involved in their treatment. For how to choose an Angelic Essence, see the section **Selection of the Appropriate Angelic Essence**.

13. To begin, mist the clear quartz crystals with the Archangel essence you have chosen to use with your client – this includes your control crystal. Place a clear quartz triangulation web of light around your client, about 18 cm distance from the body. You will be using single-terminated clear quartz crystals (or the Star of David Merkaba pieces). First place two crystals at the feet. This will act as a grounding for the client, to stabilise the crystal triangulation's energy field. Then place one crystal above the head, with the point facing away from the client, to act as a release for any negative energies. This will also prevent overloading of the client's energy field. If you use the Star of David (Merkaba) pieces, make sure they are female side up to transmit the energy.

14. Join up the quartz triangulation with your clear quartz control crystal. This is done clockwise, using your right hand. You can hold the left hand up to receive extra celestial healing energies.

15. Remove any stagnant, stuck or blocked energies anticlockwise (unwinding), using your control crystal. Start at the feet, then knees, hips, hands and arms, then work up through the seven major chakras on the body. Finish at the crown chakra. You will need to have somewhere to place the negative energy – such as a waste bin over which you can use Angel of Light spray to cleanse away the negativity. Alternatively you could use a candle and place the negative energy into the flame. You may draw out the negativity like a thread; you may sometimes need to cut this thread because of its length – use a chopping movement with your left hand – and dispose of it in the candle flame or bin, before going back, hooking the thread again and pulling out some more. Your client will very often actually physically feel this energetic thread being drawn out. Your client may also register awareness of the stagnant energy being released from the different auric levels and chakra centres. These frequently take the form of spontaneous uncontrollable body movements, facial twitches or emotional outbursts. If your client releases tears during the session, just reassure them that it is all part of the energetic procedure by asking them if they are "feeling all right" and if possible carry on with the Archangelic transmission.

16. Once all the energetic blocks and stagnant energy have been removed, use your control crystal to transmit the Archangelic energies into your client's body. You can go in a clockwise manner over the chakras; alternatively you may be guided to just allow the energy to flow into the chakra centre. Start at the feet, then knees, hips, hands and arms, and then go through the seven major chakras of the body. You must finish at the crown chakra.

17. Place your control crystal on the therapy couch between your client's feet with the termination of the crystal pointing towards your client.

18.   You will now scan your client's subtle bodies again.

19.   By scanning your client again you will decide if you need to transmit more of the Archangelic energies into your client's subtle bodies or perhaps you will feel that the therapy session is complete.

If complete, proceed to No. 20; if not, go back to No. 15 and transmit more of the Archangelic energies into your client's subtle bodies.

If it is appropriate you can now place an 'Archangel Web of Light' around or on your client's physical body. You could also use Reiki healing at this point or any other therapy that you practise, such as colour or sound therapy.

20.   When the Archangel transmission is 'complete', fill your client's energy field with celestial light until you feel physically pushed back by the energy. Then seal the 'healing' around your client clockwise. Go round your client at least seven times or more until you feel a strong wall of protective energy.

21.   Spray your client's aura with Archangel Michael Empowerment essence or Angel of Light etc. to fully seal and protect the process.

22.   Remove the crystal triangulation from around your client, taking away the quartz crystals in reverse order of placement (starting with the one above the head).

23.   Ground your client by very gently holding the ankles and directing the energy downwards – or you could use two smoky quartz points beneath the feet or use Angel of the Animals aura spray on the root chakra, legs and feet. You could also use a pair of Boji stones TM, one beneath each foot, to ground your client.

24.   Make sure that you and your client are fully grounded, centred and balanced. Allow any feelings of dizziness to dissipate.

25.   Give your client a glass of water to sip slowly.

26.   Finish by giving thanks and asking mentally that the therapy session is closed, sealed and protected with Divine love and wisdom.

27.   Give your client sufficient time to integrate the Archangel transmission session. As a general guideline it is suggested a period of twice the length of time your client was actually experiencing the transmission be allowed for integration before they resume their normal daily activities.

28.   Wash your hands and control crystal in cold water to release any unwanted energies. Cold water does not open your pores, therefore it gives protection from absorbing your client's negative energy release. Cleanse the other crystals used. You could spray Angel of Light over your crystals including your control. You must cleanse your therapy room and its contents after each client.

You may use this technique as many times as your client needs it; try using different Archangel essences for each session. As each essence will work in a different way, this will help your client to release their core energetic blocks. Try not to overdo this procedure though; remember to allow your client's body time to integrate the new flow of energy before attempting another session. Please also recognise that everyone 'heals' at their own pace. Some people choose to take the Archangel energy and integrate it very quickly, others may much take longer. We are all unique and each disease is unique, so allow the healing process to be natural to the person you are helping.

There is a growing awareness in the power of group work. So you may decide to work with other therapists, all of you using the same Archangelic transmission technique – your shared vision and intention will create a truly wonderful experience for your clients.

Crystalline Transmission

A more advanced way of using the Archangel essences on others is to transmit the vibration through your control crystal, which will amplify and enhance your client's treatment. You can replace the clear quartz point (control) with a faceted Kabalistic crystal or liquid light wand or a faceted crystal wand.

Your client can be standing, seated on a stool or lying face up on a treatment couch or massage table. You will have already cleansed your own aura before your client arrives for the therapy session. You can work in any or all of the subtle bodies. Allow your intuition and the Archangel of the essence you have chosen to guide you. The client consultation, plus the subtle body scanning, will help you to select an Archangel essence or essences which you will now use to treat your client during the crystalline transmission. You can verify the suitability of the Archangel essence with your client – very often your client will say that they have felt particularly drawn to that Archangel recently or they will relate to the Archangel energy signature and overall theme. By verifying your choice with your client it will make them feel more involved in their treatment. For how to choose an Angelic Essence see the section **Selection of the Appropriate Angelic Essence**.

Angelic Alignment

Align yourself with the source of healing energies you will be using by spraying the chosen Archangel essence on your left hand, then spreading the essence over the palms of both hands. As you do so, establish contact with the Archangelic energy. You will normally feel the energy streaming into your crown chakra and downwards to your heart chakra, before flowing down your arms into your hands and flooding out of your palm chakras. Allow yourself to be completely surrounded and supported by this energy. Then mist your pre-cleansed clear quartz control crystal with the Archangel essence. Allow the essence to flow out of the tip of your crystal. When you see or feel the energy flowing smoothly, you are ready to transmit the Angelic vibration through your control crystal towards your client.

Establishing Contact

Establish contact with your client for the energy transmission to commence by standing about 80 cm away from them. Hold your dominant hand containing your control crystal out in front of you and use your other hand to stabilise your client's energy field during the treatment. Allow your client's aura to be completely flooded by the Archangelic energy.

Auric Transmission

Spend some time observing how the energy is circulating around your client from the crystal. Allow your hands and the crystal to guide you. You may choose to go through the aura layer by layer, using circular movements of the crystal; at other times you may need to hold the crystal in one area for several minutes. There is no right or wrong way of infusing your client's aura with the Angelic energy. Just allow the process of absorption to be natural for your client. You may also find yourself using sweeping movements or be angelically guided to place specific symbols in the aura.

Remember, this whole process is intuitive, so allow your intuition to guide you as you infuse the Archangel energy and celestial light into your client's auric shell.

Chakra Transmission

When you are ready you may feel intuitively guided to work with your control crystal through the chakra centres. You could start with your client's crown chakra and move downwards through all the chakras in sequential order. Or you may be guided to work on the chakras in any order or combination. The aim is to infuse each chakra that needs it with the Archangel energy and celestial light until the chakra feels it has completed its process of absorption.

Place your control crystal on the therapy couch between your client's feet with the termination of the crystal pointing towards your client. You can now scan your client's subtle bodies again. By scanning your client again you will decide if you need to transmit more of the Archangelic energies into your client's subtle bodies or perhaps you will feel that the therapy session is complete.

Closure

When the crystalline transmission is 'complete', fill your client's energy field with celestial light until you feel physically pushed back by the energy. Then seal the 'healing' around your client clockwise. Go round your client at least seven times or more until you feel a strong wall of protective energy.

Ground your client by very gently holding the ankles and directing the energy downwards. Make sure that you and your client are fully grounded, centred and balanced. Allow any feelings of dizziness to dissipate.

Give your client a glass of water to sip slowly. Finish by giving thanks to the Archangel and the crystalline energies you have been using.

Give your client sufficient time to integrate the crystalline transmission session. Wash your hands and control crystal in cold water to release any unwanted energies. You could spray Angel of Light over all your control crystal. You must cleanse your therapy room and its contents after each client.

You can use this technique as many times as your client requires. Try using different Archangel essences for each session because each essence has a different theme and will approach your client's core energetic blocks in a different way. Try not to overdo this procedure though; remember to allow your client's body time to integrate the new flow of energetic information before attempting more sessions. Please also recognise that everyone 'heals' their dis-ease at their own pace. Some people choose to take the Archangel energy and integrate it very quickly, others may much take longer, because we are all unique vibratory beings, each with our own patterns of dis-ease.

Merkaba Transmission

The Merkaba is an ancient Hebrew word which literally translates as 'chariot'. This interpretation comes from Ezekiel's encounter in the Old Testament. The term Merkaba has been used by students of the Kabala for centuries to mean a 'vehicle' with which to travel to the different planes (dimensions, levels, spheres or emanations) of God (the ten Sephiroth of the Tree of Life). Most recently it has come into common usage as meaning a specific geometric form called a star tetrahedron, with which individuals can 'travel' in meditation to higher dimensions to raise their vibratory rate. The tetrahedron is only one of the forms the Merkaba vehicle of light can take. The way to access the Merkaba vehicle is through visualization. Kabalistic tradition dating back thousands of years teaches students to use meditation and the intoning of letters from the tetragrammaton. In ancient Egyptian (18th dynasty) the word Merkaba can also be found. The word Merkaba is made up of three sections or smaller words: Mer-Ka-Ba.

Mer translates as the 'Light of God' or 'Super-Soul'.

Ka symbolises the individual spirit which dwells in your heart centre.

Ba is the spark of life which animates the physical body and gives us our personal reality or perceptive ability.

So a Merkaba is, in reality, a multidimensional gateway or your own personal 'stargate'. This stargate can also be viewed as a portal or antenna – a receiver and transmitter linking us into a vast network of multi-level communication airways.

Quartz Merkaba

Recently clear quartz has been used to fashion Merkabas. The design, fashioned from clear quartz, is triangular in shape, with smaller triangles on each face. One face has the smaller triangle aligned with the body of the stone: this is the yang side. On the other side, the smaller triangle is inverted to the body of the stone: this is the yin side. Qi travels through the stone from the yin side, is amplified and is radiated out of the yang side.

The Merkaba cut crystals come in several sizes: the larger ones are suitable for using as meditation pieces or for room gridding and the smaller ones are often set in gold or silver and worn over the thymus at the witness point. They must be programmed first with bioinformation (energy resonance patterns). These are placed into the crystal by the focused human mind holding the intent of healing, harmony and happiness or by misting the female side of the crystal with an Archangel essence. The effect of wearing a programmed Merkaba is to protect and shield the wearer by making their aura more luminous; this stabilises the personal aura, making the wearer feel secure, focused and balanced.

The quartz Merkaba is always in a constant state of unified awareness. It teaches us how to be in a constant state of awareness by being tuned into and consciously aware of our Divine connection at all times. This helps us to become 'mindful', which means we act and react in an 'enlightened' way of being, allowing us to dance to the rhythm of our soul, as it feels its completion in understanding its connection with its Divine source. This ends the dualistic concepts of separation by stopping us attaching importance to the little ego of the self and all its deception which creates illusion. The mind is the great deceiver: by using memory and imagination, it tricks us into thinking that we can return to the past or anticipate our future; in truth we only exist in the present moment.

Body Placement Star Merkaba

We can use a star Merkaba cut clear quartz to dynamically transmit the Archangel essences into the physical body to release stagnant energy patterns of dis-ease. Using the 'Merkaba star' as a vibrational healing tool, one can place the stone on a desired part of the body (yang side down) and put an Archangel essence on the yin side (negative, magnetic inverted triangle). The subtle vibration of the Archangel essence is drawn into the star Merkaba through the yin side, amplified and radiated into the body through the yang side (positive, electric). The effect is dazzling as the star Merkaba creates a vortex of energy above and below where it is positioned on the body, allowing for a deeper absorption of the transmitted vibrational energetic information into the physical body and auric shell.

Visualisation Star Merkaba

The star Merkaba cut quartz is also a visualisation tool when held in meditation; it aids visionary abilities. This visionary ability includes understanding your own energy grid, which comprises the subtle bodies – chakras, meridians and aura. This results in greater personal healing, emotional well-being and spiritual growth. As before, just mist the cut quartz on the female side with your chosen Archangel essence.

Merkaba Triangulation Web

You can use three star Merkaba large clear quartz meditation pieces – female side upwards – to form a triangulation web of light around your client's physical body during therapy sessions. This formation of Merkabas causes negative energy to be transmuted very quickly, as each Merkaba acts as a vortex of light energy, which forms a pyramid of light around your client. Mist the cut quartzes on the female side with your chosen Archangel essence before you place them around your client.

Third Eye Merkaba

When placing the Merkaba star, yang side out, over the third eye (6th chakra) in meditation, opening and expansion are immediate, bringing consciousness evolution. For consciousness expansion you must mist the yang side with the Archangel essence of your choice. Highly recommended is Archangel Raziel's Secret – Mysteries essence or Archangel Tzaphkiel's Joy – Cosmic Contemplation essence.

Merkaba Creating a Sacred Space

The Merkaba star meditation pieces can also be used to fill your home with a powerful protective healing energy. You need four clear quartz stars; place them on the parameter of the space, in each of the four cardinal directions of the area you wish to protect and make sacred, having first programmed them using Archangel Michael's Empowerment – Angelic Protection essence.

Faceted Crystal Wand

Faceted wands are designed to focus, direct and cohere energy. They can be manufactured from any natural gemstone or quartz material. Smoky quartz wands are traditionally used for loosening pain or negative or stagnant energy, by gently unwinding the trapped obstruction. Amethyst is used for transmutation, transformation and release, being especially good for releasing addictions. Rose quartz wands are gentle, soothing and excellent for balancing the emotional level of the aura by gently nourishing the emotional body. Rose quartz is revitalising and stimulates healing by helping to maintain energy levels to protect against unwanted influences from the outside world, which many sensitive souls find overwhelming. Wands in clear quartz cohere, amplify, focus and transmit energies: it is the master healer and the only programmable crystal. Rutile quartz wands intensify the powerful quartz vibration, giving protection. Citrine wands clear and balance the solar plexus chakra, bringing personal power, spontaneity, positive mental attitudes, joy, hope and freedom from emotional hang-ups. Obsidian wands draw the quality of our Divine essence into our physical body; which purges the negativity, quickly dissolving blocks, trauma, shock and fear.

Fashioned wands are often long and have six straight sides with a small point at each end, which makes them behave similarly to natural double-terminated crystals. Others have one end rounded and smooth and these are used for deep tissue massage or as energy or blockage shifters. Then there are faceted wands with multiple facets which greatly cohere and amplify the potential energy transmission. Cutting and faceting also increase the information storage capacity. Some wands are distinguished by their faceting being very precise, with a larger yin termination; this end draws in pranic life force, which spirals down the length of the crystal, being amplified each time it comes into contact with a facet. The prana, suitably amplified, flows through the opposite yang termination. The more facets there are, the greater the coherence and power. Some innovative new faceted wands are composed of a combination of two facets. One is slender and flat and the other is wide and concave; this new generation of wands is extremely focused.

Liquid Light Wand

Liquid Light Wands are fashioned from cultured quartz crystal. Vibrational therapists are experimenting with these specimens for their flawless refined energy transmission. Although cultured quartz has recently been used for energy balancing, the process used to produce it originated in Germany some fifty years ago. While chemically identical to natural quartz SiO_2, it has a greatly refined nature, due to its flawlessness and vibrant colour (doping is the process used to add colour). Colours include blue, gold, purple and green, as well as clear. Cultured ruby, sapphire, emerald and alexandrite are also freely available to therapists. These gems are chemically the same as natural gemstones, also exhibiting the same vibrant colours as the most expensive natural gemstones and, in the case of alexandrite, a mystical colour change. They are more affordable than equivalent-size natural gemstones. The cultured crystals are cut and faceted into jewellery or sacred geometric shapes such as platonic solids, precision healing wands, the star of David, Merkaba, Star tetrahedron (this consists of two interpenetrating tetrahedrons), spheres and pyramids. Therapists are experimenting with these geometric specimens for their flawless refined energy transmission. It is advisable, if using these cultured quartz crystals for healing, to clear, charge, dedicate and programme them first and infuse them with the required bioinformation; this is because they do not contain the memory of natural devic energies. This makes them free from any outside influences and clean energetically. Some crystal purists do say that these cultured crystals are devoid of life force, which does not make any sense at all, as they are the same chemically (SiO_2) and contain a refined crystal lattice. In truth, cultured quartz is actually a purer form of quartz which has no inclusions and a more stable pattern of rotation in the molecules, which experienced crystal therapists find speeds up the energy movement within the crystal. (This is the reason why the electronics industry also uses lab-grown quartz).

Application

Using the Angelic Essences on Yourself

Many people use the Angelic essences to enhance their daily meditation practice, while others use them to gain celestial or artistic inspiration. I also know of several Reiki Masters who use them during the Reiki attunement process. However you feel drawn to use them, it is best if you do it in a conscious way by inviting the Archangels into your life to bring harmony, support and spiritual growth.

Here are some more ways you can use the Archangel essences externally:

Mist the palms of your hands with an Archangel essence before giving a therapy treatment, Reiki session, massage or Reiki, Tibetan or Karuna attunement.

Use an Archangel essence to mist your pulse points – wrist, throat, forehead, back of neck, soles of both feet – when you feel physically tired (Archangel Jophiel's Illumination) or emotionally upset (Archangel Chamuel's Embrace) or ungrounded (Angel of the Animals).

Mist the palms of your hands, then pass your hands through the aura, using a sweeping motion to cleanse it.

Mist the palms of your hands, then inhale deeply from your cupped hands to cleanse your physical body quickly. This is a useful technique for stressful situations such as a visit to the dentist, interviews, exams or after any confrontation which may leave you feeling tired or drained.

Spray your chosen Archangel essence directly into the aura, especially in any areas which may feel stuck, painful or congested. This technique is really useful when you are letting go of the past by clearing negative emotions that are impeding your future progress.

Spray your chosen Archangel essence around your room to cleanse it and make it sacred. This is especially useful if you are moving into a new home and need to clear any residual energies from the previous owners. You could even add it to your paints when you redecorate.

Spray your chosen essence into a warm bath and swirl the water with your right hand in a clockwise direction, saying the relevant Archangel's invocation. Relax for twenty minutes, focusing on the Archangel's essence and energetic theme.

Mist your washing powder or fabric conditioner with Angel of Light essence before you wash clothes or bed linen which may be holding negative or traumatic energy.

Use Angel of Light – Angelic Healing and Protection aura essence for emergency situations, because it is helpful in a wide range of stressful situations. It is our most popular essence and the one most people use first.

Add your chosen Archangel essence to your massage oil before giving a treatment.

Apply a massage oil that contains Archangel Raphael's Dream – Angelic Healing essence before and after exercise, which could reduce muscle stiffness and reduce the risk of strains.

Spray your chosen Archangel essence directly on the body to bring relief from pain. Use your pendulum to choose the essence or use Archangel Raphael's Dream – Angelic Healing or Angel of Light.

Make a hot or cold compress and add an essence such as Archangel Raphael's Dream – Angelic Healing to bring relief from bruising, bites, burns, sprains or sunburn.

Add an Archangel essence to an oil burner to fill your home with Angelic energy.

Use the Archangelic essence of your choice before you go to sleep each night. This will keep your etheric body safe and stop nightmares. If you are worried about something, you can ask for a solution to be given in your dreams. You could also spray your favourite rose, amethyst or other dream crystal with your chosen Archangel essence; this will help you remember your dreams. You could also use the Archangel essence at night so that in your dream state you can visit the Archangel Temple of your choice to gain wisdom, guidance, compassion or illumination.

Using the Archangel Essence on the Self – Dream Temple

Dreams are a fantastic way of opening the channel between you and the soul. You can use an Archangelic essence to visit an etheric Temple of Light during dreamtime, where your soul will gain instruction and help. This could be anything from spiritual growth, guidance or developing compassion to help you deal with difficult people or situations in your life.

1. Purify yourself and your sleeping environment.

2. Purifying your physical body by taking a shower or bath and putting on clean nightwear can also make you feel more receptive and in tune.

3. Select the etheric temple you wish to visit. This may be influenced by the type of spiritual work you are currently engaged in. Mist your aura with your chosen Archangelic essence.

4. You may wish to write down on a piece of paper or in your Angelic journal what you want to achieve and the etheric temple you wish to visit. Place it by your bedside so that if you receive an important experience or dream you can immediately make notes, even in the middle of the night.

5. Purify your thoughts; let go of all negative thoughts that may have lodged in your emotional body during the day. Use Archangel Zadkiel's Joy – Violet Flame of Freedom to transmute them.

6. Get into bed and relax your body; use your breath to help you relax. Allow your mind to gently follow your breath as you breathe in and out.

7. Now turn your focus to your heart chakra, where your spirit resides, and mentally call on the Archangel of your choice. You can use the word *Namaste* (a greeting of Divine love in *Sanskrit*). So it could be "Namaste Gabriel, please awaken my 'Inner Angel' and show me how to receive your gifts of hope, happiness, love and guidance."

8. Just relax and let your soul be awakened by the Archangel. You will feel your awakened-self enveloped in the power and energy of the Archangel you have decided to call. Feel it, see it, hear it, use all your senses…really fully experience it.

    If, for instance, you have called Archangel Gabriel, you will feel a joyful, light, bubbly energy, full of hope and happiness. If you have called Archangel Michael, you will feel strong, clear and focused. If you practise these dream meditations each night before you go to sleep and work frequently with the Archangels, you will soon recognise each one of them by their energy 'signature' as they become your trusted friends and guides. In fact they are your brothers and sisters, as we are all born from the same creative God force.

9. You can stay basking in this energy as long as you like…when you are ready, allow yourself to be raised upwards on a spiral of light…slowly the white or coloured light spiral raises you higher and higher…you feel yourself held in your Archangel's arms…you feel yourself transported very safely…your Archangel is carrying you to the etheric temple of light.

10. You will find yourself in the temple…here you will be able to experience or learn whatever you have asked of your Archangel.

    For instance, if you have called upon Archangel Raphael for healing and renewal, you may well find you are taken into a healing room, where you can lie on one of his special healing couches; you will be bathed in colours and crystalline healing energies…music will also bathe your body in healing vibrations…all your senses will be engaged in the beautiful experience. If you call on Archangel Metatron and you have asked for 'light body activation' you may well be placed in an ascension chamber or seated on a special ascension throne which increases your 'light' energy. Your Archangel will know exactly what experience you require.

11. Your Archangel will let you know when it is time to leave and bring you safely back into your body, to the here and now. Give thanks and write down your experiences.

12. If you fell into a deep sleep, that is wonderful too; people frequently have very strong Angelic contact in their dreams. Either way, in meditation or dreams, know that your chosen Archangel is now guiding you and your soul is visiting the etheric temples each night.

Using the Angelic Essences on Yourself – Process

The process of placing an Archangelic Web of Light around yourself is an interesting way to connect with each Archangel.

1. Cleanse, then programme, 12 clear quartz crystals with the Archangel essence mist of your choice. For how to choose the correct Archangel essence see the section **Using the Essences – Selection** (page 149).

2. Choose a warm comfortable place where you can lie down undisturbed for at least an hour. Cleanse it energetically with the 'Angel of Light' essence mist – see the section **Purification – Creating A Sacred Space** (page 158).

3. Place the programmed 12 clear quartz crystals evenly around your body, terminations pointing inwards.

4. Relax by consciously becoming aware of your breathing and heartbeat. Allow any thoughts that drift through your mind to be released. Focus your attention and use your intention to visualise roots reaching down from the soles of your feet deep into the earth...allow yourself to be cradled in the earth's vibrational gravitational field of the Great Mother...this will keep your physical body safe...now visualise yourself surrounded by a sphere of iridescent white energy...as the 12 clear quartz crystals surround you on all levels with complete Angelic protection.

5. Place the crystal web of light on the body. As an example, for Archangel Uriel you would use – black kyanite, rainbow-coated golden labradorite, malachite, opal, phenacite and ruby in zoisite. Allow 20 minutes to facilitate the integration of the energies as they are activated by the Archangel. Feel free to remove the crystal web of light sooner, if you have integrated the energy very quickly.

6. Remove all the crystals in reverse order of placement.

7. Make sure you are fully grounded, centred and balanced.

8. Cleanse your crystals using 'Angel of Light'.

9. Finish by giving thanks to the Archangel who has been overshadowing your experience and asking mentally that the session is closed, sealed and protected with Divine love and wisdom.

10. Give yourself sufficient time to integrate the session. As a general guideline it is suggested that a period of twice the length of time you were actually lying in the web of light be allowed for integration.

11. Keep a written record of the experience in your Angelic journal. Essential knowledge and personal experiences can dissipate like a dream unless they are immediately written down. Include all your experiences, however fragmented, vague or nebulous they may have seemed to you. Enter fully into the experience with all your faculties: how did it make you feel? What was the most salient, prominent or striking feature of the initiation session? Do not be overly concerned if you cannot fully understand the experience right away; fragmentary information is often referenced again in subsequent meditations. Some experiences make no sense to you for weeks, months or even years, and so your journal becomes a special way of assimilating understanding. You must record the messages exactly as they were given to you, no editing! If you are more of a pictorial person, you might decide to draw pictures of your experiences, or if you are verbal to record them in spoken form. Never be concerned with your spelling or writing style; allow yourself literary freedom.

You do not need to have all the crystals for the web of light you have chosen. In fact you can just use the 'Archangel' aura essence mist for the therapy session. For more details on this and the use of all the other essences, please turn to the section entitled **Angelic Essences** (page 171).

You could also facilitate the Archangel web of light on others. Please see the section – **Using the Angelic Essences on Others – Angelic Essence Vibrational Transmission with Crystals** (page 174).

Energy Sweep

To free (cleanse) clients from the following:

Earthbound entities (hungry ghosts)
Negative entities (astral, other dimensions and other worlds)
Entity possession (astral, other dimensions and other worlds)
Negative entity thought forms and negative entity thought form shapes
Evil that has resulted from:
Misqualified human projection
Misqualified psychic projection
Misqualified astral projection
Psychic attack
Binding ties or cords, hooks and other energy drains
Body armouring
Negative karma – You also need to invoke and use Archangel Haniel's Glory – Angelic Communication aura essence, which brings in the Lords of Karma
Forces of anti-love – You need to invoke and use Archangel Chamuel's Embrace – Angelic Love aura essence.

Energy Sweep – Using Reiki and Archangel Michael

a) Spray your heart chakra and back with Archangel Michael's Empowerment – Angelic Protection aura essence.

b)   Mist your client's aura with Archangel Michael's Empowerment – Angelic Protection aura essence.

c)   Place Reiki protection around yourself using the power symbol by drawing the power symbol on the palm of each hand. Tap the hand three times and say the name three times. Draw a large power symbol over your entire body and say the name three times. Draw the power symbol over each master chakra, saying the name three times on each, starting from the crown and working downwards. Visualise a large power symbol over your back. Draw the power symbol on the soles of your feet to ground and protect you.

d)   Say a silent invocation and ask for the assistance of the Archangel Michael and his legions of light and the Angels from the 'Halls of Wisdom' and your Reiki guides. They will open a 'vortex' for you (to pass the entity etc. through). They will assist the 'entity' etc. towards the light…you have nothing more to do……leave it to the Archangel Michael etc.

e)   Make an energy 'net' by drawing the power symbol on your left hand, then the distance symbol, then the power symbol again. Repeat on the other hand. Really *feel* the energy net between your hands.

f)   Sweep the 'net' over your client, starting at the feet and moving up the body and over the head. As you do this, ask your client to focus on the word 'release'.

g)   Go to the 'vortex' and give the entity etc. which is caught in the net to Archangel Michael and the Angels from the 'Halls of Wisdom' and your Reiki guides. You may need to do this several times, each time making a new energy net.

h)   Ask for a blessing for all involved and draw the power symbol over the vortex to close it. This will seal and protect you and anyone else involved. Then completely detach yourself from the energies.

i)   Place a power symbol over the solar plexus of the client to seal the healing and enhance the effectiveness of the treatment. This will also balance the energy in the body, to stop feelings of disorientation in the client.

Room Cleansing using Reiki and Archangel Michael

a)   Say a silent invocation and ask for the assistance of the Archangel Michael and his legions of light and the Angels from the 'Halls of Wisdom' and your Reiki guides. They will open a 'vortex' for you (to pass the entity etc. through). They will assist the entity towards the light…you have nothing more to do…leave it to the Archangel Michael etc.

b)   Draw the power symbol on all the walls, floor, ceiling and in the centre of the room. Then draw the distance symbol to connect all the power symbols together. Use the following words "I ask that this room and the contents of this room be cleansed of all earthbound entities, negative entities, entity possession, negative entity thought forms, negative entity thought form shapes, evil, misqualified human projection, misqualified psychic projection, misqualified astral projection and psychic attack, etc".

c)   Draw the mental/emotional symbol in the centre of the room, over the distance symbol, and say "I dedicate this room to love, light, peace and healing. This room is now completely protected with Divine love and wisdom". Finish by drawing the power symbol over the mental/emotional and distance symbols.

Energy Sweep –
Assisted by Archangel Michael and his Legions of Light

a)   Spray your heart chakra and back with Archangel Michael's Empowerment – Angelic Protection aura essence.

b)   Mist your client's aura with Archangel Michael's Empowerment – Angelic Protection aura essence.

c)   Say a silent invocation and ask for the assistance of the Archangel Michael and his legions of light and the Angels from the 'Halls of Wisdom'. They will open a 'vortex' for you (to pass the entity etc. through). They will assist the 'entity' etc. towards the light…you have nothing more to do…leave it to the Archangel Michael etc.

d)   Visualise or feel an energy 'net' between your hands.

e)   Sweep the 'net' over your client, starting at the feet and moving up the body and over the head. As you do this, ask your client to focus on the word 'release'.

f)   Go to the 'vortex' and give the entity etc. which is caught in the net to Archangel Michael and the Angels from the 'Halls of Wisdom'. You may need to do this several times, each time visualising or feeling a new energy net.

g)   Ask for a blessing for all involved and ask Archangel Michael to close the vortex. This will seal and protect you and anyone else involved. Then completely detach yourself from the energies.

Room Cleansing –
Assisted by Archangel Michael and his Legions of Light

a)   Say a silent invocation and ask for the assistance of the Archangel Michael and his legions of light and the Angels from the 'Halls of Wisdom'. They will open a 'vortex' for you (to pass the entity etc. through). They will assist the entity towards the light…you have nothing more to do…leave it to the Archangel Michael etc.

b)   Mist the room with Archangel Michael essence. Use the following words "I ask that this room and the contents of this room be cleansed of all earthbound entities, negative entities, entity possession, negative entity thought forms, negative entity thought form shapes, evil, misqualified human projection, misqualified psychic projection, misqualified astral projection and psychic attack, etc. I now dedicate this room to love, light, peace and healing. This room is now completely protected with Divine love and wisdom". *The energy sweep is performed, if needed, during the scanning process, if attachments are found in the client's aura.*

Distant Healing

"If the dull substance of my flesh were thought, Injurious distance should not stop my way; For then, despite of space, I would be brought From limits far remote, where thou dost stay. No matter then, although my foot did stand Upon the farthest earth removed from thee, For nimble thought can jump both sea and land As soon as think the place where he would be". (Shakespeare, Sonnet 44, v 1-8)

Distant healing, as opposed to contact healing where your client is there with you, is an excellent way to begin practising as a therapist. It is also a very powerful way of working with the Archangels and has validity in its own right, as you do not need all the 'paraphernalia' of the third dimension (therapy room, couch, etc). Distant healing is also a great way of developing your awareness of the healing energies that surrounds us all on planet Earth. In its simplest form, absent healing can be to say a prayer for the person who has asked you for help. Keep the prayer simple and unconditional.

Planetary Healing

Many people who come to my courses express a fervent desire to help others, especially after seeing the terrible situations that plague our world. With global communication being almost instant we are all constantly bombarded by these images. Many people feel burdened by these visions of unimaginable human suffering and ask if there is any action they can take to help the situation, to ease the suffering and perhaps affect the outcome. In fact, at present, the whole of humanity is undergoing an intense spiritual transformation; we are about to make an evolutionary leap. This mass mystical awakening is unprecedented in the history of the earth.

Sending Planetary Healing – Angelic Alignment

Archangel Sandalphon is the guardian of the Earth and is in charge of earth healing and planetary group work, uniting heaven and earth. By way of holding the Divine presence on planet Earth, Sandalphon teaches us to have a grounded reality and balanced spirituality. Sandalphon's presence is always in the Kingdom (the Earth plane) and he does not move between the planes of existence, for he is so vast or tall that his energy spans all levels of the Tree of Life. In the Talmud it states 'Sandalphon's head reaches heaven'. Moses described him as being the 'tall Angel'. His presence reminds us that everything and everyone is sacred, everything is God. We are not separate from God, it is only an illusion of our small egos that makes us feel separate from God and each other.

When sending planetary healing, do not suppress your emotions, as that will only cause blockages in your subtle bodies and in time affect your health. Instead, focus fully on the feelings and emotions that the haunting images created within you personally. This will ease any feelings of distress you are holding and direct the healing energy to where it is needed most. Remember, all energy comes from God, so in the end we must let go and let God direct the energy.

1. You should be seated comfortably, either cross-legged on the floor or on a chair with your feet firmly planted on the floor. Imagine roots growing out of the soles of your feet to ground and strengthen you. Make sure you are breathing easily and naturally and that your own energy circuits are open and flowing smoothly.

2. Mist your palm chakras with Archangel Sandalphon's essence and use the following invocation: "Archangel Sandalphon, guardian of planet Earth and holder of the sacred presence, please activate and support the pranic life force available to me. Guide me in helping others with planetary healing".

3. Align yourself with Archangel Sandalphon, who is the source of the healing energies you will be using, and establish contact with the energy. You will normally feel Sandalphon's energy cascading in through your crown chakra and coursing downwards into your heart chakra, before flowing down your arms into your hands and flooding out of your palm chakras. Allow yourself to be completely surrounded, supported and nurtured by this energy. You will often see it as a sphere of rainbow-coloured light. If it feels appropriate to you at this point, allow the Archangel

189

Sandalphon's energy to flow downwards from your heart chakra and into your solar plexus, sacral and root chakras too. You are now ready to transmit the Angelic planetary healing energy.

4. See the energy as a swirling rainbow of light moving outwards from you towards the area of distress where you have chosen to direct it. See the situation and all the people involved absorbing this energy – you will see the area becoming illuminated with iridescent rainbow light. As you continue watching, become aware of all the other healers and planetary healing groups who are also sending out rainbows of hope. They are the children of light – the rainbow warriors of light. Allow your energy to fuse with theirs. Feel how the power intensifies as you all join together. Many of these rainbow warriors meditate every day and send out healing energy in the form of rainbows; they know instinctively that the planet and those in need will receive it in whatever form is appropriate to them. You will now feel as if you are part of this powerful angelically-guided rainbow energy. If you were to leave your body astrally and view the earth, you would see it etherically surrounded by millions of multicoloured lights that combine to make a brilliant rainbow web of light.

You may now choose to send healing energy to a client, family member or loved one, knowing that the energy they receive is blessed many times over because of all the other healers and healing groups who are also sending unconditional healing.

When you feel you have accomplished all you can in this session, allow yourself to detach from the energy of Archangel Sandalphon and ground, centre and focus yourself in the present moment, giving thanks for the experience.

You could also use your control crystal during the planetary healing session by misting it with the Archangel Sandalphon essence and directing the rainbow healing energy through the tip of your crystal.

Distant Healing – Client

For this technique you could use a clear quartz crystal with single termination to amplify the energy. If you have a control crystal, so much the better. Have a regular time and place to practise distant healing, the most effective times being dawn and dusk. Try to have a special room for distant healing work and keep it free from other vibrations and influences. Purify it with Angel of Light essence or have a large amethyst cluster to focus and cleanse the energies.

Client Responsibility

When people ask you to send absent healing for themselves or their loved ones, make sure they give you feedback on the situation and how it is developing. Weekly updates will be required for you to fully monitor the situation. This puts the responsibility on your client and further empowers them. Your client should also make themselves available to 'receive' at the same time as you are 'sending' the distant healing. They should join in the session by making themselves comfortable, lying or sitting down and asking their Guardian Angel to make them as receptive as possible. Tell them the session will take 30 minutes. They can play soothing music if they wish to.

1. You should be seated comfortably, either cross-legged on the floor or on a chair with your feet firmly planted on the floor. Imagine roots growing out of the soles of your feet to ground and strengthen you. Make sure you are breathing easily and naturally and that your own energy circuits are open and flowing smoothly.

2. Mist your palm chakras and control crystal (if using a crystal) with Archangel Sandalphon's essence and use the following invocation "Archangel Sandalphon, guardian of planet Earth and holder of the sacred presence, please activate and support the pranic life force available to me. Guide me in supporting (person's name) unconditionally with distant healing".

3. Align yourself with Archangel Sandalphon, who directs the source of the healing energies you will be using, and establish contact with the energy. You will normally feel Sandalphon's energy cascading in through your crown chakra and downwards to your heart chakra, before flowing down your arms into your hands and flooding out of your palm chakras (and out of the tip of your control crystal if you have chosen to use one). Allow yourself to be completely surrounded and supported by this energy. You will often see it as a sphere of swirling rainbow-coloured light. You are now ready to transmit the Angelic distant healing energy.

4. Sit quietly meditating on the energy flowing through you and begin to focus your intent on your client – the person to whom you are sending the distant healing. Having a picture of them or a piece of their hair, or maybe just their name on a piece of paper will help you focus on them even if you have never met them. See the energy as a swirling rainbow of light moving outwards from you towards them. Continue focusing on your client and you will feel a definite contact being made with the person. This may take a few minutes to happen, but it will happen if they really want to receive the healing energy. Once contact is made, take a few moments to gain energetic rapport and attunement, then allow the rainbow light to make a very strong positive connection with your client.

5. Now you have made the contact, just allow the rainbow healing energy of Archangel Sandalphon to flow through you to them. This usually takes 30 minutes. Hold your concentration on the person; the more you focus on them, the stronger the distant healing session will be. Be mindful of any insights into the reason for your client's dis-ease. You could also send your client positive loving thoughts, such as "You are perfectly healed on all levels with Divine unconditional love and wisdom" or "You are a beautiful being of rainbow light, take all you need from this distant healing session for your perfect mind, your perfect body, your perfect health".

6. When you feel you have accomplished all you can in this 30-minute session, allow yourself to detach from the energy of Archangel Sandalphon. Ground, centre and focus yourself in the present moment, giving thanks for the experience. If using a control crystal, retract the rainbow light back into the crystal.

Grounding

When I have taught how to send distant healing on my courses (I have been teaching these courses since 1986), I sometimes see students swaying back and forth during the 'sending' part of the session. I have also observed this occasionally in certain students during meditation sessions. The reason for the swaying and rocking motions that happen spontaneously to some people during certain forms of meditation is entirely due to them being ungrounded. They have not earthed themselves properly before the session and are unable to actually channel the energy outwards towards the 'receiver'. If you find yourself swaying back and forth with the energy, simply stop the absent healing or meditation session and ground yourself down into the earth, otherwise you will be overloading your nervous system and chakras.

To ground yourself, just imagine etheric roots growing from the bottom of your feet; feel them reaching deep down into the earth. Allow any excess energy or tension held within your body and subtle bodies to just simply drain away.

191

To conclude the grounding process, go through your seven master chakras in sequential order, starting with the crown, and feel each chakra suitably closing and sealing. When you feel sufficiently grounded and centred, feel your chakras and aura being protected by a large sphere of golden light. To complete the grounding session, stamp your feet.

Karuna

There are numerous other absent healing methods which we need to explore further. But first, what is distant healing, how does it work and why does it work?

Sending a distant healing session to your client is really meditation in action. It is an act of compassion also known as *Karuna*. The word *karuna* comes from the *Sanskrit* language and literally means any action which you consciously take to alleviate the suffering of others. This is the most important step you can take on the path to enlightenment and spiritual transformation. *Karuna* causes the *Bodhichitta* to flow, which then resides in your innermost heart where it becomes "the path of service" until one day you find you are a fully fledged *Bodhisattva* – just like Avalokiteshvara, who could be described as the quintessential Bodhisattva, for he is the Bodhisattva of Compassion and compassion is the distinguishing mark of a Bodhisattva. His mantra is *'Om mani padme hum'*. He appears in many diverse forms; you may have come across him as the white-robed Kwan Yin.

Universal Connection

To understand how and why distant healing works we can look at the philosophy of the ancients, in particular the Chinese. The Chinese see human beings as a microcosm within the universal macrocosm. The principle demonstrated by the inner workings of humans is reflected in the universal relationships of energetic flow. They call this energy qi or chi; they give its explanation as a unique substance which flows from the environment into the physical body. The Chinese feel that qi is an energy of both nutritive and cellular-organisational characteristics which supersedes the energetic contributions of ingested food, water and air. Therefore this qi is a type of subtle energy which permeates our universe. As everyone exists on several levels of reality at the same time and all energy comes from the Source (God) and since the Source is outside the reality of space and time and is on all levels simultaneously, 'it' is not subject to 'normal' scientific laws. When we, as individualised aspects of God, raise our consciousness through meditation from the purely physical plane we can step outside the rigid physical patterns and influence the flow of qi instantaneously within the universe. This is why the power of prayer is so effective; it is a method of influencing the cosmic currents to flow in a particular direction. Harmony and health are not just of the physical body, but rely on harmonious cosmic currents. When we become dis-eased, we block the flow of energy on all levels of our being. Distant healing, or any form of healing, allows energy to be redirected by the healer, which clears the client's patterns of dis-ease which have blocked their harmonious flow in relationship to the universe. Researchers in the field of psychoneuroimmunology are examining the subtle-energetic links between emotions and immunological function. It has already been established that physiological links between human emotions and illness do exist. Various researchers who have examined the link between emotions and illness have found a strong association between depression, grief and the overall suppression of immune functioning.

Distant Healing – Client Physically Absent

Prepare for and give a full Archangel healing session, just as if your client was actually with you in the therapy room. You will be amazed at what happens. Always send the distant healing without any attachments to the outcome – just allow your emotions to soften and be in the energy of compassion. You may also find yourself transported to your client. Or your client may report later that you have visited them in their dreams and given them some form of healing or instructions. Your clients may also have visions of you in their waking state. My clients and students have reported my 'visitations' to them so many times that it seems absolutely 'normal' to me and them.

Distant Healing – Crystal Web of Light

Use a photograph of your client and place it into the centre of a crystal web of light in a triangular configuration using three single-terminated clear quartz points. The terminations should all point towards the photograph. You should mist the crystals with your chosen essence – Archangel Raphael or Archangel Sandalphon essences are very good for absent healing and you could use Archangel Michael if your client felt protection was needed. Leave the Angelic web in place for as long as your client requires absent healing or protection.

Distant Healing – Pyramid Energy

Write your client's name on a piece of paper and place your distant healing crystal on top of it. This works best with a clear quartz pyramid or clear quartz standing point. The point upwards will channel the positive energy towards them. You should mist the crystal pyramid with your chosen essence – Archangel Raphael or Archangel Sandalphon essences are very good for absent healing and you could use Archangel Michael if your client felt protection was needed. Leave the pyramid in place for as long as your client requires absent healing or protection.

Distant Healing – Etheric Temple

By creating a sacred space on the inner planes you will be taking a vital step in the evolution of your soul. By constructing your 'Etheric Temple' you must understand it is not just some pleasant exercise in your imagination, but a necessary step upwards in your evolutionary development, so you must approach it with due reverence and care. You will eventually build the 'tower without foundation' which will give you access to all levels of the reality we call God. You exist on several planes of reality concurrently (as does everyone else), but because of the path you have chosen of personal or spiritual development you will have raised your vibrational rate through self-reflection and meditation to a point where this sanctuary of transformation is the next step.

We will use guided visualisation to create our 'Etheric Temple', so you need to think before you begin this exercise what is sacred to you personally; hopefully you will have already created a sacred space on the earth plane where you keep your Angelic altar, so that will have already given you some valuable insights and inspiration.

When you are guided to your temple you can either become the architect of your temple and use your imagination to construct all aspects of it, including any sacred objects you wish to place within its walls, or you can allow your subconscious to unfold it for you, including any scenes or events that need to take place. This can include meeting your Angelic guides. Either method of constructing your 'Etheric Temple' will reflect your soul's evolution up to this point in time, just as your sacred space on the earth plane reflects your soul's evolution on the physical plane. Your 'Etheric Temple' will evolve over time, just as your sacred space on the physical plane has, as you

193

have added more sacred objects and removed those which no longer have meaning or feel right for you.

If at first you find it difficult to visualise, keep practising, as this is an important step in developing your imagination and ultimately becoming the architect of your own spiritual home.

Your 'Etheric Temple' will be your sacred space, a place you can go to receive or send healing or even momentarily during your day when you need your own 'space'. Your angels and guides will meet you in your temple and your 'physical' clients can also visit you by invitation, unless you are a very gregarious individual who has an 'open house' policy.

You could select an Archangel essence to support you in this exercise; choose one that feels intuitively right for you at this present moment in time. It is also fine if you choose to do this exercise without an essence.

I will give you instructions for using an essence, as it will give you valuable insights, as will the whole exercise into your present level of awareness and spiritual growth. Remember, in this exercise there are no right or wrong choices, only pathways for you to explore on your journey.

Etheric Temple Visualisation

1. Sit in a comfortable steady posture with the spine and neck held erect but not tense. This means that the base of the spine needs to be higher than the knees, thus tilting the pelvis forwards to a position where the spine naturally remains upright when relaxed. The easiest way of doing this is to put a small, firm cushion beneath the base of the spine. The psychic current must be able to flow unimpeded from the base of the spine to the top of the head.

    Alternatively, sit in a straight-backed chair with your feet firmly planted on the ground.

2. Command the mind (ego) to be still for a specific length of time.

3. Forget about the past and future, come alive in the eternal now.

4. Align yourself with the source of Angelic energies you will be using by spraying your intuitively chosen Archangel essence on your left hand, then spreading the essence over the palms of both hands. Then sweep your hands through your aura. As you do so, establish contact with the Archangelic energy.

5. Consciously tune in to your normal breathing pattern.

6. Allow your awareness of your breathing to expand effortlessly.

7. In the middle of your breathing, experience your heartbeat.

8. Experience your sense of balance as gravity pulls on your body and your muscles respond with perfect precision to keep upright; feel your connection to the earth by sending down etheric roots if needed.

9. Allow your awareness to expand to encompass the whole of your body and aura.

10. As you inhale slowly, consciously focus upon the sensation of energy flowing up from the earth into your root chakra and then on upwards in sequential order through each chakra...now as you exhale slowly, open up to receive a spontaneous flow of energy from above...experience a downflow of light, insight and power into your body...moving through each chakra in turn until all seven chakras have been illuminated from above...and

you are empty of air...then again, without effort, let your breath spontaneously come rushing into you...allow energy to flow up from the earth into your chakras...all the way to the crown...rather than just visualising this, see if you can actually feel this experience happening inside you...

11. Again, after the full inhale, reverse the experience...opening to the downflow of universal energy into your personal energy system...continue with this pattern for a number of breaths...

12. Once you have cleared the energy in your spine and chakras and feel you have a good earth connection and Higher Self connection (the downflow of light) you are now ready to begin to focus on your third eye chakra; this will improve your visualisation abilities.

13. Allow your third eye chakra to open and feel receptive. You are now ready to start the visualisation.

14. Visualise a star cluster set against the background of a dark velvety night sky. Perhaps you recall seeing a photograph of deep space taken from a high intensity telescope...notice how colourful the stars look in their swirling patterns...feel how familiar they seem to you...from somewhere deep inside your subconscious you remember seeing them before...you notice that one of the stars is twinkling very brightly...and you feel yourself irresistibly drawn towards that star...as you gaze upon it, it begins to grow in size, colour and intensity...until the light fills the whole of your vision...slowly the light becomes less bright as your eyes get used to gazing upon it...and you become aware of the particles of light energy moving and dancing...slowly the clouds of energy particles separate and you see before you two huge ancient stone pillars...walk towards them...stand between them and place each of your hands on a pillar...as you activate the sacred energy... you see the temple which has been in ruins awaiting your return begin to re-build itself before your eyes...you can now allow it to rebuild naturally from your subconscious cellular memory or use your focused intent to rebuild the temple to your own design.

15. Once the etheric temple is rebuilt, or your experience is over, allow yourself to return to your normal consciousness by closing, sealing and protecting your chakras and aura. Ground, centre and focus yourself into your normal everyday waking reality.

Write down immediately in your Angelic journal all you have seen, sensed or felt throughout the whole experience. Do not leave out any details.

Part Seven

A–Z of Crystals

Agate (Blue Lace and Botswana) – Agate is used for general strengthening, grounding, stabilizing and centering of physical energies. It can be used for universal healing, bringing vitality, balance and inner harmony. It is slow to work, but agate is especially good for animals, plants and children. In historic times, agate was used in drinking water to heal the body; it also eliminates thirst. If you are using agates 'magically' they should have appropriate or special natural 'markings' on them appertaining to and pertinent to their use. Blue lace agate is also known as 'Avalonite': it facilitates clear and truthful verbal expression. Self-empowerment is accomplished through voice. Blue lace agate provides willingness to express thoughts and feelings, known or unknown. Botswana agate is strengthening and generally healing to the physical body by bringing stability. The chalcedony enhydros, or water agates, have a unique significance; they are masses which consist of a shell of cloudy-white chalcedony within which is sealed a quantity of water. This can often be heard splashing about when the pebble is shaken. Sometimes the water is visible. These enhydros are mostly found in Brazil. They are very useful for healing emotional trauma; this is facilitated by holding the enhydro in the receptive hand, or placing it over any painful area of the body until all painful sensation has stopped. Enhydros can be used to heal all fluid functions of the body. They work quickly and have been successfully used in the treatment of liver disorders. The cleansing effect is very beneficial on all organs of the body. Enhydros have a cleansing, supportive, watery, female energy. They equate to the primeval waters, the symbol of the collective unconscious. They have been carried as talismans by pregnant women since the dawn of civilisation.

Ajoite – Ajoite is turquoise in colour and occurs as an inclusion within quartz. It is an exceedingly beautiful, sweet, gentle, feminine, nurturing crystal. It is a healer for the emotions of the heart. It teaches you to talk from the heart. It loves the sharing of emotional wisdom and heartfelt communication; it loves togetherness and family. It brings kindred spirits together and gets them communicating. It soothes the nerves and 'nourishes' the central nervous system; thus it is helpful in healing situations of nervous stress, tension or breakdown. It can help to stop panic attacks and emotional shock. The colour turquoise subdues fevers and cools inflammation of the nerves; it is particularly good for the pain of neuralgia. Ajoite helps you strengthen your voice: a person's voice is a good indication of overall health and emotional well-being. It gently purifies and cleanses the throat chakra; you can tell if someone's throat is blocked, as they have to keep clearing it every few minutes. Ajoite teaches true communication: not idle chatter, but purposeful thought-out communication. It is about personal expression combined with personal responsibility. It aids focused meditation and communication with the Angelic realms. Its peaceful turquoise blue colour is measureless. It embodies the essence of shunyata, the vast blue emptiness, stretching in all directions, absolutely clear, pristine and radiant. By this blue sky stretching into infinity we can gain an understanding, a feeling for the expansiveness and freedom which could be ours if we did not allow our horizons to become narrow, clouded and limited, if we did not permit our minds to become fixated and hypnotized by cravings and worries centred on what really are empty passing phenomena. Physically it has been used therapeutically to ease fatigue, weight problems, allergies, diabetes, the digestive system, muscle cramps, heart disease, high blood pressure, cancer, shallow breathing problems, sore throats, neck-ache, thyroid problems, hearing problems, asthma, headaches, nervous complaints, nightmares and dizziness.

Alexandrite – A vortex crystal, alexandrite will, if you let it, transform your life into a joyful Angelic experience. It has to be said that I am talking about the very rare colour change natural chrysoberyl called alexandrite which, when faceted, is pure Angelic magic, pure joy, pure transformation! The colour in daylight is green and under incandescent lamp red. You can also get lab-grown gems which have very similar properties and a magical colour change of magenta-red indoors and deep blue-green in sunlight. There are also alexandrite crystal clusters, but these do not have a colour change. Natural alexandrite which displays a colour change and is pure enough to facet is very rare. Alexandrite is used for dissolving fear and guiding us through life changes, instilling the energy of hope and optimism: this it teaches by the incredible energy change it displays through its own colour transformation. It teaches us to 'shift frequencies' and move into a higher octave of awareness, so we can go on inner and outer journeys to discover the higher self. These soul explorations, though intense, will bring enlightenment. Its vortex energy also awakens our inner angel that resides within our hearts by igniting the Divine flame that dwells in each and every one of us. By connecting us back to our Source, we soar into the highest possible dimensions of love. Alexandrite helps you to interpret your dreams and visions, especially when combined with danburite; in fact, when combined with danburite it gives not only dream recall but lucid dreaming. Alexandrite is a crystal which must be taken very seriously though, because in using it one can easily be caught up in the energy field of pure rapture, pure joy, pure bliss – this is where we must be aware of others on this planet who are not in this energy field – we must take responsibility for our actions and bring the high, joyful, ecstatic energy down and anchor it on the earth plane to facilitate mankind's evolution into the higher realms of love and light.

Amblygonite – A very rare mineral. Energetically amblygonite is soothing and inspiring to the mental body, giving a flowing graceful energy of calm and peace. It is very suited to those of an artistic or theatrical nature and gives Divine inspiration to those of us who need to, or wish to, express ourselves via writing or poetry. Indeed it is so inspirational that you may find you are almost overwhelmed by the passionate experience, as the ideas and information flow so fast as to cause 'overload'. Using these stones for inspiration is like being tuned into the creative force of the cosmic universal mind of God/Goddess. Amblygonite will, with conscious direction, clear the etheric body and can be used to activate any chakra, especially the higher centres above the head. It brings the consciousness of the higher self into the spiritual body and sends your intent out into the universal streams of energy. This crystal will also balance your emotional body and is wonderful to work with when you wish to be heart-to-heart with someone you love. Its message is 'follow your heart, for that is where true joy lies'.

Amethyst – Amethyst aids comprehension and enhances the faculty of judgement by stimulating the spiritual body, which ultimately brings detachment from worldly mundane concerns. It is a transformational healer, which will bring spiritual growth and Divine understanding. It purifies all the chakra centres and can be used anywhere on the body and on all levels of the aura, giving relief from addictions and addictive traits within the personality. Amethyst works as an amplifier of healing and spiritual energies. When consciously directed, it will break down and transform blocked or stuck energies. Its pain-relieving properties have been demonstrated over and over again, so much so that it never seems to fail in drawing out pain.

Angelite – Used for conscious connection to the Angelic realms via attunement to the heavenly vibration of this blue stone. Angelite brings peace, tranquillity, calm and focus to the highest realms of light. This makes it easier for us to focus our energies towards the heavenly realms and find within our hearts the peace that passes all understanding.

Apatite (Yellow) – These wonderful yellow crystals can be used to energise the solar plexus chakra, which then eases any problems associated with an underactive solar plexus. Blocked, stuck or stagnant energy in the solar plexus is exhibited in a myriad ways, the most common being a lack of energy, depression, M.E., feelings of low self-worth, nightmares, soul-loss, poor digestion and food assimilation, lack of concentration, poor learning abilities, low stamina, restlessness, memory loss and a short attention span. Yellow apatite is the great eliminator; it cleans and removes waste from the system. Faulty elimination is the cause of the beginning of most disease. Apatite also works on the pancreas, liver, gall-bladder, spleen and middle stomach. The liver is known as the seat of anger, where our emotional upsets and hurts are stored; yellow apatite can help with the release of this stored anger.

Aphrodite – Also known as sphaerocobaltite or cobaltocalcite or cobaltian-calcite. Although this ravishingly beautiful gem species has been around for some time, it is becoming very popular as of late. This hot-pink gem that many crystal healers and jewellery designers are attracted to has become better known as Aphrodite, after the Greek goddess of love. It is found as crusts and small crystals. Large crystals are rare. Aphrodite is a extraordinary gift of love from Mother Earth. It is a true love stone, healing all old heartaches from all lifetimes – past, present and future. It helps with the formation of new friendships, especially when trust in other human beings has been damaged. It fully activates the heart chakra – in fact this crystal emanates love. Just being in the energy field of this crystal brings about powerful realisations of the true vibration of love, the truth being that every soul on the planet is part of ourselves, so as we do to others, in all our relationships, whether by action, word or thought, it is projected at ourselves. This is because every soul is a 'fragment' of God/Goddess and how we relate to others is how we relate to God/Goddess…if we project hate, anger, resentment, bitterness etc. at others we directly project it at God/Goddess, the original creative force in the universe. Only by treating others with unconditional love and compassion can we ever hope to heal ourselves into wholeness. Physically, it induces states of deep relaxation, releases stress, aids healthy cellular development and is excellent as a meditation stone.

Aquamarine – The 'gem of the sea' derives its name from 'sea water'. Legends say that it is the treasure of mermaids, with the power to keep sailors safe at sea. The ancients also believed aquamarine gave protection against the wiles of the devil and to dream of aquamarine meant that you would meet new friends. Aquamarine gives freedom from the impressions and influences of others. Calming, soothing to the emotions, cooling and an excellent meditation stone, it helps you go with your own 'flow', finding your perfect karmic path with courage, fortitude and, most of all, compassion for yourself. It will shield the aura from anger, hatred, envy, jealousy, hostility and the fearful emotions of others. It opens the gateway to understanding the archetypal realms, gives mental and emotional stability, promotes greater understanding of the dramas we may be caught up in and facilitates being able to step out of the drama to see the underlying emotion. Archetypes are universal themes, or models, of the 'human condition'. They are illustrated through myths, legends, fairy stories and even modern plays and films; they serve to provide us with an understanding of our emotional experiences – both what we are and what we would like to become. Once you understand your 'drama' or 'life role' you can then change it for one that is more in harmony with the life you really desire. Aquamarine also identifies the underlying patterns or miasms we may have embedded into our neural pathways, which are outwardly projected as particular behaviours; we can choose at any moment to discard those which no longer serve us. Aquamarine teaches us to take up our emotional reins and the emotional challenges that face us every day, in order that we can choose a different direction and move into a new stage of authentic development. Aquamarine is very stimulating and we find we can safely use this stone on any area of the body; it will release stored stress, induce peace and healing resonance. The stillness of aquamarine calms the panic that can follow emotional shock. It stops the person running away from their hurt self, humiliation and the painful situation. It is a good stone to use when encountering problems in relationships. It encourages you to be able to speak what is in your heart. It is useful in overcoming self-sabotage and in centering oneself.

Azeztulite – Azeztulite is among the highest vibrations in the mineral kingdom. It activates the third eye and crown chakras, as well as the chakras above the head in the etheric body. It stimulates the three ascension points. Azeztulites are stones which are said to have been engineered etherically to carry the energies and communications of a group soul called the 'Azez', who are in non-physical form and station themselves underground in power spots.

Beryl (Red) – Red beryl is extremely rare, vibrant and beautiful. With conscious attunement this crystal facilitates, activates and supports the pranic life force available to you by reclaiming your original soul mandala, your genetic blueprint, and activating latent DNA strands. Thus, by increasing your own personal energy through conscious evolution, you are able to reclaim and balance your personal and sexual power through the integration of karmic lessons and clearing of miasms that may have lodged in the root and sacral chakras. It helps you view and remove curses, psychic hookups, negative entities, negative entity thought forms, implants, misqualified human projection, misqualified astral projection, psychic attacks, binding ties and ghost prints. It heightens your awareness of the devic energies of the planet and facilitates sacred pathworkings with the crystal, plant and animal kingdoms. It also increases awareness of higher vibration interdimensional and galactic beings who have consciously chosen to work with mankind at this pivotal point in human evolution. These beings can help with your positive evolution and teach you to close the negative portals to the lower astral realms which have been causing the unprecedented lowering of humanity's vibration during the last decades. These tears in the etheric web of the earth have mostly been caused by pollution on all levels, including pollution from human minds, especially by those who are not spiritually clean or those who are spiritually manipulative.

Calcite (Pink) – Sometimes referred to as manganese calcite, this is perfect for the heart, releasing old fears and grief, bringing in the essence of unconditional love. Pink calcite, when consciously directed, works dynamically on the heart chakra, gently cleansing and then transmuting all stored putrefied negative issues of self-worth, self-confidence, self-acceptance and so on. It will allow the integration of positive energy within all levels of the chakra system, the positive energy being love, compassion, understanding of unity within diversity, bringing tolerance, forgiveness and ultimately the complete expression of universal love and self-love to every corner of the microcosm and macrocosm. We are all a reflection of the whole and the more love we can hold within our own being, the more will ultimately be reflected outwards to all life and returned to us magnified. Pink calcite relieves all stress, tension and anxiety, especially about our physical body. Its energy is such that it just melts and dissolves our resistance to loving ourselves enough to honour our body as the temple of our soul. This means taking care of ourselves and choosing food that nurtures us, rather than listening to the negative ego, which only seeks instant gratification, regardless of the long-term detrimental effects. Pink calcite is also useful after a person has been assaulted in any way, or if they have had an operation or dentistry.

Calcite (Yellow) – Joyful, agile, uplifting and expansive, yellow calcite activates, cleanses and aligns the solar plexus chakra, which aids mental clarity and concentration. It will balance your will power by the right use of your Divine will. It brings wisdom, honesty and expansion to the thought processes. Its energy is penetrating and cleansing. Cleansing means purification which induces healing. Yellow calcite is the great eliminator, thus it can aid digestion and cellular regeneration.

Celestite – This will be your guardian and celestial contact initiator. It will teach you to 'journey' freely to the celestial realms and find inspiration and vision that will refresh your life. It even dares you to become authentic and dance in intense ecstasy with your soul. Celestite allows you to discover your soul connection with your guardian angel: it will bestow faith in yourself and the confidence to move ahead with grace and ease. This helps you to formulate a plan to improve your life and recreate your future with ease, learning new perspectives and reaching your highest potential.

Celestite (Bi-coloured) – The bi-coloured celestite tabular point from Ohio will be your guardian and celestial contact initiator as it elevates your vibrational rate. It will teach you to 'journey' freely to the celestial realms and find original inspiration, inner joy and exquisite visions which will refresh your life. It even dares you to become authentic by releasing your fears and feelings of separation, so that you dance in intense ecstasy with your soul as you align to the rarified currents of the Angelic domain. Celestite allows you to discover your soul connection with your Angels: it will bestow faith in yourself and the confidence to move ahead with grace and ease. This helps you to formulate a plan to improve your life and recreate your future with ease, learning new perspectives and reaching your highest potential as a 'Member of the Family of Light'.

Charoite – Charoite is a stone of vast spiritual transformation and deep personal healing; it activates the *Bodhisattva* energy. Whatever methods one uses to bring it about, the *Bodhichitta* can arise and establish itself firmly within one's innermost spiritual heart. Here it grows and becomes the 'path of service'. There are aspirant Bodhisattvas, who are people trying to 'act' as Bodhisattvas, keeping the Bodhisattvas' precepts, which basically are to *solely pledge to be the unfailing champion and guardian of all life in its battle to overcome suffering'*. Bodhisattvas normally compose their own vows or can use a formula used by previous Bodhisattvas. However, it is one thing to 'feel' the Bodhichitta arise and a great leap of faith and love to 'live' the Bodhisattva vows. Charoite can activate and balance the crown chakra. It has also been known to fully activate and integrate the heart, third eye and throat chakras. This stone has also been used to facilitate past life recall. Charoite helps infants to sleep peacefully and will give protection from nightmares and insomnia. It releases deep hidden fears. Soothing to the body, it will reduce heat and fevers. Charoite transmutes the symptoms of dis-ease.

Cinnabar – Cinnabar activates the kundalini energy and enhances the pranic life force. It teaches us that challenges are merely encounters for us to use as positive learning experiences. It helps with the sudden shifts in human consciousness and evolution that are very prevalent at this pivotal point in human evolution. Cinnabar really helps you rise above the mundane world and see through the veils of illusion into the heart of the matter. It strengthens the heart chakra and allows for the downflow of energy known as Divine grace. As the heart chakra becomes more open and free-flowing with cosmic pranic energy, the capability to unconditionally love oneself and others is substantially increased, along with a greater flow of life force or chi to all the organs it supplies. At a psychological level, the heart chakra deals with the emotions that bind individuals in various loving relationships. The act of nurturing is fed by the different emotional feelings generated by the heart chakra. Feelings of love, compassion and empathy are a direct outpouring of spiritual growth, therefore the heart chakra is important in developing higher levels of consciousness. When these elements are lacking in the personality, it indicates a severe dysfunction or energy block within the heart chakra.

Coral (Red) – Coral is known in Sanskrit as prawal and moonga in Hindi. Generally expressed as being the axial skeleton of the coral polyp, which gives the impression of being an internal skeleton, similar to the bones of our bodies, coral is better described as being a scaffolding upon the surface of which boneless animals live as a colony. The composition of coral is almost wholly calcium carbonate with about three per cent magnesium carbonate and possibly a trace of iron oxide. Red coral is to be used for virility, fertility, courage, physical strength and stamina, endurance and fulfilment of goals, passion and vitality. It is said to strengthen the immune system, healing the skeleton and muscular systems. It balances the bladder and kidney meridians, providing beneficial healing for the emotional cleansing system. It instills the qualities of leadership and self-confidence when suitably worn or carried. It will speed up the healing process of wounds or bruises, purify the blood and help reduce fevers. Wearing coral is said to bring good fortune and one is never possessed by evil spirits or bothered by ghosts, nightmares, storms, lightning or bad vibrations. Evil spirits cannot affect the wearer, nor will they suffer from the bad effects of the evil eye. It heals the muscular system, blood and immune system and helps with fertility and night sweats.

Danburite (Blue) – Blue danburite is a product of advanced twentieth century technology. In high-temperature near-vacuum conditions, atoms of pure gold are pyroelectrically bonded with top grade clear danburite, creating these highly energized crystals. The bonding process of the danburite and pure gold co-mingles the two substances in a permanent way, which results in the dazzling original colour and unique therapeutic properties which can help one to swiftly connect to the communication currents of the Angelic domain. It will also promote lucid dreaming and give a joyful connection to the Angelic realms during dream states, giving one access to the serenity and inner wisdom that can be obtained by journeying to the Angelic Temples. Danburite can facilitate one's ability to act with a compassionate heart and an activated mind, guided by the true wisdom of one's connection to spirit. In meditation, blue danburites are powerful aids to the attainment of higher states, because of their natural resonance with the higher frequencies of the human vibrational spectrum.

Danburite (Clear) – The brilliance of danburite carries a very high vibration of the supreme ray; it works to stimulate the third, fourth, fifth eye and crown chakras, plus the 8th to 14th chakras in the etheric body: this connects you to the communication currents of the Angelic domain. Danburite can activate the heart chakra and integrate it with these higher energies. It will also promote lucid dreaming. The brilliance that danburite carries is not a colour, it is the original light; not an earthly vibration, but cosmic light that clears away any cloudiness in a person's aura to add lustre and beauty. Danburite can facilitate one's ability to act with a compassionate heart and an activated mind, guided by the true wisdom of one's connection to spirit. It is said to be useful to those who wish to consciously access inner guidance. In meditation, danburites are powerful aids to the attainment of higher states, because of their natural resonance with the higher frequencies of the human vibrational spectrum. We use this stone when we want to bring about change, major or minor, in our lives. Danburite allows us to wipe the slate clean, to start again. The energy of pure danburite will allow us to move on in a new direction. This can be on any level: physical outer changes, emotional changes or spiritual changes. It is good for those who are making the transition from life to death

Danburite (Pink) – This can help one to connect to the communication currents of the Angelic domain. It will also promote lucid dreaming. Pink danburite has the purity of the trinity, love, power and wisdom. It clears away any cloudiness in a person's aura to add lustre and beauty. In everyday use, when worn or carried, danburite will give a joyful connection to the Angelic realms, giving one access to serenity and inner wisdom in one's daily encounters. Danburite can facilitate one's ability to act with a compassionate heart and an activated mind, guided by the true wisdom of one's connection to spirit. In meditation danburites are powerful aids to the attainment of higher states, because of their natural resonance with the higher frequencies of the human vibrational spectrum. We use this stone when we want to bring about change, major or minor, in our lives. Danburite allows us to wipe the slate clean, to start again. The energy of pure danburite will allow us to move on in a new direction. This can be on any level: physical outer changes, emotional changes or spiritual changes. It is good for those who are making the transition from life to death

'El Chorro', the Spanish Azeztulite – Each azeztulite carries its own energy, but links in to all the other azeztulites. Each is etherically engineered and guided by a group of interdimensional, extraterrestrial beings collectively called the 'Azez', which roughly translates in the language of light as 'the nameless light' or the light from the 'Great Central Sun'. The El Chorro area the azeztulite comes from is a 'power vortex' and above it is anchored Archangel Sandalphon's etheric temple/retreat. Initial working with El Chorro azeztulite would suggest it tunes you in to the energy stream of the 'Great White Brotherhood'. This life stream (dimension) is inhabited by Ascended

Masters, Archangels and other beings of Love and Light who are also collectively known as the 'Hierarchy'. In group work each participant had an activation of bright white light all round, inside and above their head. This activated the silver cords from everyone's crown chakras as they were gathered up and stretched upwards through the white light. Others who have worked with the El Chorro azeztulite have experienced profound life-changing encounters with Angelic beings. Sleeping with the El Chorro azeztulite brings profound lucid dreaming.

Fluorite (Purple) – Purple fluorite is an excellent meditation stone, due to its colour and crystal nature, very often revealed as the double pyramid formation. The purpose of meditation is to calm and focus the mind. But what is the mind? The mind is neither visible nor tangible. It does not exist in the physical body, as does the brain, but in the astral body. Its magnitude cannot be measured, for it carries all feeling, ideas and impressions for this life and from previous lives. Meditation practice will unleash your immense potential; it helps you to clear your mind and improve your concentration. This improves your health and can rejuvenate your body.

Gem Silica – Also known as druzy chrysocolla, it is a combination of chrysocolla and quartz. The colour is the most amazing Mediterranean sky blue. Gem silica is a rock composed of agatized chrysocolla with a crust of small sparkling quartz crystals. This wonderful crystal, with its unique synergy of powerful crystal energies, offers us the superb potential for past life healing of deep hidden problems related to negative emotional states and deep fears associated with personal power and how we can misuse it. Therefore it is a most beneficial cleansing crystal which, when laid on the witness point, will release karmic miasms – crystallized old patterns of dis-ease and decay which we may have carried over from previous lives. It is also a good 'witness' stone for group work and will bring the energy of living in universal harmony as brothers and sisters, sharing our Mother the Earth with every living creature. In this way we will be able to witness the birth of a new world of love, beauty, trust, wisdom and harmony.

Goethite in Amethyst – Deep purple amethyst is a transformational healer which will bring spiritual growth and Divine understanding. It purifies all the chakra centres and can be used anywhere on the body and on all levels of the aura, giving relief from addictions and addictive traits within the personality. It works as an amplifier of healing and spiritual energies. When consciously directed it will break down and transform blocked or stuck energies. It also helps protect from over-indulgences which have lodged in the emotional body, it calms the mind and thereby aids spiritual and personal growth, giving understanding into the cause of the indulgence. Amethyst aids comprehension and enhances the faculty of judgement by stimulating the spiritual body, which ultimately brings detachment from worldly concerns. It helps you to achieve self-discipline and high standards in life. Amethyst encourages you to become your own leader and master. It is full of originality and inspiration and is a great teacher. Combining power and humility, it will instil these qualities in those who wear it and work with it. Amethyst brings spiritual dedication, which makes it a powerful and positive meditation stone. The goethite is strengthening and empowering. It advances latent channelling abilities. It clears the pathway for necessary action by exposing flaws, corruption, negativity and shams. It sustains life and the vital life force. It is used to restore a person's vibrancy and vitality, which will lead to the resonance of perfect health, harmony and balance. Goethite in amethyst can provide the energy to break down barriers which have held up your spiritual progress. It helps you to conquer anxieties and phobias.

Gold – Pure gold helps you access higher knowledge. It has always had an association with wealth, money, energy, power, status and the sun. Gold indicates treasure: the higher treasure of the soul's experience of indestructibility. It never tarnishes and always remains pristine beyond corruption. It reminds you of your true immortal self, which not only lives for ever but is beyond the mundane day-to-day pettiness and corruption of the physical plane. Parasites are unable to hang on to the energy of fine gold, which makes it very useful in healing. It helps you overcome, subdue and release any kind of parasitic entity or infestation on all levels. It is strengthening, comforting and uplifting, which makes it beneficial for depression, both physical and psychological. It eases suicidal tendencies, it raises your feelings of self-worth and aids you in using your personal power wisely.

Herderite – Herderite is very expansive and can elevate your vibrational rate exceptionally quickly, which can immediately activate out-of-body experiences. The golden herderite has a strong focused pulsing quality that can be too powerful for some sensitive souls. It is not recommended to be worn or carried on the body; it is best kept as a meditation stone. But the pale blue to lilac herderite activates the crown and third eye chakras and will enhance clairvoyance, telepathic abilities, channelling and trans-channelling. For those who can attune to and integrate crystal energies with ease and responsibility, this stone can be very joyful! It is excellent for those interested in exploring the universal web of life. It has been used for past life work, as well as soul retrieval, after someone has suffered soul-loss or soul-fragmentation. Physically it can make us aware of our personal power and vitality and what causes our personal energy drain or power-loss. Knowledge brings us the power to change, so understanding our personal energy field is very important if we are to work effectively and harmoniously with the myriad energies that are present on this planet.

Indicolite – Also known as blue tourmaline, indicolite is an emphatic heart healer; it is used on the heart chakra to dispel old fears and hurts. It may even show up fears and hurts which have been totally suppressed, events which were so traumatic that you lost them deep within your subconscious. It has helped those who feel emotionally fragmented. Use it on any chakra that needs the soothing healing blue ray of this mollifying stone. The blue ray of this stone is a must for anyone who uses crystals on others, as it protects them from any negativity they may encounter. It is used to stop insomnia and night sweats. Indicolite is helpful for sinus pain and congestion (unshed tears from childhood); its soothing ray is one of nature's pain-killers. It can be used directionally to remove pain and aid healing. It can be applied to any area of the body that is holding dis-ease patterns, miasms, pain and congestion.

Iolite – Iolite can exhibit the properties of extreme pleochroism. Gem quality iolite, which was used in the Archangel essences, has different colours in different directions in the crystal. A cube cut from iolite will look a violetish-blue, almost like sapphire, from one side, clear as water from the other, and yellow from the top. Iolite has a very high vibrational rate. It is ideal for the awakened 'star children' on the earth plane: a vision-prophecy stone. Often we choose to be blind to the potential illuminated by our third eye. In its connection with the higher functions of consciousness, the third eye is a psychic tool reminding us that everything we see, hear, smell, touch or taste started as an inner vision or in-sight. Iolite teaches us not to get too attached to ritual, but to look for our own path via a balanced third eye chakra; it takes us into the realms of personal inner knowing. It brings the passionate expression of our true potential – 'rather than society's expectations and stereotypes'.

Jasper (Sea) – The variety of quartz known as jasper is a heterogeneous mass of micro-crystallised quartz which is heavily pigmented with colourful minerals. The colours of jasper are mainly due to iron and are usually yellow, red, brown, black or green. Sea Jasper is grounding and stabilising to the whole body. It strengthens the will to survive. It is also a good, slow, steady healing stone. The energy is also very protective and may be used in stressful situations when it is important to retain one's own boundaries or when you want to have no outside influence interfering with your energy. It also helps with the release of toxins from the liver and large intestine. It will support you during the releasing process by gently stabilising your energy field, easing the discomfort normally associated with toxin release.

Kunzite – Kunzite carries the energies of the pale pink to lilac ray, which is the ray of spiritual love. It works on all parts of the body, mind and spirit. It is used for the newborn to help them integrate their energies into the earth vibration, for birth and re-birth, for new beginnings and for mid-life crisis as a heart opener. It is also used as a heart consciousness wakener. It comforts and heals the heart and old 'heartache'.

Kyanite (Black) – Black kyanite will bring guidance and faith, giving great encouragement to break loose from the chains of ignorance, desire, fear, anger and hatred. It will aid you in your struggle towards the light of your soul and your soul purpose: it will help you fulfil your *Dharma*. Kyanite integrates the bodies' energies into the head and so, with conscious attunement, can align all the chakras. It is the seeker of truth and will combat fear of speaking the truth

Kyanite (Blue) – Kyanite is also known as disthene. It contains the royal colour of integrity and is uplifting to the soul as it searches for its maturity. It will bring guidance and faith, giving great encouragement to break loose from the chains of ignorance, desire, fear and hatred. A kyanite blade has a very focused swift action: it holds the keys to higher knowledge and understanding the sapphire blue ray of sincere communication. Kyanite integrates the bodies' energies into the head and so can, with conscious attunement, align all the chakras, so it is good for people who intellectualise everything or can only deal in grandiose throat chakra concepts. Kyanite is the seeker of truth and will combat fear of speaking the truth. It will aid you in your struggle towards the light of your soul and your soul purpose. Kyanite works with Archangel Michael and his sword of truth; it is more powerful than *Excalibur*, the legendary sword of King Arthur. Use it to cut away the wrong mental, emotional and spiritual attitudes that have held you captive. It is a double-edged sword, so you can cut away duality and dualistic concepts which have blinded you to the truth. Use it wisely; once you have picked it up, it is very hard to put down until you have ended not only your own suffering (ignorance) but the suffering of all sentient beings.

Labradorite (Golden – Rainbow-coated) – Truly an enchanting, fascinatingly beautiful mineral. When faceted golden labradorite is coated with precious metals it really comes alive. Labradorite is metaphysically known as the 'bringer of light', the illumination on the path. It works by dispelling darkness. Enchanting labradorite is connected to mystery: it points to magic and esoteric knowledge. It is a gateway to other worlds and dimensions. Rainbow-coated golden labradorite is a shape-shifter; it plays with the light, it moves it and bends it and plays with illusion. It skilfully removes the 'hooks and ensnarements' of other people's mental projections, allowing one to completely clean the auric shell of other people's emotional debris. It removes negativity and depression that have been caused by disappointments in life. It teaches you to look beyond the visible world, to use your sixth sense. Its energy can see beyond the illusion of time and space. It can see right through you – it will expose all your flaws, shams, corruptions and shame, then it teaches you to heal them. It is a powerful, mesmerizing, bewitching female ally and guide. Labradorite is here to offer you insight, clairvoyance, truths to the questions of the universe. It teaches you to exercise your third eye, by letting your intuition guide you daily.

Lapis – Lapis contains a pure, high etheric nature. It frees you from fear-based concepts. It contains the energies of royalty, wisdom, patience, truth, mental attainment, good communication, contentment, artistic inspiration, deep meditation, spiritual and philosophical contemplation, personal integrity and loyalty. It is the 'Spirit of Truth'. Lapis lazuli will heal an unbalanced throat chakra. How do you tell if the throat chakra is unbalanced by being too open, by spinning too fast or being damaged? The person is over-talkative, dogmatic, self-righteous, arrogant, aggressive or holds entrenched views. If the throat chakra is too closed, restricted or spinning sluggishly, the person is capricious, fickle, holds inconsistent views and holds back from self-expression. Lapis teaches you the power and potency of the spoken word. It teaches you to 'give voice to your truth'. It counteracts harshness and rigidity. If somebody is acting insensitively in a situation, lapis will help them become more compassionate. Lapis gives relief from pain, both physical and psychological, and combats cruelty and brutality. Lapis is an interesting stone to meditate with, as its high intensity etheric nature means you really have to reach high to bring your energy into line with its refined vibration. It contains a higher order of intelligence and wisdom, 'intellectual integrity'. Lapis aids discrimination of wisdom; it is very penetrating and does not suffer fools gladly, or those who are fooling around with other people's spirituality. Lapis teaches you to reach for the stars and looking at lapis reminds you of a summer night's sky. The small crystals of pyrite, which are always present in lapis, and the streaks of white calcite produce starry pictures, which will aid your intuition. The white calcite brings in the energies of the crown chakra and the yellow pyrite brings in the energies of the solar plexus chakra to activate, energize, align and integrate the throat chakra. Lapis also teaches the mastery of active listening by integrating the full faculties of hearing. It is a sad fact that active listening is totally neglected in our society. We need to fully develop the outer ear, before the subtle inner ear can be available to us for inner guidance. All too often Divine guidance is not heard, because of not truly listening to the 'wisdom' behind the words.

Larimar – Etherial in its nature, with an other-worldly feel, this beautiful heavenly blue stone contains an energy of peace and tranquillity. It gently transmits pure spiritual substance into the higher chakras above the head. Larimar contains 'Grandmother Earth' energies and will assist you in finding your true path in life. It will also assist you in removing the blocks you have placed on your path to personal power. For women it will activate your own Goddess energies, bringing understanding of the Divine maiden, mother and crone. It is useful for connecting those who feel disorientated and out of step with the earth. It has been called the Dolphin stone, due to its watery energy, though this is another aspect of 'mystery' about this stone, as its birth is definitely fire in nature. It is best worn as a pendant for long periods of time; this facilitates its magical properties, allowing them to fully manifest in your life. The best way of understanding larimar's fire is through our own fiery emotions, which very often are released through our watery tears. Our tears are our very own ocean, which has been gifted to us to facilitate our personal cleansing process. The dolphin energy contained within the stone is also playful in nature and it will activate a deep healing of our emotional inner child or, as has been observed, activate our own Angelic inner child.

Lithium Quartz – Lithium in quartz contains an extremely high vibration which activates the gift of prophecy. It is serene and calming to the mind and works on the brain's pain centres, which helps with addictions and addictive traits within the personality. It gives you your own space back, so you can heal, so it is good for convalescence. Lithium purges anaesthetics and pollutants from the system. It facilitates the energy of no mind, thus relieving stress. It is also useful for integrating the personality by balancing both sides of the brain. In meditation it feels like a gentle wave of energy flowing through the mind. Lithium quartz is especially good for insomnia. The 'spirit' keeper or Angel of lithium quartz facilitates its use as a 'dreamtime' crystal, an astral guide. It changes our way of consciously viewing the world, by accessing other dimensions and realities. Lithium, when amplified by inclusion in quartz, is a good space clearer; it can emit an immense force field that will keep anything negative at bay. It has been used to clear the mind of unwanted debris before meditation, so it aids deep meditation practice. It can fully activate and integrate the crown chakra, bringing alignment to the higher transcendental chakras above the head. It stops depression, obsessional thinking and confusion. It alleviates symptoms of sensitivity to pollutants, chronic exhaustion, epilepsy and Alzheimer's. Lithium quartz also strengthens the immune system and has great healing powers. It gives a rest to the troubled heart and brings inner peace and emotional healing.

Malachite – Malachite can balance and bring harmony to the heart chakra. It brings the ability to experience wholeness and love. It is very restorative and tunes you in to the plant kingdom, helping you understand environmental issues and giving you a social conscience. Malachite gets to the core of the problem, the very heart of the matter: it fact it will leave no stone unturned in doing so. This makes it a very strong and powerful crystal. Malachite is also a practical idealist and it will help you release the negative aspect of the heart chakra, of coping with unquestioning acceptance, hopelessness, of self-denial and self-suppression; a refusal to live life to the full.

Marcasite – Marcasite swiftly dispels despondency, despair and lack of energy. It is a must for those who display tendencies of low self-worth and inferiority. Marcasite is a protective stone that will keep your energy field clear of unwanted outside influences. It will stop energy leaks and energy drains from the physical body and auric shell. It will support and strengthen the meridian system.

Moldavite – It has no crystalline structure: this means it can take you beyond your self-limiting belief system into uncharted realms of infinite possibilities. Moldavites are the rarest of gems, perhaps rarer than diamonds, rubies or emeralds. Since their origin is not of the earth, the discovery of new deposits seems unlikely. Metaphysically, we have within us the light body and this contains encodements of information like files. When we hold the beautiful green moldavite this data is released. Very often many people are not consciously aware of the information being unlocked, they just feel what has commonly been called 'the moldavite flush', a huge wave of powerful energy which actually flushes through the body; this can cause sweating or a bright 'red' face. Interestingly, red is the green ray's balance colour. Others experience the decoding or download as heat surging up their spine. Still others experience the download as an emotional release of tears, joy or laughter. Others find the vibrational download shift and the resulting rise in their vibrational rate too intense and they may become fearful. Others experience it as dizziness or headaches. There is no doubt, though, the download does cause massive spiritual growth and healing. It can take years to fully integrate the download of information. In fact the more people resist the integration of their Divine blueprint being decoded from the Akashic records, the longer it takes. Moldavite is very fast, hot and cosmic. It was sent here for the awakened 'star children', to help their ascension into the higher realms of cosmic consciousness. This massive vibrational shift is happening right now, that is why so many people feel a magnetic attraction to the cosmic transformational tool of moldavite. The 'Grail Stone' is another name for moldavite: it is its 'spirit' name. Legend has it that anyone who touches the 'Grail Stone' will have a spiritual transformation.

Morganite – A stone of interdimensional connections, it assists those who desire to attain the guidance offered from the higher planes. Morganite facilitates universal love and compassion; the love of humanity, of honouring each being for their own unique expression of their intrinsic Divinity; of unity within diversity. Morganite contains the energy of high affection – affection without ulterior motive. It melts any resistance you may have to being truly in love or truly giving love freely. Morganite clears the way, by preparing the body to receive 'healing'. It soothes the physical body, making it more open and relaxed. Morganite's signature is very special: it holds the emotional body stable as you let go of pain and painful memories; this is the key to its use.

Opal – Opal is absorbent; it picks up your emotional energies, positive or negative, and works with the karmic law of return: what you send out is returned amplified. The reason the energy is magnified is very simple: like attracts like. The universal law of resonance is that whatever you focus on attracts even more of the same energy; this law makes you very aware of your every thought, word and deed. This law can cause havoc when you consider all the 'black' spots on the planet. We have all had enough of killing, of chaos and confusion. Opals are wonderful emotional healers when you are ready to accept responsibility for owning your own emotional energies and vibratory pattern. Opal is also used for 'soul star' activation: the brilliant flashes of light frequency emitted by the opal cause a significant vibrational shift in the chakra immediately above the crown chakra. Although the 'soul star' chakra is not actually located on the physical body, its influence and activation will cause a download of 'light vibrational information' that can greatly induce emotional healing and deepen the spiritual results of meditation practice.

Papagoite – Etheric blue in colour, papagoite occurs as an inclusion within quartz. It is an exceedingly rare and beautiful mineral, coming from only one 'extinct' mine in the world, as does the ajoite crystal that it frequently grows with. It is a 'master healer' which has the ability to transform negative energy into positive life-supporting beneficial energy. It appears to keep the energy of the throat chakra cleansed, energised and aligned with the highest communication possible to the Angelic realm. It brings feelings of peace, tranquillity, harmony and emotional upliftment which are so euphoric they are beyond anything that one can ever experience without spending many hours in deep meditation practice. In fact papagoite enhances meditation practice, allowing one to merge with grace and ease with the Divine feminine watery aspect of creation. Papagoite has the power to nurture all things and gives us glimpses of other realities. It enhances the ability to be compassionate towards others, as well as expanding our horizons, allowing us to gracefully let go of our limitations and weaknesses.

Petalite (Pink) – This crystal makes us gentle yet strong; there is no question of pliability or giving in, regardless of any outside pressure that wishes to manipulate our energy field for its own selfish gain. It strengthens the emotional body by activating the Kundalini energy within the root chakra. This allows us to stay strong, focused and grounded whilst maintaining a balanced, open, compassionate heart chakra. Pink petalite is warming to the whole body. It clears the heart meridian, which in turn releases stored emotional baggage. It also releases us from worry and helps discrimination: thus it aids wisdom. Pink petalite teaches you to avoid fear, anger, hatred, greed, desire, ego manipulation, pride, boastfulness and laziness. It will, with conscious direction, activate higher states of cosmic consciousness, where you realise that 'powers' such as clairvoyance and clairaudience are not worth striving for, because far greater illumination and peace are possible beyond them.

Phenacite – Phenacite is a dynamic activator of the upper chakras, particularly the crown and the non-physical 8th to 14th chakras above the head. The soul star chakra, which is located just above the crown chakra, becomes especially energised into complete alignment with the higher self; this brings Divine inspiration. Phenacite helps you to activate the light body and to consciously experience your existence in higher dimensions. It encourages you to become a spiritual hero in the worldly battlefield: to be brave, be undaunted, be a spiritual soldier; to conquer the inner war with the mind and senses, for it is more terrible than the external war; to soar high into the higher regions of bliss. Clear phenacite from Madagascar especially brings this conscious awareness of the universal law of resonance, like attracts like. It teaches you to be aware of every thought, word and deed, to purify and refine your vibration until your whole system on every level is full of pristine light and glory and you become a conscious channel for the light, a force for good. It encourages discipline, humility, wisdom, understanding, truth, dispassion, discrimination, serenity, self-restraint, one-pointedness of mind, purity, forbearance, fortitude, patience, forgiveness, the spirit of service, sacrifice and love for all. Phenacite is a multi-dimensional energy device: it can teach you astral travel. It knows the gateways to other realms and worlds of infinite bliss. Initiation into the ancient mysteries are stored within its vibrational structure. Phenacite gives the full activation and initiation of the ascension process by downloading the information stored within your Divine blueprint on the Akashic records into your energy body. When used to clear the chakra system it is a healer of the soul, heralding the soul force into the vibration of ascension.

Pink Lazurine TM – This carries the purest energies of the pink to lilac ray, which is the ray of deep spiritual love and discernment born out of insight and understanding. It is the ray of the Divine Mother, which helps us to understand our relationship to the feminine principle, both in ourselves and others. All of us, regardless of being in a male or female body, have a feminine aspect. It is this side of our nature that is intuitive and sensitive. We all have the ability, if we choose, to nurture others. Pink lazurine makes us look very carefully at how we nurture our own soul and the soul of others. It also helps us to look at our relationship to our human mother, the one who gave us life. Pink lazurine gently works on all parts of the body, mind and spirit. It is used for the newborn to help them integrate and consolidate their energies into the earth vibration, for birth and re-birth, for new beginnings and for mid-life crisis as a primary heart opener. It is also used as a heart consciousness awakener. It comforts, soothes and heals the heart and old 'heartache'. Pink lazurine has a perfect balance of compassion, reconciliation, harmony, peace and emotional freedom and has chosen to make itself available at this time to teach the lesson of spiritual love. It makes us look at our hidden agenda to loving fully and unconditionally ourselves and others; it then teaches us to love unconditionally by opening our heart and third eye chakras in perfect unison. On our path to enlightenment the most important energy is spiritual love. By truly being able to fully hold this energy within our own personal energy system we attract the energy of the Divine Cosmic Mother, who instantly perceives our shift in consciousness towards the highest spiritual goal; in fact it is as if "God has smiled on us". This quickens our energy field even more, allowing the energy of God to 'uplift' us. This can remove karmic miasms and deeply entrenched negative neural pathways which no longer serve our highest good.

Pyrite – Pyrite has a very strong, powerful male yang energy that will induce intellectual superiority when worn or carried. It is ideal for students and those who wish to improve their academic prowess and memory. It is also ideal for those people who feel subordinate to others or who have an over- abundance of the female yin vibration. It can make those who are very male or yang act almost too aggressively, so they need to be aware of its potency, being conscious at all times to use this mineral in a balanced holistic way. Pyrite is totally focused and will act like a swift arrow, going straight to the physical, mental or emotional disease. There it will facilitate healing but, more than this, it will also make you aware of the cause of the illness or disease and bring about favourable circumstances to find 'cures' for the 'cause' of the dis-ease. This process is facilitated by a synergy of the higher self and the improved concentrated mind action of the pyrite mineral as it interacts with your energy field. It will swiftly dispel deep gloom, lift despondency, despair and the drudge mentality. It is also ideal when you feel a severe lack of energy. It is a must for those who display tendencies of low self-worth and subservience. Pyrite teaches you to honour and accept yourself, to work towards self-empowerment, personal freedom and joy. Pyrite is a very protective stone and will keep your energy field clear of unwanted outside influences. It will stop energy leaks and energy drains from the physical body and auric shell and will strengthen the meridian system.

Quartz (Clear) – Clear quartz is the 'master healer' or 'cure all' because it contains the full spectrum of the visible 'white' light (iridescent rainbow cosmic light) and as such it will work on every level of our being, physical, emotional, mental, astral, spiritual, etheric etc. It is acknowledged as the only 'programmable' crystal. Clear quartz also contains the double helix spiral of Universal Life Energy. Working with, holding or meditating with this 'master' energy of the supreme ray will unlock not only deep memories but facilitate healing by quickly removing the 'blocks' or stagnant energy which may cause or have caused illness or distress within any level of the body. It is also used for amplifying one's concentrated attention and intent. When healing energy is directed through the clear quartz crystal, it is transmitted into the body of the patient and distributed to the areas most in need of energy balancing. There is an intelligence contained within this focused energy that always directs it to the areas displaying a lower vibration or 'block'. Quartz crystal allows for easy access to altered states of consciousness and it will assist the movement of energy flowing between the chakras. It can also be used to bring about 'Kundalini' activation. Use clear quartz crystal when you need to bring clarity and light to a situation, or when you need to bring about a change, major or minor. Clear quartz is considered a cure all by many crystal therapists. There are many types and uses.

Quartz (Black Druzy) – Black druzy quartz is grounding and gives psychic protection. It purifies the physical body and releases body odours. It is especially useful for people who lack faith in their own judgement and who are easily swayed by other people's opinions and belief systems. It stimulates the imagination, aids meditation practice and enhances the ability to use and maintain positive affirmations as a way of changing negative behavioural patterns which may have lodged in the neural pathways.

Quartz (Rainbow Aura) – A product of twentieth century technology, just as aqua aura quartz, opal aura quartz, rose aura quartz and ruby aura quartz are. The beauty of these quartzes is apparent as the 'new' technology enhances the extremely powerful properties of the master healer, clear quartz. Rainbow aura quartz is clear organic quartz combined with gold and titanium; this combination produces the most amazing deep metallic rainbow colour. Titanium is a master healer. The energy of titanium is activation; activation of all levels and energy centres. It works by clearing a pathway for the vital life force to flow. Titanium works on the endocrine system. Titanium supports the life force within all the bodies, physical, emotional, mental, spiritual, etc. and the surrounding auric field, allowing for a greater abundance of vital life energy. Rainbow aura quartz is very energizing and enlivening to all the chakras; it will awaken and activate any energy centre, dispelling sorrow and replacing it with unlimited joy. It can ignite and activate the inner rainbow body of light. Rainbow aura quartz also helps to heal stressful relationships. All our interactions with others only serve to reflect an aspect of ourselves. This gives us the opportunity to see ourselves more clearly. Taking this into account, using rainbow aura quartz can speed up the personal learning process in life. There is also the value of working through conflicts that brings us to opening to wider possibilities. Those who can let go of old belief systems and ways of relating will be rewarded by transformation and regeneration and will find life can flow much more smoothly without pain, resentment and conflict. Wearing or meditating with this dazzling gemstone will also give new insights to your relationships on all levels; even with your guides and Angels you will find new ways of relating which you may not have thought possible. These could also include hidden talents and Divine gifts.

Quartz (Rose) – One of the most pleasantly seductive varieties of quartz, rose quartz is gentle, soothing and excellent for balancing the emotional level of the aura by gently nourishing the emotional body. Rose quartz is revitalising and stimulates healing by helping to maintain energy levels to protect against unwanted influences from the outside world, which many sensitive souls find overwhelming. Natural rose is highly tuned and sensitive; it carries the promise of spiritual fulfilment. It is used to attune to the love vibration. The rose quartz ray works dynamically on the heart chakra, gently cleansing and then transmuting all stored putrefied negative issues of self-worth, self-confidence and self-acceptance. It contains within its beautiful pink mandala the ray of hope. The pink warmth melts and dissolves resistance to allowing the full manifestation of love into every corner of the heart. It will allow the integration of positive energy within all levels of the chakra system, the positive energy being love, compassion and understanding of unity within diversity, bringing tolerance, forgiveness and ultimately the complete expression of universal love and self-love to every corner of the microcosm and macrocosm. The guardian or angel of rose quartz is very affectionate, deeply understanding and non-judgemental. Many people who tread the angel path are passionately aware of the potent force of this Divine pink manifestation. It is ideal to carry and wear in stressful situations.

Quartz (Rutile) – A semi-precious stone that has been used as a talisman since ancient times, rutilated quartz was thought to be 'captured sunlight'. It is known as the illuminator of the soul. Titanium or rutile needles within the clear quartz structure produce an extremely potent synergy of crystalline vibrations which can be used not only for vibrational healing but unprecedented spiritual growth. Rutilated quartz has a perfect balance of cosmic light. Use it for illumination and channelling the Universal Intelligence to provide power, wisdom and Divine guidance. It clears the pathway for necessary action by exposing flaws, corruption, negativity and shams. It sustains life and the vital life force. It is used to restore a person's vibrancy and vitality, which will lead to the resonance of perfect health. Rutile quartz can provide the energy to break down barriers which have held up your spiritual progress. It helps you to conquer fears and phobias. Use rutile quartz to bring about a change, for rejuvenation and new directions. It activates the aura and fills it with light. Rutile quartz is used for healing and balancing the aura by repelling negative energy. It works on the physical, etheric and astral bodies and dispels unwanted interference from both the physical and spiritual worlds.

Quartz (Smoky Phantom) – Smoky quartz phantoms have experienced many lifetimes of learning, through eons of time, while continuing in the same physical configuration. This crystal is a 'living' example of the evolution of consciousness and the ultimate continued growth of the eternal towards total perfection of the being. This crystal is without a doubt very useful for those of us who feel we have reached a 'brick wall' and do not know how to continue, or even if we have the strength and courage to continue to 'evolve' and grow. The smoky quartz phantom teaches you the right use of power and keeps you 'grounded' in fearful situations. It stops destructive power that is used out of selfishness, greed, manipulation, evil or weakness. It is very protective. It stops depression and restriction. Smoky quartz phantoms contain hidden riches; they can also throw up energetically a smoke-screen of protection which will temporarily hide you – nothing permanent though, just a breathing space while you gather your scattered emotions and ground yourself or 'go to ground'. Smoky quartz is a great teacher: it can take you deep inside the earth to work with the elementals for healing. It is stimulating and purifying to the first chakra, so it is good for meditation practice. Smoky quartz can bring you back to earth to everyday normal waking reality. It eases despair, despondency, gloom, melancholy and suicidal tendencies. It can help you bring your dreams into reality. There is nothing weak about smoky quartz. It enhances the survival instinct, it is a life-saver. Smoky quartz allows for clarity of thought and contemplation. It will balance the male/female polarities; it relieves headaches and congestion of the intestines, helps heal the feet and legs and eases lower back pain. It also relieves muscular cramp – not just physical cramp, but soul cramp too. Its pain-relieving properties are wonderful: it just draws out pain. It has been used against the negative effects of radiation, including electrical equipment negativity.

Quartz (Spanish Red) – Spanish red quartz holds a vigorous, vibrant, positive energetic charge which clears miasms from the root and sacral chakras: this enhances life force. It encourages originality and spontaneity. As a member of the quartz family it has the usual healing energetic signature. It is used for general strengthening, grounding, stabilizing and centering of physical energies. It connects you to the Goddess and earth healing energies. It can be used to stabilize the root chakra, attuning you to the positive force of gravity, allowing for your interconnectedness to the earth, your past and childhood.

Quartz (Sunshine Aura) – A very bright, garish, odd, unnatural-looking crystal, sunshine aura quartz is also attractive in a very lively sort of way; it isn't easy to ignore. It seems to 'jump' out at you shouting 'I can help!' Many people have been attracted to its vibrational healing properties. It is almost hyperactive as crystal energies go! It appears to be the ultimate cleansing crystal, the great eliminator. As we all know, cleansing means healing – out with the old rubbish, as it cleans and removes toxins and waste from the system. On a physical level it removes toxins and promotes the flow of gastric juices, as well as stimulating the lymphatic system. Sunshine aura quartz really cleanses the system and relieves constipation. Constipation represents holding on to past unresolved emotions. On the emotional level sunshine aura quartz clears low self-esteem and issues of low self-worth and the fear of responsibility. On a mental level it clears and stimulates the mind, activating the intellect and intuition. On a spiritual level sunshine aura quartz is very active and expansive. It can really get communication started; it is also good for releasing fears and phobias. Sunshine aura quartz is also protective, because its energy is so vast, fast and intense; it just shakes off parasitic energy on all levels and increases the wearer's capacity for laughter and joy. It appears to be the 'cosmic clown' of healing crystals. It says the best medication as an antidote to illness and disease is a joyful heart.

Rubellite – This is a powerful heart stone which connects you to higher truths. It strengthens your wisdom, empathy, compassion and will-power. Your creativity is enhanced as you open yourself to the beauty that surrounds you. You will become aware of the many etheric levels of consciousness and Divine joy. Rubellite (pink tourmaline) will help heart and lung conditions. It is also helpful to those who have a problem with their femininity. It brings spiritual beauty; it is also a good crystal to give your client before a therapy session, as this crystal really makes you feel relaxed, receptive and open to the experience of healing. It helps heal a painful broken heart by releasing the blocks that have formed there. With conscious use you will soon discover that your ability to find forgiveness for others is enhanced.

Ruby – The superb scarlet variety of corundum, ruby is the second hardest natural mineral known. It was said to be the most precious of the twelve stones God created when he created all things and this 'lord of gems' was placed on Aaron's neck by God's command. The Bible says that wisdom is "more precious than rubies". Ruby instills in the wearer a passion for life, truth, courage, wisdom and perseverance. It introduces dynamic leadership qualities. It emits the energy of optimism and originality. Ruby is for the pioneers, those who must go first, bravely, into uncharted territory. Ruby is raw power, drive and will-power. The bright red, scarlet, crimson and flame are clean, pure, pristine forms of ruby; when used spiritually, it is devotion that transfigures Divine love into Divine will. Ruby will stimulate the heart chakra when consciously directed, raising – then transforming – the raw power of the root chakra into devotion, reverence and enlightened religious zeal. Ruby works very well with those who have a strong 'spiritual devotional' energy to the 'ultimate liberation' of the human race from suffering and ignorance into enlightenment.

Ruby in Zoisite – Ruby in zoisite manifests the beauty of the body and spirit in perfect harmony through a balanced, harmonious, peaceful heart chakra.

Sapphire (Pink) – Pink sapphire is magnetic: it manifests that which you need into your life, so personal life-lessons can be learnt swiftly. It teaches you mastery of your heart chakra and emotions. It frees you of emotional turmoil and aids the digestion by allowing the integration of cosmic affection. It is a gemstone of the Divine Mother, as it contains within its vibratory signature universal harmony and cosmic love, which will open the door to your innermost heart. Pink sapphire can, with conscious attunement through dedication, allow us to work with her to heal our psyche and really forgive ourselves and others, which will bring healing and peace to the earth. Many people die in a state of anger, refusing to forgive themselves and others. We must make peace with others who we perceive have hurt or harmed us, otherwise the anger and resentment will be carried on to the next life. This will bind us in chains of ignorance and for all eternity to that person until we do truly and freely forgive them. Pink sapphire therefore works with the body-mind connection. Every thought you have influences your body. Negative thoughts weaken your immune system. Positive thoughts strengthen your immune system. So by forgiving others and releasing negative thoughts such as anger, resentment, etc. you will strengthen your physical body and release emotional turmoil and your etheric body will move into a higher vibration, which brings peace and tranquillity. You will have started on the upward spiral towards enlightenment of the soul.

Sapphire (Yellow) – Mentally and spiritually stimulating, yellow sapphire is very expansive to the mental body and works well to activate and balance the solar plexus chakra. Its vibratory signature balances the pancreas, liver, spleen, gall-bladder and middle stomach meridians. It also energizes the nervous system and digestive system. It is good for removing cellulite and stored emotional waste and toxins. Elimination is the law of life, faulty elimination is a vital contributing factor to the beginning of most diseases. Yellow sapphire teaches you to clear your mind of negative thoughts, so it aids concentration and meditation. Emotionally it clears low self-esteem. It also stimulates the lymphatic system. It brings joy and a sunny positive disposition, originality, tolerance, personal honesty and spiritual abundance. It is the most important crystal to work with for improving your manifesting abilities and spiritual growth through the power of infinite abundance.

Selenite – Selenite is a stone of communication and communion with the past and present; this includes communication with our guides and angels. It aids telepathic links with others by enhancing intuitive and remote viewing skills. With regular use it increases sensitivity, perception and telepathy.

Seraphinite – A beautiful deep green gemstone with feathery silver iridescent markings, seraphinite activates Angelic contact of the highest realms of love, light and especially healing. This alone makes it a powerful heart healing stone, but it is also a dynamic purifier of the two major conduits through which energy rises up the spine. These are the female *Ida* and the male *Pingala*, the yin and yang. This purification process quickly causes old blocks and stagnant energy to simply dissolve, so that new pristine energy is quickly integrated into the chakra system and spiritual spine. Seraphinite brings balance and stability to the heart chakra and aligns it with the crown chakra. It therefore aids discrimination of the heart. Seraphinite's magic makes you feel it is good to be alive; it helps you succeed without struggle by harmonising the desires of the heart into perfect alignment with your soul's true heartfelt desire for enlightenment. If your heartfelt desire is for enlightenment, this will bring alignment and healing on all levels of the body and aura.

Sugilite – Sugilite *is* the third eye activator; it works on the pineal gland, the top of the head, the crown and heart chakras, as well as the brain and scalp. Sugilite has a potent mature Universal Consciousness. It is very nurturing, giving the 'star children' feelings of security and protection against the harsh climate of the negative earth vibration of hostility, rage, anger and fear, so it is good for those who feel abandoned and disconnected from their 'home' and source of emotional nourishment. It has also been used by very gentle sensitive souls who find it difficult to screen out the negativity and hostility of others. It is very protective as well as gently grounding. It can integrate the spiritual body with the physical body, which is very helpful for those amongst us who 'space out easily' or are 'walk-ins' or soul or twin flame exchanges. Many people on the spiritual path have utilised sugilite for grounding their spiritual experiences into their everyday life, which can sometimes be difficult, as these mystical trips into other dimensions and altered realities can become dreamlike and easily dissipate if not fully integrated. At the present time it is very important that those of us who can move between realities or are aware of multiple realities or multiple selves hold this vibration within their innermost being at all times, thereby allowing for an easier transition for all sentient life on earth as she makes her energetic shift into the higher dimensions of love and unity. Above all, sugilite brings peace, dignity, humanitarianism and mental creativity. It really does develop psychic abilities, allowing for mystical experiences. It can develop faith and inner strength. It teaches you personal mastery, that you have a Divine right to your own point of view and inner truth. Sugilite also contains the spirit of mercy and is very dignified; it allows you to work with the highest levels of thought and gives a thorough understanding of the thought process. Velvety sugilite is the aristocrat of the purple gemstones; it commands respect as it guides you towards spiritual perfection. It has a richness and quality about it that lead to refined mystical psychic perception. It is good for those who meditate and teach meditation and healing disciplines: its vibration can produce great mystical leaders and enlightened gurus.

Sunstone – The orange sunstone is used to bring in vibrant solar energies in meditation and body layouts, for connecting with one's own source of light and transmuting dark or negative energies into positive healing energies. It is very yang in nature and emits a strong energy of leadership and positive personal empowerment. It works on the sacral chakra, lower back, lower intestines, abdomen, kidneys, bladder and ovaries. Orange sunstone is very magnetic and attracts the energy of making things happen now. It makes you take action in your life; the time for procrastination and hiding your light away is past; rather than just dreaming of the life you would like, live the life you want to live right now – no more postponement, deferral, delay or stalling. It is a strong stone, which links you into your intuition. It removes inhibitions, sexual hang-ups, self-imposed constraints, repression and emotional hang-ups, even emotional hook-ups. The emotional hook-ups from others are energies other people have placed within your energy field to control or manipulate you in some way. They can be very debilitating and draining on your energy field. Sunstone gently removes these emotional snares and transmutes them into positive loving energy. It really makes you look what sacrifice you make to suit others. Dysfunctional relationships are detrimental to both people involved.

Tanzanite – Those crystals which exhibit the full tanzanite spectrum of pleochroism – violet-blue, purple and bronze – are very potent in their healing application, as they contain a vast spectrum of possibilities and applications. Poorer quality stones may have a only brownish colour. Metaphysically, tanzanite is mesmerising. The pleochroism facilitates altered states of reality. These can cause radical permanent shifts in consciousness, by raising the vibratory signature of the user; this expands their personal mandala or 'original Divine blueprint', allowing for 'downloads' of information which is activated from the Akashic records. Tanzanite is then used for inner/outer journeys. Your raised vibratory rate will cause you to see a thinning of the veil between the various planes of consciousness, allowing for clear communication with Ascended Masters, Angels, spirit guides and other enlightened beings from dimensions not usually available to your normal conscious awareness. With dedicated use, tanzanite facilitates deep meditation, astral journeys, materialisation and alchemy. It can activate and integrate the energies of the base, sacral, solar plexus, heart, throat, third eye, fourth eye, fifth eye and crown chakras, as well as the chakras eight to fourteen above the head, facilitating a situation in which the mind and psychic abilities are activated and guided by the wisdom of an enlightened heart. The energized throat chakra allows for clear communication of this integrated understanding.

Topaz (Blue) – Legend has it that topaz dispels all enchantment…it inspires and uplifts. It assists your soul in its search for truth. It contains purity and innocence and is very soothing and calming. Blue topaz is of a very high vibration, it simply lifts you above the stressful energy by raising your vibratory rate; what was once perceived as stressful, you now rise above. It is a witness stone! Whenever you feel outrage at an injustice, or feel on the receiving end of a 'perceived' wrong, be it on any level, just ask Archangel Michael and the Lords of Karma to act as your witness. The only rule is that you must then in no way, word, thought or deed behave in a negative manner towards the 'cause' of the injustice. You must be beyond karmic energy and just allow the situation to 'play' itself out; allow the full 'drama' to manifest, as you are merely a silent pristine witness 'viewing' the situation. Using this stone is very useful: it will allow you to see what 'movies' you have got caught up in, in the 'theatre' of life. Natural pale blue topaz is a wonderful 'channelling' gemstone. It can connect you to the Angels of truth and ancient wisdom. Blue topaz teaches you the 'energy' of selfless love; it is a universal healer; it reminds you that you can overcome all obstacles. It helps you to remain calm and composed. It teaches you to speak your truth in a dignified manner. It is a very dignified crystal. If you can remain calm and focused in any situation, you will have learned the lesson this crystal is here to teach: detachment.

Topaz (Golden) – Golden topaz is revitalizing; it has the energy of the ancient Egyptian Sun God Ra. It brings a feeling of energy, power and vitality to the user. It is used for any problem that is associated with the mental body, toxins and elimination, including negative mental attitudes which have stopped emotional or spiritual growth. It is a powerful stone and, when worn, carried or used in meditation, will bring personal power and self-mastery. Golden topaz can activate contact with your higher self, your Divine aspect, which dwells within each and every one of us. It brings immortality – you are already immortal, but you may have forgotten that you are! You are an eternal being of infinite light, love, compassion, wisdom, truth and joy. This crystal can encourage you to go towards the infinite dazzling, incomparably brilliant light of the void and find the connectedness with God/Goddess that is your true spiritual evolution.

Vanadinite – Vanadinite instantly increases prana, which aids vitality and brings mental clarity. Overall, personal creativity is greatly enhanced. Vanadinite swiftly clears blocks in the meridian system and helps the full integration of prana; this ensures the correction has not only been fully assimilated into the meridian system, but the body has stabilized to a balanced sustainable level. Vanadinite also strengthens the auric integrity, which is vital in maintaining overall health, emotional well-being and spiritual cleanliness – otherwise your auric shell could be breached by low level negative vibrations, low level astral entities or misqualified human projection.

Archangel Pendulum Chart Quick Reference Guide

Angel of Light – Archangel Seraphiel – Healing and Angelic Protection – Creates a harmonious, sacred, safe, healing environment. Clears and releases spaces with built-up negative emotional, psychic and mental energies. Use for healing, Angelic attunement and meditation practice. The essence has also been successfully used for clearing crystals of stagnant energy.

Angel of Ascension – Archangel Metatron – Cosmic Consciousness and Light Body Activation – Creates a vortex of energy which aligns all the chakras on the physical body and activates the 8th to 14th transcendental chakras above the head. Used for meditation, light body activation and spiritual evolution.

Archangel Shamael's Sacred Sound – Sound Healing – Utilizes the transformational healing energy of sound in its sacred aspect. Shamael carries the colour vibrations of indigo, violet and gold. He represents the first impetus of creation and is depicted as an aspect of Archangel Metatron in Western spiritual mystical tradition (the Kabala).

Archangel Raziel's Divinity – Secret Mysteries – Raziel is the Archangel of the secret mysteries, who bestows Divine information by allowing us to understand the enigma of God. Our crown chakra is opened, the flames of enlightenment descend and we transcend normal reality.

Archangel Tzaphkiel's Contemplation – Cosmic Contemplation – Tzaphkiel is the Archangel of deep contemplation of God, representing the Divine feminine watery aspect of creation. Tzaphkiel has the power to nurture all things and gives us glimpses of other realities.

Archangel Zadkiel's Transformation – Angelic Violet Flame of Freedom and Joy – Archangel Zadkiel, whose name means 'Righteousness of God', is the guardian of the violet flame of transmutation, transformation, joy and freedom. This transforms lower energies into positive life-affirming energy. Zadkiel is the Archangel of mercy, who teaches trust in God.

Archangel Jophiel´s Illumination – Angelic Wisdom – Archangel Jophiel, whose name means 'Beauty of God', connects you to your higher self, bringing wisdom, intuition, perception, joy, bliss and soul illumination.

Archangel Chamuel´s Embrace – Angelic Love (God's Love) – This Divinely-guided essence ignites and expands the flame of pure unconditional love within your heart. Its warmth melts and dissolves all resistance you may have to allowing the full manifestation of unconditional beneficial love into the heart and chakra system.

Archangel Raphael´s Dream – Angelic Healing – The blessings, mercy and compassion of Archangel Raphael and his legions of healing Angels gently bring healing into wholeness for body, mind, spirit, soul and relationships.

Archangel Haniel´s Glory – Angelic Communication – A warrior energy, providing spiritual armour to protect your soul when faced with obstacles and negativity, assisting in the fulfilment of your life's mission through Divine communication.

Archangel Michael´s Empowerment – Angelic Protection – Brings freedom, releases fears, strengthens your faith, provides inner fortitude and courage. This essence brings immediate practical assistance, giving you protection from physical and spiritual dangers. It strengthens the immune and meridian systems and activates the Hara centre.

Archangel Gabriel´s Call – Angelic Guidance – Awaken your 'Inner Angel' and receive Archangel Gabriel's gifts of hope, happiness, love and Angelic guidance. This essence creates a vortex of energy that will transform your life into a joyful Angelic experience.

Archangel Uriel´s Initiation – Angelic Peace – Archangel Uriel brings wisdom to our 'Earth walk' and illuminates our 'path through life'. This essence is vital for those who feel lost, abandoned, rejected or alone. Peace and harmony are restored with Uriel's illumination.

Archangel Sandalphon's Presence – Guardian of the Earth – Sandalphon, Archangel of the earth, is in charge of earth healing and planetary group work by uniting heaven and earth. By holding the Divine presence on planet earth, Sandalphon teaches us to have a grounded reality and balanced spirituality.

Guardian Angel Initiation –Attune to Your Guardian Angel – An amazing joyful encounter awaits you. This unique essence invokes the presence of your Guardian Angel by activating your Angelic chakra. This attunement brings love, warmth and an overwhelming sense of peace and well-being. Angelic communion is enhanced.

Angel of the Animals – Animal Healing – This Angelically-inspired essence provides a supportive and nurturing space for those working to heal the Animal kingdom.

Archangel Pendulum Chart

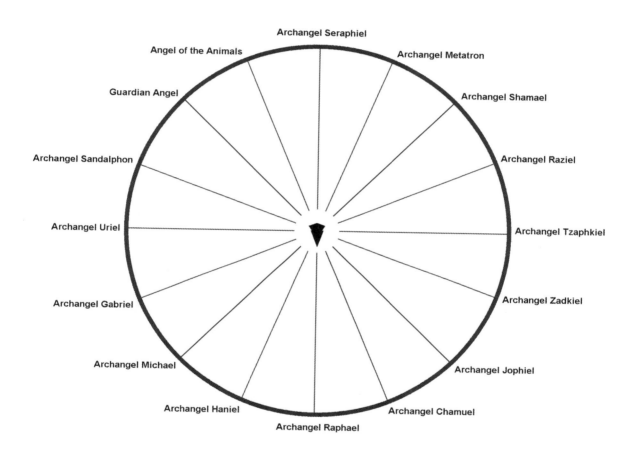